THOMAS CARLYLE

THOMAS CARLYLE

BY

IAN CAMPBELL

HAMISH HAMILTON

LONDON

First published in Great Britain 1974
by Hamish Hamilton Ltd
90 Great Russell Street London WC1

Copyright © 1974 by Ian Campbell

SBN 241 89005 5

Printed in Great Britain
by T. & A. Constable Ltd., Edinburgh

to D. C.

CONTENTS

ILLUSTRATIONS

INTRODUCTION

WHEN CARLYLE died in 1881, there was a general consciousness in Britain that a really major figure from the Victorian age had been lost. The *Saturday Review* called him '. . . in the opinion of many capable judges, the greatest writer of his time', and also '. . . a living teacher, or, as he has often been called, a prophet'. Walt Whitman in North America acknowledged that 'As a representative author, a literary figure, no man else will bequeath to the future more significant hints of our stormy era, its fierce paradoxes, its din, and its struggling parturition periods, than Carlyle.'

Certainly it was more than a chorus of praise, for even in the obituaries there were dissident voices. Yet Dean Stanley maintained in a funeral sermon that Carlyle was '. . . an eminent instance of how a man can trample on the most cherished idols of the market-place if yet he shows that he has in his heart of hearts the joys, the sorrows, the needs of his toiling, suffering fellow-creatures'. It was more than oratory: Carlyle was a figure of enormous importance to his time, and his death was to many the end of an era.

In the 1970s the force of emotion felt at the time of Carlyle's death seems strangely out of proportion. Carlyle's works in their many volumes are little read, and after a long period of neglect he is only now becoming again the subject of criticism among academics. The publication of his letters, the re-editing of his works, the recent assessments of the major figures who contributed to the 'spirit of the age' in the nineteenth century have all contributed towards a restoring of Carlyle's popularity. Yet this falls far short of the emotion generated during his lifetime, and at his death.

The purpose of this introduction is to convey to the reader who may share neither the emotional involvement, nor the close acquaintance with Carlyle's works, of his nineteenth-century predecessor, an insight into Carlyle's life and writings, and the interaction between writer and society in a long literary career of great complexity.

In his own lifetime Carlyle succeeded in keeping his private affairs remarkably private. Coming from an intensely clannish family in Scotland, he kept in close touch with them by letter throughout the fifty-odd years he spent in London after moving to Chelsea in 1834. He kept carefully all letters received, throwing away nothing. More remarkably, his letters so impressed the people who received them that they tended to preserve them as well: the biographer has access to a unique and extraordinary two-sided correspondence through which Carlyle's evolving thought can be traced alongside the day-to-day experience of a man who lived through the stormiest years of Whitman's 'stormy era'. His wife, Jane Welsh Carlyle, was a letter-writer of scarcely less talent than her husband—her letters, too, are a mine of information which has been too little used in previous works on 'the Carlyles'.

After their deaths, their private lives became public property through the publication of reminiscences and journals, selected letters and biographies, some of which were of such quality (notably Froude's) as to make their material wide-spread throughout the English-speaking world. The idol of the nineteenth century could not survive such intimate scrutiny of his privacy: he ceased to be the ideal of his times, and with the discrediting of his status as idol came the shift of public opinion away from his historical and social writings which seemed increasingly out of date and illiberal.

As his life became more an open secret, so his writing became more a closed book. Carlyle continued to fascinate biographers, from David Alec Wilson (author of the monumental six-volume act of piety in the 1920s and 1930s) to literally hundreds of pamphlets and short tributes to Carlyle, or attacks on his writing. The disputation over Froude's unhappy decision to publish freely the family papers left in his charge at Carlyle's death led to ludicrous and overheated controversy which is one of the *causes célèbres* of Victorian studies. Only now, close to a century later, is it possible to look at the Carlyles and try to attempt an estimate of their life and works.

The materials used in this study are principally the letters and collected works of Carlyle. Some half of the letters remain unpublished, scattered throughout the libraries and collections of the world, though the long-term aim of the Duke-Edinburgh edition of the letters of both Carlyles is complete publication. The letters, published and unpublished, are indispensable in the study of the lives of the Carlyles.

The *Reminiscences* were written by Thomas at moments of especial strain in his life, on the death of his father (in 1832) and his wife (in 1866). Under stress his memory spontaneously recalled scenes as distant as half a century with extraordinary clarity, and he relieved the feelings of the moment by committing these memories to paper. They survive to illuminate any attempt to understand his thought.

The literature produced on Carlyle's life and his writings is already vast. To provide documentation throughout these pages would be an undertaking of some magnitude, and would interfere with the nature of what is essentially an introductory essay. A chapter on sources and reading at the end of the book offers further information to those readers who may want to follow up this introduction.

My thanks to the libraries and institutions who have welcomed and helped me in the preparation of this work: in Scotland to the University Libraries of Edinburgh, Glasgow, Stirling, St. Andrews and Aberdeen, to the Trustees of the National Library of Scotland, by whose permission many manuscripts are quoted, to the Mitchell Library in Glasgow and the public libraries of Dumfries, Edinburgh, Aberdeen, Kirkcaldy and Montrose; in England to Carlisle Public Library, Manchester Public Library and the John Rylands Library; the British Museum, Victoria and Albert Museum and London Library; to Cambridge University Library; to the National Trust for Scotland and curator of the

Carlyle House, Ecclefechan and the National Trust and curators of the Carlyle House, Chelsea; to Mr and Mrs Armour of Craigenputtoch and to many relatives of the Carlyles who have helped with manuscripts and information; to the Bibliothèques Universitaires et Cantonales de Genève et Lausanne; in Canada to Miss Carlyle of Brantford and to the University Libraries of Guelph, Toronto and Waterloo; in the United States to the Houghton Library, Harvard, the Pierpont Morgan, Columbia University and Public Libraries of New York, to the Library of Congress in Washington, D.C., and to Duke University Library in Durham, North Carolina; to William and David Hutchison, especially to the latter who helped to see this book through the press; to Alec Cheyne; to scholars and friends too numerous to list, but with especial gratitude to the general editors of the Carlyle Letters, Charles Richard Sanders and K. J. Fielding.

Edinburgh, 30 *January* 1974

CHILDHOOD

THOMAS CARLYLE was born in 1795 in the Dumfriesshire village of Ecclefechan. In 1881 he died, famous as the sage of Chelsea; but the formative years he spent in Scotland, particularly in this remote part of Scotland, should not be overlooked in any study of Carlyle's intellectual history. He lived there almost to the age of fourteen, and spent his vacations there frequently for almost twenty years after this, so its importance is considerable.

Ecclefechan stood then, as it stands now, on the main route of communication between Glasgow and the South. Now, it is by-passed by both road and rail; then, it was an important coaching stop, where the mails changed horses, and where carriers stopped for refreshment. A network of carriers, local and long-distance, linked it with the outside world. Carlyle's years in Edinburgh were closely associated with the carriers who brought clothes, food and letters to and from his home. Ecclefechan in the closing years of the eighteenth century was in no sense isolated—it was a centre of local transportation, and a stop on the long-distance routes. It was also the scene of local fairs, when village life around stopped for the day while everyone went to Ecclefechan to buy or to sell, to meet friends, or to enjoy the booths and sideshows which Carlyle was to recall in his unfinished fragment of novel, *Illudo Chartis*. Its population was growing steadily. When Carlyle was born, 1,198 people lived there; by 1821 the figure was 1,640.

Ecclefechan was also, to some extent, a centre of industry. Though set in a predominantly agricultural area (of the 5,727 acres of land in the parish, 5,143 were devoted to farming), it derived most of its income from 'the manufacture of ginghams', and later of straw hats, an industry which Carlyle helped foster. The crude wood-and-leather 'clogs' which were the inexpensive but robust footwear of the district were also a speciality of Ecclefechan. Weaving was really the backbone of the village economy, and there were 108 families in the village engaged in 'trade or manufacture' as against only 71 in agriculture. A picture emerges of a village which was no sleepy hollow, but survived on industry and service to the agricultural community, and which obviously was thriving at the time Carlyle grew up there.

The home in which he was born is the main theme of any study of Carlyle's early years. His father was a part of the village life as described so far, a small tradesman who with his brothers carried on a stonemason's business, either contracting out or else building on his own enterprise. The house he occupied at the time of Thomas's birth he had built himself, and it still stands as the Carlyle Museum in Ecclefechan. His first wife, Jannet, had borne him one son before her early death; she was buried in Hoddam Churchyard, and the son (John) later emigrated to Canada. James Carlyle then married a poor but pious girl, Margaret Aitken, and the eldest of their large family was Thomas Carlyle. The family was to move house, sometimes almost once a year; the father was to leave the stonemason's trade and set up as a small farmer; they were to know real hardship, as well as moderate prosperity, as the national economy fluctuated in the difficult years following the Napoleonic wars, but Carlyle's loyalty to his parents and family was unshakable, his interest in them consuming. The family bond was of the greatest importance to the Carlyles, who were an exceptional family, and knew it.

Carlyle's early years emerge from scattered references in *Reminiscences*, from the letters, from remarks he made to other people in later life. What runs like a ground bass through the various accounts is the importance of his father's influence in these early years. When Carlyle heard of his father's death in early 1832, in far-off London, he realised he could not attend the funeral (railways were in their infancy) and so as a form of tribute he wrote the first of the *Reminiscences*, 'James Carlyle', an eloquent tribute not only to the personality of his father, but to the importance of his father's example in his own formative

years. In many ways this is the best of the *Reminiscences*, un-
marred by the studied grief which often disfigures the later work
of the 1860s. It recalls, with a memory sharpened by sorrow and
remorse, his earliest recollections of home, inevitably bound up
with his education. He strains his mind back to 1800, when his
father taught him the elements of arithmetic; by 1805 he was a
good enough arithmetician to be considered better than his uncle,
who was a businessman. Reading and writing, on the other hand,
are things he cannot remember having learned. He later remarked
(to William Allingham) that he had taught himself to write, but
his earliest signatures and scraps of writing are so similar to those
of other boys in his age and class that this statement is very
improbable. His own parents read only with difficulty, and his
mother taught herself to write in adult life so that she might have
the pleasure of corresponding with her favourite son in Edinburgh. It is very possible that Tom picked up scraps of education
at home and at school, and the two blended in his memory.

He attended the village schools; his earliest memories were of
'Tom Donaldson's school', a poor building recently demolished
in Ecclefechan, where a struggling Divinity student kept a
private school in order to raise money for his own studies. The
parish school was decayed, maybe because of the ridiculously low
salary paid to the master, and 'those parents who can afford it
almost universally prefer sending their children to the other
schools, where the fees are larger'. The local minister, noting this
in his *Statistical Account*, did not mention the shortcomings of
the other schools, shortcomings which no amount of good home
background could remedy.

Tom Donaldson probably performed the forgotten task of
teaching Thomas to read and write; in due course he moved on to
pursue his own studies, and Carlyle had to go to the broken-down
village school, where one 'Sandy Beattie' taught him 'English'
studies; he was proficient by the age of seven. At this point
(as Carlyle was to note sixty years later) Beattie's resources
failed him. He told Carlyle's parents that the boy must 'go into
Latin', or waste his time, but alas Beattie himself was incompetent
to teach Carlyle the Classical studies which were the essential

prerequisite to any education at the time. 'The poor Schoolmaster did not himself know Latin; I gradually got altogether swamped and bewildered under him'.

At this point, his family's reputation for piety saved him, for the minister of his father's Church, John Johnstone, rescued Carlyle, and gave him private tuition. It was under him (and Johnstone's son, also a minister) that 'the first grounds of the Latin tongue began to dawn on me', as Carlyle later recalled. Johnstone senior was a remarkable man, cultivated, the only man in the district to know Hebrew; he declined an academic career in order to devote his life to the ministry of the Burgher Secession Church of Ecclefechan, and to do good works, such as rescuing the children of local men from the deficiencies of the education they might receive in the parish school. Johnstone, 'the venerablest and most venerated Clerical Person I have ever seen', was to play an important part in Carlyle's life, but none more important than in this instance. By teaching Carlyle Latin he opened the door to the nearby Annan Academy, and from there to University, and the world of learning. James Carlyle may have been an elder in Johnstone's Burgher Church, and Sandy Beattie was to become a minister of the same Church, so between them their influence was used to procure Carlyle this essential early help. 'To the end of his life', as David Masson testified of Carlyle, 'he was a fair Latinist'.

As Carlyle admits in *Sartor Resartus*, much of which is semi-autobiographical, he was miserable at Annan Academy. He had left a close background in Ecclefechan, he had been a bright boy in a Church-dominated society, the son of an outstandingly pious man, and had been patronised by the Minister. To move to a nearby town, and be submerged in the rough-and-tumble of the Academy, was an unpleasant shock, and he hated it. Two masters, however, may be conjectured to have made a strong impact on him. One is Adam Hope, again a member of the Secession Church. In the early 1800s, Hope had operated a private school in Annan, and among others had taught Edward Irving, who was later to become one of the most celebrated ministers of the 1820s and 1830s, and also Carlyle's intimate friend. Hope closed his school in 1804, to join the staff of the Academy, where he taught Irving and Carlyle successively. The headmaster (Dalgleish by name) was a distinguished classicist, but Carlyle makes no mention of him in his recollections. The people who remained in his memory were the English master, Hope, and the mathematics master. It seems a fair inference that they taught the subjects which interested him, and occupied the forefront of his mind. In English, he admired (and feared) Hope, but he began his lifelong habit of miscellaneous reading; the local library was a good resource for him, and he borrowed frequently, with a special taste for Smollett.

Morley, the mathematics master, 'whom I loved much, and who taught me well', stirred interest in his pupil too. If, as the *Reminiscences* suggest, Carlyle was a very competent arithmetician before attending school, this shows that he was likely to do well in this class, and so to enjoy it. If he read widely, it was also a probable indication that he would do well in English, and would enjoy it. The pattern of his education was set. If he enjoyed a subject, he did well in it; if he did well, he worked at it very hard, and improved himself. His Classical learning was slow and painful at Ecclefechan, and so it can be conjectured that the Annan headmaster's class did not inspire him, for he found it difficult. On the other hand he found himself at home in English and Mathematics, and so enjoyed them and improved himself.

The standard curriculum of high school education at the time was followed: French, the Greek alphabet, Latin, Geography, Algebra, Arithmetic. The books used, if the surviving French primer preserved at Chelsea is any guide, were good and up to date—the French grammar had been published only one year when Carlyle was using it. Inevitably, the standard varied between subjects, and Carlyle wryly recalled that Latin was mechanically taught as a language, without much regard to poetical technique— 'quantity was left a frightful chaos'. Nevertheless the schooling must be placed in perspective; the intention was to prepare large classes, at low cost, for University entrance at the age of fourteen. Universities were often hampered in Scotland by the necessity of taking large classes trained to a very scanty extent, particularly in classical studies. Annan Academy prepared large classes of young men for a University education which followed on naturally from its curriculum, and as such it seems to have offered Carlyle a good schooling, which caused him no difficulty through deficiency when he went to Edinburgh University in 1809. If he was unhappy in the company of other boys, he was happy in the company of English authors, and on his weekend visits home.

The family circle in Ecclefechan was notable for more than loyalty, and piety. The Carlyle parents were quite remarkable people in the sense that they were strong-minded and had unusual powers of self-expression, which they passed on to their children. Biographers of Carlyle, in the 1880s, who enquired zealously in Ecclefechan for details of the family, found a universal testimony that they were sharp-tongued and vivid in their speech. James Carlyle was accounted 'a good scholar; he could do his ain business well; and was looked up to as a knowing bodie. He had old-fashioned works, like nobody else. He read muckle; he was a great talker . . .' The local gossip which gave this account to Frederick Martin had saved the most important point to the end—another gossip recalled that servants of the family were literally frightened of the Carlyles, as when roused their tongues could lash bitterly. All accounts agree that the Carlyles *were* great talkers. James Carlyle was exceptional.

'Measured by quantity of words, he was a talker of fully average copiousness; by extent of meaning communicated, he was the most copious I have listened to. How, in few sentences, he would sketch you off an entire Biography, an entire Object or Transaction: keen, clear, rugged, genuine, completely rounded in! His words came direct from the heart, by the inspiration of the moment: "It is no idle tale," said he to some laughing rustics, while stating in his strong way some complaint against them; and their laughter died into silence. Dear good Father! There looked *honesty* through those clear earnest eyes; a sincerity that compelled belief and regard.'

Margaret Aitken Carlyle was not a copious talker (though she could talk to effect when necessary); she reserved her intimacies for when she was alone with her son (they smoked together, clay pipes, from his very early youth) and for her brief, trenchant postscripts to letters to him from other members of the family.

Again and again in the *Reminiscences* Carlyle stresses the untutored nature of his parents' ability—an idea which was to affect his later writings on other subjects. 'My Father's Education was altogether of the worst and most limited. I believe he was never more than three months at any school . . . A solid knowledge of Arithmetic, a fine antique Handwriting; these, with other limited *practical* etceteras, were *all* the things he ever heard mentioned as excellent: he had no room to strive for more.' Thus, though his self-developed talents might be considerable, they were bound to impose certain limitations on his son's development. 'Poetry, Fiction in general, he had universally seen treated as not only idle, but *false* and criminal. This was the spiritual element he had lived in, almost to old age.' The resulting ban on his family's enjoyment must have hampered Carlyle's earliest years. The theatre, of course, was unheard of. Carlyle's lifelong favourite author was to be Shakespeare, yet he had not heard a line of the plays until he went to Annan. Prose fiction was condemned as 'downright lies'; when Carlyle sent home his *Specimens of German Romance* in 1827, he added in the covering letter to his mother that 'I have inscribed [it] to my Father, tho' I know that he will not read a line of it'. Poetry suffered the same fate; his father had the opportunity to meet Burns, but did not take it. 'My Father went to the door too from curiosity . . . and after looking at him for a minute or two went back into the house and to his business and thought no more about him.'

Again the modern reader feels Carlyle must have suffered from this, and indeed it is very possible to trace back to this source Carlyle's lifelong insensitivity to what William Allingham called '. . . the technique of Poetry—*i.e.* the form and body of it', which Allingham found 'astonishing, and by me inexplicable'. The explanation may be found in the stern atmosphere of the Carlyle home in Ecclefechan, but the deficiencies of Carlyle's mind in the appreciation of poetry were remarkable, and commented on frequently. In 1846 a visiting American heard him harangue for two hours on the subject of poetry, and summed up the experience as 'one eloquent proclamation of the defects of his own mind'.

The home background may have cut him off from certain areas of experience, particularly those of poetry and drama, at an early age, but it gave him in exchange the privilege of growing up in a stable, powerfully religious background, and in a community where the young man acquired powers of self-expression which were to astonish his student friends. His father runs, a firm and unshakable source of admiration, throughout Carlyle's life. His mother lived for many years as a link to this stable home atmosphere. The one immovable foundation for the Carlyle home in Ecclefechan was religious belief; it explains the impoverishment of Carlyle's early experience, but it at leasts compensates for it by the early and ineffaceable teaching of the Burgher Secession community.

In the late 1730s, dissension within the established Church of Scotland had led to the original 'Secession' Church, and in the 1750s the 'Relief' Church also separated from the parent body. In 1747 the Secession was itself split by internal argument into the 'Burgher' and 'AntiBurgher' wings; later these two wings were again split, each into 'Old Light' and 'New Light' branches, according to the doctrinal beliefs of the members. The Carlyles belonged to one of the thriving branches of the New Light Burgher Church, probably the least extreme of the various combinations possible, and this was a major formative influence on Thomas.

The Church was growing rapidly; the original 32 Secession charges were to multiply to 262 by 1820, when the Secession Church was reunited. Annandale had been a notable centre of the Church's activity, crowds of 10,000 and more gathering for 'sermon' in the 1730s. By 1744 the Annandale congregation had a minister, by 1746 a church in Lockerbie. In 1747 came the split between the AntiBurghers (who remained in Lockerbie) and the Burghers, who established their own community in Ecclefechan. By 1760 they were a thriving congregation, and in 1761 called John Johnstone to be their minister. In 1766 their meeting-house was built, and the fact that it seated 600 shows to what an extent the Ecclefechan Burgher Church was a focus for the surrounding parishes. People walked to service there from many parts of South-West Scotland (Edward Irving and Adam Hope walked regularly from Annan), and even from Carlisle, in England, could be seen parties of 'pious weavers' who thought nothing of walking to Ecclefechan to 'hear sermon'. This reflects partly on the energy of the Ecclefechan congregation and partly on the integrity of Johnstone's ministry; inevitably offshoots were formed in Annan (59 members) and four other parishes. This separation took place in 1805, when presumably the activity of the parish was at its height, and when Carlyle was attending, regularly, with his parents. 'Rude, rustic, bare, no Temple in the world was more so;—but there were sacred lambencies, tongues of authentic flame from Heaven, which kindled what was best in one, what has not yet gone out.' This was Carlyle's view of the services there, in retrospect. The emphasis in the Secession Church was very much on the preaching of the Word, and its application to the individual life. As was natural in a Church which had owed its existence to strong personalities insisting on their right to independence in all matters relating to faith and ecclesiastical life the stress on individual behaviour, on the relation of the Bible to morality in each person's life, and on the duty of the individual in the universe dominated by a Transcendent God (the most important of Calvin's ideas which Carlyle would have heard in early youth) would have been very strong.

The Ecclefechan Church was a stern moral breeding-ground; it was no assembly of religious fanatics. Its members saw themselves as people apart, particularly apart from the Established Church whose shortcomings were obvious. Annandale, as Carlyle was to recall in his *Reminiscences*, was 'more given to sceptical free-thinking than other places', particularly as in Annan itself the minister was weak and drunken. Members of the Church of Scotland, then, were in Carlyle's eyes given to a mere 'decent form of devoutness, and pious theoretically anxious regard for things Sacred', rather than to the weightier problems of life and individual behaviour which the more sternly independent

Secession Church regarded as all-important. As one ecclesiastical historian of the time remarked, 'strong individuality is a feature that might be expected in those who, though but a small minority in a Christian community, believed the cause of God was in their hands'. Although outnumbered ten to one by members of the Church of Scotland in Ecclefechan, the Burghers were well respected, and the local minister noted of them in the *Statistical Account of Scotland* that 'This is one of the oldest dissenting congregations in the south of Scotland, and some of its members are very respectable in their station, and easy in their circumstances.'

This was Carlyle's early religious background, a minority congregation with a secure foundation, a long history and an excellent minister. In a Church where preaching was so important the minister was bound to be crucial to the success or otherwise of the parish life, and Carlyle had always the strongest respect for the Burgher ministers, men he described as 'Evangelists in modern vesture, and Poor Scholars and Gentlemen of Christ'. Carlyle certainly attended Church with his parents, and from an early age. In Dumfries Public Library a note survives, pencilled by Carlyle in the margin of a book he read many years later. This note describes a certain blind poet of Dumfriesshire: 'He lived in *Annan*, about 1804; & had died, or gone quite across to England (*died*, I rather think), before 1806. I remember well once sitting *beside* him in the Ecclefechan meeting-house through a sermon, and gazing with terror & *fascination* at his hideously protrusive blind eyes, or the one of them next me. Poor old soul, he was listening so seriously.' So, no doubt, was Carlyle. His letters and writings are so saturated with Biblical and preaching language that he must have paid very considerable attention to it in his formative years. But what is interesting about this note is the date, for if Carlyle saw this James Fisher before 1806, then he was sitting through 'sermon' in Ecclefechan well before the age of ten.

The picture which emerges of Carlyle's early years is necessarily a sketchy one, yet it is much more than the few hints of Teufelsdröckh's youth in *Sartor Resartus*, which are so often accepted by biographers as sufficient indication of what happened to Carlyle early in his life. Three main influences which must be followed through this study can already be clearly defined.

The first is that of the family; in terms of affection and loyalty, this is of the very greatest importance. Carlyle knew his mother's character intimately, and she his, and the reader of the *Letters* cannot avoid the suspicion that Carlyle shared many more intimacies with his mother, even in letters, than he did with his wife. And as the *Reminiscences* testify, James Carlyle remained throughout Carlyle's life an unattainable ideal of manhood, strong Christian faith, and near-perfect adaptation to the exigencies of his life and environment. The parents were not only strong and loving, they were of exceptional talent in speech and expression, a quality important for Carlyle's own development.

Second, the Church to which they unswervingly belonged dominated Carlyle's youth, shaping the choice of his reading and the use of his leisure, and guiding his moral choices and the background ideas of his universe from a very early age. The Church, moreover, was a minority one, very conscious of its minority status, and therefore self-conscious, to the extent that its members were never allowed to forget the Church and its place in their lives.

Third, in education, a pattern was early formed which is to be followed throughout Carlyle's further education, both at University and in the unhappy years which followed. His first love was for reading, and for mathematics; in these he was content. He did well at school, and where he did well he was happy. If an unfortunate beginning made him less good at classics than at mathematics, then he worked harder at mathematics; at University he was to make much more of an impression in the areas where we know he excelled at school than in the more obvious classical studies which he encountered, or the philosophies. Annan Academy, it may be supposed, also fostered his great delight in self-education by solitary reading, since he so disliked the experienced and feared bullying of the bigger boys. This, too, was to have a significant effect in his later life.

The Carlyle who lived through this early period, and who in the autumn of 1809 prepared to go to Edinburgh University as a student of Arts, maybe later of Divinity, was therefore a fairly typical product of his environment, but a young man whose background had certainly given him strength of character, power of speech, and strong religious conviction. He was not in any sense rich (he walked to University, like all other poor boys), but he had a rich background and certain assets which the next five years at Edinburgh were to see developed in a way which shaped his whole life.

UNIVERSITY

WHEN THE glaciers swept over the plain which is now the Lowlands of Scotland they encountered an immovable obstruction in the shape of Edinburgh's Castle Rock. The ice flowed around and past the rock, and in the wake of the rock there grew a pile of rubbish, earth and rock, which was pushed ahead of the glacier, and deposited when the ice had to flow around the obstruction. This 'tail' of material stretched, and stretches, eastward from the rock, and on it there gradually appeared the Royal Mile of Edinburgh, a tall, blackened cliff of houses, many storeys high, stretching on each side of the narrow street which runs from the Castle down to the Royal Palace of Holyrood.

As a setting Edinburgh's Royal Mile is superb, and travel writers throughout the eighteenth century were moved and astonished by the grandeur of the tall buildings marching down the slope. But the same writers noticed, too, its smell. Dr Johnson grumbled to Boswell that he could smell him in the dark, and indeed this was no exaggeration, for the evening ritual of emptying the household slops into the open street below was still commonplace. The other factors of an uncertain and primitive water supply, and an abundance of dark closes and common stairs, led to the fabled insanitary conditions of a city where life could be short, and always disease-ridden; the youthful Sir Walter Scott lost six brothers and sisters while his family lived near the Royal Mile.

In the decades before the close of the eighteenth century, the character of the city was changing. The insanitary conditions had not prevented a most brilliant social and cultural life from springing up in the city, and in the 'golden age' of the eighteenth century many of the most distinguished scientists, philosophers and literary figures of Great Britain were resident in the city. Not only were they resident, but in a cramped city like Edinburgh they saw each other frequently, and exchanged ideas in the taverns and closes, and the informal soirées of the Old Town. Smollett's mythical tourists in *Humphry Clinker* could not help noticing how difficult it was to be incognito in Edinburgh; by the same token, when a bright young man came to town, or a new work was published, the word spread quickly, and the cross-fertilisations of interest and discipline contributed notably to the remarkable width of the 'golden age' and its achievement.

While the city flourished intellectually, it became increasingly aware of the physical limitations of its surroundings. The mood of the times was for improvement; foreign travel (even were it only to London) became more commonplace, and the citizens of Scotland's capital were increasingly sensitive about their backwardness, real or imagined, in an age of European elegance. Some of them took lessons to iron out their Scottish accents, some (like Boswell) tried hard to emigrate to London and become good citizens of the culture-capital of Great Britain. Others stayed at home, but tried to improve their city. From this came the golden dream of the 'modern Athens', which was slowly coming to reality when Carlyle first arrived.

Modern Athens was primarily an escape from the picturesque filth of the Old Town. The New Town tried first to expand in the classical southern squares on open land near the city, George Square, Brown Square, Argyle Square; much more important, however, were the developments in the green fields situated to the north of the Castle. Beyond the Castle there lay unsavoury marsh, the Nor Loch, and although there was much building land to the north it was unpleasant to have to climb down to this marsh, cross it somehow, and then climb to the fresh territory. A bridge was the obvious solution, and the opening of the North Bridge in 1777 led to a rapid expansion of the city in the parks, squares and crescents of the New Town. In many ways it was a Modern Athens; great architecture, golden stone, and a clever use of a sloping site created a city which was visually beautiful, and which still attracts world-wide attention. It grew steadily during the last two decades of the eighteenth century, and the first three of the succeeding one.

With the New Town came a rapid polarisation of city life. Those who could afford to, gladly moved from a cramped and insanitary flat in the Old Town to spacious and fashionable quarters in the New. Some, as Lockhart noted in his *Peter's Letters to his Kinsfolk*, preferred to remain in their familiar quarters, but these were few. The vacated properties suffered a swift decline, first in social status, then in condition. They were filled, and later over-filled, by the poorer classes, whose living conditions, and mortality rates, are equally appalling to contemplate, and were sufficiently gruesome to call for special mention in Engels' *Condition of the Working Classes in England*.

At the same time, however, certain institutions remained located in the Old Town, even if those who worked there might have moved their private residence. The Law continued to operate in Parliament Square, the Advocates' Library remained nearby and the University continued to function from its premises close to the Square. Thus Carlyle, entering the city in November 1809, was attending an institution which was situated near what was a rapidly declining area; his view of Edinburgh was one of an area 'infested with hordes of mendicants', as one historian has described it. A schoolboy who walked the same streets at this time wrote in his diary of crowds of thugs 'running after the people on the pavement, and striking them with their sticks and making a great noise'. Certainly Carlyle, who walked much alone, narrowly escaped a beating from footpads, and saw two such publicly executed just off the High Street. 'Before that', he told William Allingham much later, 'I had seen a man from Liddesdale, Armstrong by name, hanged for horse-stealing. He was a strong man, grimly silent. His body spun and twitched horribly. I saw it before my eyes in the dark and in daylight for weeks. At last I drew the horrible figure on paper as exactly as I could, and thenceforth it ceased to haunt me.' Carlyle's Edinburgh was far removed from the elegant terraces of the New Town. For lodgings he went to Simon Square, then as now a poor area of the city. The University buildings stood nearby, and his world would be divided between the two. The Law Courts were something he regarded as mere diversions for the tourist (his own visit is recorded in the *Reminiscences*), the Church deserved a weekly visit. The literati of Edinburgh, the circles of Sir Walter Scott and Francis Jeffrey and Sydney Smith, were another world. Carlyle's world was the University.

Edinburgh University was then the youngest in Scotland, and in the throes of a rebuilding programme which had been halted by the Napoleonic Wars. In a city aspiring to the condition of Athens, the old 'Tounis College' had seemed insufferably cramped, dirty and inadequate, described by William Robertson, the historian, as 'extremely unsuitable, both to the rank which this University has for several years held, and to the present advancing and improved state of the country'. Parts of the old fabric were demolished, and work begun on a superb quadrangle designed by Robert Adam. From 1789 till 1793 work proceeded, but funds ran out, and the new and old stood uncomfortably together for the next twenty years—including the time during which Carlyle studied there. Contractors' materials lay everywhere, making still duller a building which Carlyle saw only in the winter months. Thirty-four professors taught in only eleven classrooms, five old and six new, and crowding was acute.

It has already been mentioned that Scottish High Schools prepared large classes of boys to what would be to-day regarded as a low standard, for early University entry. In fact Carlyle was not considered as unusually youthful when he entered Edinburgh University at thirteen, nor were his classical accomplishments thought to be inadequate even when (we believe) he knew no more than the Greek alphabet. The University's standard of entry was lower, and account was taken of this in preparing the classes. The intention was to give a general education, at minimum cost, to a far higher percentage of the population, and cross-section of society, than would have been the case in England. Lockhart's condescending descriptions in *Peter's Letters* emphasise this point very acutely; the very poor did succeed in attending University, particularly if their previous summers had been spent working in order to save enough. One of Carlyle's closest student friends,

Thomas Murray, records in his *Autobiographical Notes* that he had
conducted a school in his native Kirkcudbrightshire until he had
the money to support himself very meagrely at University, and
this is doubtless what Carlyle's two teachers in Ecclefechan did
as well.

The University's fees were two, maybe three guineas per year,
plus a matriculation fee of five shillings, and a library deposit of a
guinea. Otherwise, lodgings were the sole expense, and these
were sometimes very poor indeed. The carriers often supplemented students' diets with supplies from home (Carlyle's
mother used this resource frequently) and so students could live
on very little. It was quite feasible, and not unusual, to exist on
£20 a year. Thomas Guthrie, son of the leading merchant (and
provost) of Brechin, lived at this time in Edinburgh on only £10
per session, plus fees: a friend of his lived on one chest of oatmeal
for three months. Three months of porridge took their toll,
however, and he lost his reason. Yet another student recorded
that he lived on two shillings and sixpence per week.

Carlyle, having no recorded exceptional expenses (his personal
library contains no great number of books acquired at this time),
probably lived on £20 a year or less; even this bulks large in a
family like his whose annual income never exceeded £100.
Carlyle's education meant financial sacrifice for the family, yet it
was a sacrifice gladly undertaken, for it was expected that Carlyle
would eventually become a minister of the Church, the dearest
ambition of many parents at the time.

David Masson, in *Edinburgh Sketches and Memories*, has
provided a pioneer sketch of the kind of education Carlyle
received at University, but it is a sketch which requires a good
deal of supplementing. The 'arts' education of the time was a
standard, general process shared by all students. Specialised or
vocational training followed the 'M.A.' course, and so it was
naturally on this that Carlyle embarked in 1809.

In his first year, Carlyle studied the normal curriculum of
classical languages. Professor Dunbar taught a large class the
elements of Greek, his lectures described by one student as 'grave,
dry, and without interest'. His task was unenviable, with some

200 ill-prepared students, but his teaching methods are unanimously condemned by those who wrote of them. Very different
were the classes in Latin, under Professor Christison, who
although a language professor was also distinguished as 'a very
diligent and delighted student of the higher mathematics'. A
description of his lectures is of value to this study.

'Mr C. did not either in the first or second class deliver any
formal set of lectures on general criticism, or on Roman antiquities. This had been the practice of his predecessors. But his plan
embraced a much wider range. Whatever occurred in the course
of reading in the class, whether it regarded the language or the
sentiment, he illustrated in a very miscellaneous way, calling in to
his aid the writings of the most celebrated critics, poets and
philosophers, ancient and modern. He also made frequent
allusions to the sciences and even to the arts, all of which he
occasionally laid under contribution, and ingeniously pointed out
to the students what reference they bore to the passage to which
their attention might happen to be directed.'

Here we come across something which may be an unrecognised, but an important early source for Carlyle's writing and
style. We know that his Latin was sound, if uninspired; he would
not have had to struggle to keep up with his teacher, but rather
he could have sat back and listened with pleasure to the width of
the professor's reading and reference. A cultivated mind, well
versed in the sciences and arts as well as his own subject, cannot
have failed to impress the eager but little-informed student from a
small country town. Indirectly, we have evidence to suggest that
Christison and Carlyle did have some contact, for although there
is no proof that Carlyle was an outstanding Latinist at University,
Christison recommended him, unasked, to a good teaching
position in 1816. This suggests that Christison had had occasion
to get to know Carlyle, and to appreciate Carlyle's original mind
which, if not as well-stocked as the professor's, was as interested
in a bewildering variety of subjects from all fields. Certainly we
can imagine that Carlyle found interest and excitement in these
classes, rather than in the 'snores, protracted yawns, and other
indecorous noises' which punctuated the Greek lectures.

It was not a year of academic challenge; the challenges lay in readjustment, and in the natural reflex of loneliness and long hours in an unlovely part of town—solitary reading. From the moment of his arrival at University, Carlyle began to exploit the library facilities of the University to commence a course of voracious reading and self-education. 'What I found the University did for me', Carlyle was to tell the students of Edinburgh in 1866 when they installed him as Lord Rector of their University, 'was that it taught me to read in various languages and various sciences, so that I could go into the books that treated of these things, and try anything I wanted to make myself master of gradually, as I found it suit me.' A quick, impatient man, Carlyle liked to find things out for himself, and the University Library seemed ideal for this. True, its organisation seemed dreadful, in a cramped building which was part of the condemned old college; but as Teufelsdröckh recalls in *Sartor Resartus*, from its chaos 'I succeeded in fishing-up more books perhaps than had been known to the very keepers thereof. The foundation of a Literary Life was hereby laid.' Chaos is perhaps a hard word, but the library was ill-housed, and when in 1827 the 70,000 volumes were finally rehoused, 3,000 were found to require rebinding, and 13,000 repair of some sort.

Service was slow, and hours of opening were meagre. In 1794, readers had access for only four hours a week, but newspaper advertisements suggest that by the 1820s the premises were open for three hours per day on five days of the week. Carlyle's energy was certainly adapted to the opportunity. 'He read through Chalmers's edition of the *British Essayists*, forty-five volumes', recorded a student contemporary with awe: '... His reading was miscellaneous; but he preferred works of sentiment, such as the British Essayists, Shakespeare, the English poets, Burns, etc. He was not given to history or metaphysics . . .' His memory was now being stocked for the incredible range of allusion and quotation with which all Carlyle's writing is adorned; clearly Carlyle had read very widely in English literature in his youth, and the lonely years at Edinburgh University must have given him ample opportunity.

B

The earliest recorded description of Carlyle comes from his friend Thomas Murray, who knew him at the very end of his first year at University. The picture which emerges is one of a self-made man, very much the product of his home environment as we know it; Murray's description is written in 1849, but he writes of Carlyle as: '. . . distinguished at that time by the same peculiarities that still mark his character—sarcasm, irony, extravagance of sentiment, and a strong tendency to undervalue others, combined, however, with great kindness of heart and great simplicity of manner. His external figure, though then only about fifteen years of age, was similar to what it now is—tall, slender, awkward, not apparently very vigorous. His provincial intonation was then very remarkable, and it still remains so; his speech was copious and bizarre. With this gifted and ingenious person I lived on terms of affection as long as he remained in Scotland.'

The story of the remainder of Carlyle's period at Edinburgh University is one of development along the lines described so far.

Three professors taught Carlyle in his second session; Professor Dunbar continued with Greek, although Carlyle did not find it necessary to go any further with Latin. Instead he began Logic and Mathematics.

The University system of Scotland at the time, as Dr George Elder Davie has brilliantly described it in *The Democratic Intellect*, was one which made the centre-piece of its fundamental Arts course the study of philosophy—whether mental philosophy, or the natural philosophies—the scientific subjects. All branches of study revolved round philosophy, and so an approach like Christison's which used all other disciplines to illuminate lectures in Latin were quite in keeping with this thinking. It was an approach to learning, and to knowledge, which was soon to be displaced by a more rigorously scientific one, based on the teaching of Cambridge University. But Carlyle was subject to the older system. His first contact with Logic, then, was an all-important one, for any attempt to comprehend a philosophical system must necessarily include a competence in logic. In fact Carlyle reacted violently to the personality of the professor of Logic, and so to some extent at once sealed the doom of any attempt to mould him to this conception of knowledge, as practised in Edinburgh University at that time. Carlyle failed completely to become interested in logic; for the rest of his life he showed his dislike for the dry, mechanical side of the subject by his caustic references to 'logic-choppers', people whose approach to life was too unimaginative for Carlyle. To Carlyle, Professor Ritchie of Logic 'professed logic, was great at curling, no ingenious contriver of neat little partitions of the divine spirit of man'. The sarcasm points clearly to Carlyle's dislike both of man and method. Contemporary descriptions of Carlyle's professor suggest that indeed Ritchie was more distinguished as curler than as scholar; certainly Ritchie's task was an unenviable one, teaching a very young and large class the elements of Logic, but his approach was not original, indeed it has been described as '. . . a diluted form [of] the psychology of Thomas Reid and the logic of Watts and Duncan'. Ritchie succeeded both in repelling Carlyle at the time from the study of logic, and in creating in Carlyle a state of mind which led him later in life to equate logic with an excessively mechanical approach to life.

The other professor Carlyle encountered in his second year was in the greatest possible contrast. Although fat and unpleasant in outward appearance, John Leslie was an acute and original physicist and mathematician, and in some circumstances a good teacher. Certainly, in the case of Carlyle, he aroused in a wayward and bored student an intense interest in his subject, and there is every indication that Carlyle's first spiritual awakening came long before the 'Rue St Thomas de l'Enfer' of *Sartor Resartus*. It came in the dingy mathematical classroom of Edinburgh University.

Carlyle was touched by the interest Leslie took in him. He had been prepared for these classes by an early arithmetical training at home, by Morley in Annan, and by Christison's lectures, so he was ready for the challenge they offered. But he needed the spur of personal attention from the professor, which had been lacking in the other classes. This achieved, he worked hard and well, and his lecture notes for the class (which are preserved in the Carlyle House in Chelsea) are written up with care, and well illustrated. Leslie's classes were small, some of them numbering only forty, so

Carlyle had the opportunity to be seen and recognised; his class certificate is unusually warm in its testimony that he 'applied himself with the greatest diligence and success, [and] . . . appears to possess talents peculiarly fitted for mathematical investigation'. He won first prize in the class, and his room-mate in lodgings claimed it was without effort, though Carlyle later denied this.

Mathematics came to dominate his life, particularly geometry, which, as he was to write, 'shone before me as undoubtedly the *noblest* of all sciences' at that time, till 'far more pregnant enquiries were rising in me, and gradually *engrossing* me, *heart* as well as head'. Leslie obviously liked quick, alert people—students complained that he had 'shorthand ways of working', and that he 'gave his hearers credit for powers which they did not possess', but Carlyle managed to keep up, and like Christison, Leslie was later to pay him the compliment of offering him a lucrative position after he left University.

Mathematics, as taught by Leslie, was part of the University system which comprehended the universe by a series of philosophical studies; mathematics was one of the means of studying the universe, and the relationship of its parts, described by the Edinburgh philosopher Sir William Hamilton as 'the transition study from the concrete to the abstract, from the science of matter to the science of mind'. Carlyle at this time was not merely becoming a mathematician, he was studying all available subjects, and in his ferocious reading on the subject soon found himself studying Newton till long past midnight, overwhelmed by 'differential calculi, secondary quadratics, and systems of pneumatics, ontology theology and cosmogony'. This came to be one of the most important aspects of his life.

'Of his progress in the learned languages he himself made little account; nor in metaphysics did he find any light, but, rather, doubt or darkness; if he talked of the matter it was in words of art, and his own honest nature whispered to him the while that they were only words. Mathematics and the kindred sciences, at once occupying and satisfying his logical faculty, took much deeper hold of him; nay, by degrees, as he felt his own independent progress, almost alienated him for a long season from all other studies . . . He gloried to track the footsteps of the mighty Newton, and in the thought that he could say to himself: Thou, even thou, art privileged to look from his high eminence, and to behold with thy own eyes the order of that stupendous fabric ...'

The passage comes from *Wotton Reinfred*, an unfinished fictional fragment in which Carlyle tried to embody some of his own adolescent experiences; the hero (Carlyle himself) is trying to express the sudden liberation of the spirit, coupled with a feeling of pride at self-recognition, which was felt when he first achieved some understanding of the 'higher mathematics' which Leslie's lectures opened out to him. Carlyle went to University a competent mathematician, if we can believe the scattered evidence of his schooling, and the sudden freedom which Leslie's classes offered was not the discovery of a competence in the mechanical skills of the subject. Rather Leslie, and the tradition of mathematics and philosophy which he adhered to, first opened Carlyle's eyes to the possibility of metaphysical speculations which now, in the second year at University, began to excite and fascinate him. As the passage above implies, the effect was to be merely a temporary one, but while it lasted it was exciting, and it offered more glamour, more excitement and certainly more original knowledge than logic or the classical languages. Carlyle's letters were to be full of mathematics almost till 1820; it is certain that this first taste of the subject, in 1810-1811, was a new awakening for him.

The new excitement inevitably pushed older interests and preoccupations aside; from this time onwards the very stable religious faith which had dominated his childhood played less and less important a part in Carlyle's life. Mathematics gave him the chance to find things out for himself, rather than to accept ready-made systems, however good their authority, and a split began to form between the very strong background described in the previous chapter, and the maturing thought of the University student.

The excitement of the second session was continued in the third. Leslie's second class offered a continuity both in subject and in study method, and in the smaller class the chance of still more

personal attention. Another novelty was offered, in the shape of
the Moral Philosophy classes of Thomas Brown, who had in 1810
inherited the chair from the very famous Dugald Stewart. Brown
was young, but already he had built up some reputation as
Stewart's assistant; he was not famous as an original thinker, but
as an uncommonly clear lecturer whose elegant illustrations from
English literature, particularly poetry, were very much admired
by the audience. Potentially this was something important for
Carlyle—a subject less mechanical than logic, taught by a young
man whose aptitude for (and knowledge of) the use of literature
was acknowledged. If Christison had fostered Carlyle's literary
interests incidentally while lecturing on another subject, so might
Brown. This was not to be. 'The originality, the depth, and
eloquence of the lectures had a marked effect upon the young men
attending the University in leading them to meet physical
speculations', wrote one historian, and Carlyle's friend Thomas
Murray noted that these same lectures were 'eminently distinguished for polish, ingenuity, and eloquence'. Carlyle loathed
them. He found the delivery too affected and precise (and he was
not, to do him justice, alone in this), and he could not make
sufficient allowances for this to take the subject-matter seriously.
He mocked him for many years afterwards, 'a finical man they
called Brown, or Missy Brown, that used to spout poetry'. The
Carlyle described at this time by Murray is a gauche, extraordinary figure of rough delivery, and he would have found
Brown's courtly, almost feminine delivery repellent. He also
objected to the matter, in so far as he took it seriously, describing
it as 'unprofitable utterly & bewildering & dispiriting', a technique
which 'neatly divided the spiritual life of man into faculties and
states' but which did not really tie in with real life. The Brown
Carlyle described was a man who was in demand for tea-parties, a
man far from Carlyle's earnest but rough-and-ready style. And
so another chance for Carlyle to come to grips with the philosophical interests of his teachers was lost. Logic and moral
philosophy were both quite rejected, and his interest remained
firmly in mathematics.

This interest continued in his fourth session. This year

unfortunately contained another of the personality clashes which marked Carlyle's career at Edinburgh University. Although he continued to derive pleasure and instruction from Professor Leslie, he failed completely to share the popular and prevalent admiration for John Playfair, whose lectures in Natural Philosophy were his other class in this fourth session. A fragment of *Wotton Reinfred* which has recently come to light shows Carlyle incorporating into an early version of that book a satirical portrait of Playfair as Sir Gideon Dunn, a calm and courtly man who fails to make contact with Wotton (the earnest but rough young mathematician and philosopher). In particular he refuses to take life, and the problems of society, seriously, but shelters behind a polished and amused manner. Sir Gideon Dunn is unmistakably Playfair, just as others of the characters in *Wotton Reinfred* are recognisable caricatures.

Playfair was generally liked in society, and people spoke of the 'fine old Archimedes with his reposed demeanour', whose teaching style, 'so simple, unaffected, and sincere in manner, so chaste in style, so clear in demonstration' attracted many admirers. Carlyle should ideally have derived great pleasure and value from these lectures; educational theorists of the time pointed out that natural philosophy demanded an exceptional mathematical talent in the student if its teaching was to be fully effective, and this Carlyle seems without doubt to have possessed. And he did certainly try. 'For years', he told Moncure Conway many years later, the years perhaps leading to the exaggeration of which he was plainly guilty, 'I attended his [Playfair's] lectures, in all weathers and all hours. Many and many a time, when the class was called together, it was found to consist of one individual—to wit, of him now speaking; and still oftener, when others were present, the only person who had at all looked into the lesson assigned was the same humble individual.' Playfair did not ignore Carlyle—indeed, he asked him to perform some translation for him—but the only reward for a year's diligent attention was a slightly more fulsome class certificate than usual. It is difficult to tell how much of Playfair's influence remained with Carlyle. Henry Cockburn records that Playfair's dying wish was to be read to, not from the offered Scott novel, but from Newton's *Principia*, so perhaps this admiration may have affected Carlyle. There is indirect evidence, also, in the surviving lecture-notes in the University Library of Edinburgh taken by a classmate of Carlyle's, beautifully written and illustrated, and continuous enough to suggest diligent attendance at lectures. By all accounts Playfair was an engaging teacher, and Carlyle's knowledge of the natural sciences was considerable, and remained with him all his life. Even in old age a scientist who travelled with him recorded that 'his questions showed wonderful penetration', and found the old man quite capable of keeping up an intelligent conversation on physics.

In fact, Playfair's influence was probably mainly an indirect one; he taught not physics, but natural philosophy, the philosophy of nature and natural phenomena, in keeping with the overall education theory of the time in Edinburgh, and his teaching inevitably complemented the earlier work of Leslie. In this way Carlyle's voyage of self-discovery and self-education was furthered by Playfair's teaching, even if the ostensible reason for attending the classes was not fulfilled. In short Carlyle was an assiduous student, but the good the classes did him was submerged in the general excitement he felt in the mathematical and philosophical studies.

With the end of the fourth session Carlyle's 'Arts' course was complete; he had shown himself more than competent to survive the lectures and tests, but very selective, with the originality of a strong and talented mind, in what he drew from the courses which the educators had prepared for him. What he had appreciated was the library, and the peculiar value of University in allowing a strong-willed mind to select from a body of knowledge, and educate itself by intensive reading. Carlyle did not make the attempt to appreciate the world-picture and the philosophy behind the Edinburgh system. He was interested in certain things only, notably in literary reading and in mathematics, and these he pursued relentlessly. He certainly was at fault in cavalierly rejecting so much, and particularly in allowing personality conflicts to alienate him so completely from parts of the system. But we know that he received an enormous stimulus from what he did accept, and that even if he did not receive in any sense a complete or rounded education, he succeeded (like his fictional Wotton Reinfred) in establishing a lifelong habit of intensive reading and self-education in what interested him—even at the cost of ignoring what lay behind. The example of his dogmatic father must have been strong in this—James Carlyle simply ignored what did not interest him, if this comprehended poetry, music, art. His son's blindspots were different, but the approach was significantly like that of his father.

In 1813 Carlyle was far from ready to face the world, even had he taken his degree. Few at the time bothered to graduate, merely succeeding in their courses and passing on either to further training, or to teaching or other work. Carlyle's next few years, in fact, were to be consumed in further training.

UNCERTAINTY

TEUFELSDRÖCKH, HERO of *Sartor Resartus*, is made to suffer spiritual agonies before attaining a state of tranquillity which Carlyle describes as the 'Everlasting YEA', a state where the doubts and uncertainties of a precocious boyhood and a patchwork education culminate in religious doubt, and are then transcended in a new faith which is more powerful than any doubt. Carlyle suffered very similar agonies; he passed through his 'Everlasting NO' and his 'Centre of Indifference' in Edinburgh, before achieving his new amalgam of faith; and the history of the years which followed his University Arts education is one of doubt, false starts, frustration, growing ill-health and real suffering. Above all, these are years of uncertainty.

The uncertainty which most immediately faced Carlyle lay in the choice of a career. He was, of course, destined for the Church, but his own personal doubts made him view the prospect with less and less enthusiasm. His Arts training complete, he was faced with either three full sessions of University training in Divinity (which would have been financially out of the question) or the 'partial' attendance which he in fact chose. This latter course was the only practicable one for poor students; after a year of full-time attendance at the college, they were able to spend the following six years in employment, continuing their education in the evenings, and appearing in Edinburgh only once per year to deliver a trial sermon. Carlyle chose the latter course, and it is possible that the advantages it offered might have been more than mere economy—it gave him a breathing space in which to consider the future, before finally committing himself to a career whose attraction was fast fading.

Biographers have not enquired why Carlyle, a Burgher

Seceder, should have attended the Divinity Hall of Edinburgh University rather than his own Church's Divinity Hall in Selkirk; there was an acute shortage of ministers in the rapidly expanding Burgher Church, and his parents would have been eager to see their son trained to the Burgher ministry. The answer may lie in David Scott's *Annals of the Secession Church*, in the passing note that students attending the Burgher Hall were expected not only to have completed an Arts curriculum, 'but also to possess a competent knowledge of Hebrew'—which Carlyle assuredly did not. Indeed, he himself admitted that only Johnstone, the venerable minister of Ecclefechan, knew Hebrew, alone in the whole district of Annandale, so Carlyle would be excluded from Burgher training without further rigorous preparation. The memory of the difficulties with which Latin had presented him would doubtless discourage any such idea.

Very little trace of Carlyle's year of formal training in Divinity Hall survives. This in itself is mute testimony to how little impact the experience made on him, but his reaction to the classes he had was really hostile. The reasons for this are a continuation of the whole unhappy relationship between Carlyle and Edinburgh University—a hostility to the subject-matter of the classes, and a temperamental dislike for the professors.

Professor Ritchie's Divinity classes were unmemorable, so much so that Carlyle could only recall, much later, the forceful delivery of the speaker. 'The Devil, after succeeding in his vile machinations retires to his infernal den and grins with horrid satisfaction!' This sentence he repeated to William Allingham much later, but could recall no more. Professor Meiklejohn, although well-known (according to contemporary newspapers) for his attention to his students' well-being, was a bland and undistinguished figure, with '. . . no name in general learning or theology'. Professor Brunton of Hebrew was much more impressive as a man, and much more repulsive too. A particularly successful city minister, University professor, University librarian and social figure, he yet managed to spend more than six months of the year in his country house; and he played well at University politics. Carlyle noted this at the time of Brunton's appointment (1813): 'Brunton, I hear, has got the Hebrew chair . . . aye! aye! "kissing goes by favour" [is] true yet, I see'. Brunton, and to a lesser extent his colleagues, repelled Carlyle by representing as nearly as possible the exact antithesis to the unworldly, selfless ministry he had seen exemplified in the Burgher Seceders of Dumfriesshire. The worldly wise and successful men of Edinburgh knew how to fill fine pulpits, how to hold lucrative University chairs without apparently doing much to fire their students' enthusiasm for what Carlyle had been brought up to recognise as the most important subject in the world. In short, they seemed trivial and irreligious by Carlyle's severe standards. What they taught did not interest a young man whose family had inculcated in him a world-picture where religion was equated with stern instructions on how to live, and how to prepare for the judgement of an all-seeing, omnipotent and omnipresent God. The more academic subjects taught at Divinity Hall seemed trivial and disgusting, and by 1817, a mere two and a half years after leaving it, Carlyle was describing it in very unflattering terms:

'I have not been within its walls for many months—& I know not whether I shall ever return, but all accounts agree in representing it as one of the most melancholy & unprofitable corporations, that has appeared in these parts for a great while . . . It may safely be admitted that tho' the Drs Ritchie junior and senior [i.e. Professors of Logic and Divinity], with Dr Meiklejohn, Dr Brunton & Dr Brown were to continue in their chairs, dozing in their present fashion, for a century, all the knowledge which they could discover, would be an imperceptible quantity—if indeed it sign [sic] were not negative.'

The student gossip, the bantering tone, cannot disguise the boredom and disillusion which lie behind this savage paragraph. Carlyle had plainly lost his vocation for the Church, and in 1817, on finding the Professor out when he went to re-register for the coming session, '. . . My instant feeling was, "Very good, then, very good: let this be finis in the matter." And it really was.'

This point marks a real crisis: Carlyle's whole life, as described so far, was theocentric, and the vocation to the ministry one of its most sacred features. To abandon the ministry, not with the anguished doubts of Mr Hale in Elizabeth Gaskell's *North and South*, but on the paltry pretext of not finding the professor at home on the first visit, is a grave step, and open to obvious danger not merely to Carlyle's own frame of mind, but to his important relationship with his parents. Fortunately the parents rose nobly to the challenge of what must have hurt them deeply.

'I told my Father and they were much grieved; it must have been a sore distress to them, but they bore it nobly—and my Father said to me that notwithstanding, his house would always be a home to me and that no one in that house should ever speak or act with severity towards me on account of what I had done.'

In this gesture, the Carlyles made possible the continuing warm relationship their son enjoyed with both parents, which meant much to him while he was in this troubled adolescent period, and afterwards.

His parents' decision was one bright spot in an otherwise very unhappy period of Carlyle's life: principally he chafed at the employment by which he had, almost inevitably, to sustain himself at this time—schoolteaching. First at Annan Academy, where he himself had been taught, and where he had been so discontented, then at a better school in Kirkcaldy, Carlyle suffered the torment of a shy and intolerant young man forced to keep discipline, and instil the rudiments of English, classics and mathematics into young heads. He loathed it, and related his loathing in letters to his friends throughout the years (1814-1818) between leaving University, and quitting the 'schoolmaster trade' in November of 1818.

The appointment to Annan was gained simply by making an impressive show at interview, but the Kirkcaldy post was an interesting sidelight on Carlyle's character at this little documented period of his life. The Town Council of Kirkcaldy were anxious to procure a bright young man to rejuvenate the Burgh School, slumbering under an ageing and incompetent man, and they sought help from among the professors of Edinburgh University. The man they were recommended, by Professor Christison, was Carlyle, and the correspondence and council minutes which survive in the National Library of Scotland are a mute witness to the favourable impression Carlyle must have made on his teachers. The Kirkcaldy appointment was well paid, with an annual salary of £80, and had the additional advantage of being close to the capital, where many of his friends were still living. Friends were something Carlyle valued, for in the two years he had spent in Annan he had found the absence of friends a real burden. His letters to college acquaintances harp on the theme of loneliness, and although he resolutely tried to banish loneliness by hard study he obviously longed for the intellectual stimulus of the friends he had made at University. His family were nearby, but they were separated from him by a gulf of education and literary taste, as well as by the shadow of his growing religious doubt.

At Kirkcaldy Carlyle made two very important friends. One was Edward Irving, also an Annandale man, teacher in a competing private school, who had preceded Carlyle by several years in the familiar pattern of schooling at Annan Academy and Edinburgh University. Irving and Carlyle were two really remarkable characters, strong-minded, of powerful intellectual and verbal potential, and emerging from a rigidly pious childhood into intellectual freedom, ranging freely through the riches of literature and science. They shared many interests, as well as a common background, and each recognised in the other a man of powerful and original mind. Irving's welcome was characteristically frank and sincere. 'You are coming to Kirkcaldy to look about you in a month or two: you know I am there; my house and all that I can do for you is yours;—two Annandale people must not be strangers in Fife!' His house was a useful asset, his library an even better one for Carlyle, who at the time could afford few books of his own. 'From the first we honestly liked one another, and grew intimate; nor was there ever, while we both lived, any cloud or grudge between us, or an interruption of our feelings for a day or hour. Blessed conquest, of a Friend in this world!' Kirkcaldy was made more pleasant by this meeting, far more so than Annan and his '. . . solitary *quasi-enchanted* position' there.

These passages, from the *Reminiscences*, underline the sharpness of Carlyle's memory, also the importance of companionship to him, in that he could still recollect fifty years after the bright shock of making Irving's acquaintance. Carlyle needed the moral support of an 'elder brother', the position Irving filled: Carlyle had all the nervous insecurity in him which Thomas Murray's description suggested, and although he had considerable talent of expression by this time (as his earliest newspaper letters of this period show) he was very unsure of himself, except in the privacy of letters to his family. He knew he had made some progress in the world, by the fact of his appointment in Kirkcaldy, but this was not enough. He knew he had made progress in study at University, but the lonely nights at Annan had merely shown him the vast quantity of knowledge he still wished to conquer. Irving's friendship, his willingness to talk and argue far into the night, were important: when they were not talking, they were sharing the results of their reading, and Carlyle read with voracity, as well as buying several books for his private library.

'Irving's Library was of great use to me: Gibbon, Hume, etc., etc., I think I must have read it almost through;—inconceivable to me now, with what ardour, with what greedy *velocity*, literally above *ten times* the speed I can now make with any Book. Gibbon, in particular, I recollect to have read at the rate of a volume a day (twelve volumes in all); and I have still a fair recollection of it, though seldom looking into it since. It was of all the books perhaps the most impressive on me in my then stage of investigation and state of mind. I by no means completely admired Gibbon, perhaps not more than I now do; but his winged sarcasms, so quiet, and yet so conclusively transpiercing, and killing dead, were often admirable potent and illuminative to me; nor did I fail to recognise his grand power of investigating . . .

'. . . We had books from Edinburgh College-Library too (I remember Bailly's *Histoire de l'Astronomie*, ancient and also modern, which considerably disappointed me); on Irving's shelves were the small Didot French Classics in quantity, with my appetite sharp: I must have read (of French and English, for I don't recollect much Classicality, only something of mathematics in intermittent spasms) a great deal during those years.'

The opportunity for reading and talking, and the delight of a secure intellectual companionship made these two years in Kirkcaldy a happy period for Carlyle: schoolteaching was dull, but otherwise the possibilities were exciting. Carlyle was aware of the excitement, but perhaps he was unaware of a struggle which was taking place in him and which Irving's company did something to affect.

This was the time of Carlyle's failing ambition to enter the ministry of the Church of Scotland: it was also the time of his reading Gibbon, and wincing at the 'winged sarcasms' which killed dead. It was the time of the spiritual convulsion which his parents nobly tolerated, and it was an epoch of his life where the secure underpinning of youth, the faith in religion and in the example of religious men, were shaken to their foundations. Irving knew all the circumstances of this struggle, for after all he had shared Carlyle's education and to a large extent his reading, and he attended worship in the Ecclefechan Burgher Church when he was in his native Annan. Irving knew Carlyle as closely as anyone would ever be able to do. There was the essential difference of faith, for Irving was almost ready to present himself for licensing as a minister of the Church, to serve his trainee years before full ordination. Irving's faith was more steady than Carlyle's, and survived the disillusion of Divinity Hall, of cosmopolitan thought on a provincial mind, and of forbidden worldly reading and trivial worldly enjoyment. Irving was destined for the Ministry, and he was not to be diverted. The two argued and talked endlessly, and Carlyle testifies in the *Reminiscences* that they made no secret of religious differences. Carlyle may well have been saved from total despair, or from total atheism, by Irving's boisterous determination: Irving must have been strengthened for what was to be a very troubled and doubt-torn ministry by his nocturnal walks and arguments with Carlyle. Certainly both were gifted speakers, and their arguments would have been remarkable in their potency and powers of expression. Neither was, as far as we can tell, moved by the other's views, but both drew spiritual strength from the exercise.

The other friendship of these years is important. Biographers

Ecclefechan: the Arched House on the left was built by Carlyle's father (see *Reminiscences*), and Carlyle was born in one of the upstairs rooms in the half further from the camera

Annan Academy: Carlyle was a schoolboy here, and later a teacher. He hated both experiences

Carlyle's lodgings in Moray Street (now Spey Street), Edinburgh, now ruinous. They were his happiest lodgings, and he was living in them when he experienced the 'Everlasting NO' of *Sartor Resartus*. They lie half-way between Edinburgh and Leith

The Grassmarket, Edinburgh, with the Castle. The carts in the
roadway are similar to those by which Carlyle kept in touch with
his family while he lived in Edinburgh: the scene is little changed
from the one he knew

Craigenputtoch. The house survives virtually without alteration

Thomas Carlyle.
Pencil drawing by Daniel Maclise, 1832

have tended to assume that the brief romance in Kirkcaldy between Carlyle and Margaret Gordon was the first serious affair which Carlyle had had, although the recent publication of the early letters suggests that there was an enigmatic 'Miss Merchant' in Edinburgh who crops up from time to time, but who drops out of sight as Carlyle's Edinburgh friends leave the city to begin employment around the country. It is impossible to tell how seriously to take these hints, nor how seriously to take the suggestion, made in some Dumfriesshire local histories, that Carlyle was in love with the daughter of his Ecclefechan minister, Johnstone.

Margaret Gordon lived in Kirkcaldy, and she there became acquainted with the gauche but interesting schoolteacher whose gift of speech was matched by a shy but intense friendship for her. Margaret Gordon was of good family; she was later to become Lady Bannerman. Her aunt, with whom she stayed, did not approve of Carlyle as a suitor, and put an end to their friendship, but only after it had given Carlyle much pleasure over several years. The parting scene, where Margaret confessed to Carlyle that they must meet no more, was a painful one, and forms the basis for such scenes in both *Wotton Reinfred* and in *Sartor Resartus*. Carlyle was deeply hurt, for the experience of female company had moved and excited him, and he saw no reason for his rejection. He was not rich, but he had good prospects. He had appeared in print, and in 1817 was mentioned in Professor Leslie's *Elements of Geometry* as 'an ingenious young mathematician, formerly my pupil', who had devised a new answer to a problem. His teaching was firm and effective, and he was patronised in Kirkcaldy by Provost Swan. In short, he thought that at last he was making a name for himself, and this rebuff was doubly unwelcome. At Christmas 1818, for instance, after he had resigned from his teaching position, he was able to enjoy a most pleasant visit to Kirkcaldy, and his reticence in a letter barely disguises the reason why:

'I forgot to say (what was indeed of no consequence) that I spent, along with Irving, the Christmas holidays in Fife. They were the happiest, for many reasons which I cannot at this time explain, that for a long space have marked the tenor of my life.'

Succeeding Christmases and New Years were spent in this way, till (probably in 1820) the fateful parting took place. Carlyle was quickly resigned, writing to one friend of his lost love as belonging to the class of '. . . shadows, radiant shadows, that cross our paths in this dark voyage; we gaze on them with rapture for a moment; and pass away—borne onwards by the tide of Fate'. Margaret Gordon, too, had to become reconciled, though her final letter to Carlyle shows that she fully understood her lover, strong and weak.

'One advice, and as a parting one, consider—value it— *Cultivate the milder dispositions of your heart, subdue the more extravagant visions of the brain.* In time your abilities must be known; among your acquaintances they are already beheld with wonder and delight; by those whose opinion will be valuable, they hereafter will be appreciated. *Genius* will render you *great*. May *virtue* render you *beloved*! Remove the awful distance between you and ordinary inferiority, and be convinced they will respect you as much and like you more . . .'

These, judging by the later Carlyle, were shrewd words. He could not be at rest, even with the woman he loved.

Unrest, then is a keynote in these years. In 1818, prompted by the establishment of a rival school in Kirkcaldy, he seized the opportunity to abandon his teaching, and move back across the Firth of Forth to Edinburgh, which had been tantalisingly in sight throughout his two years at Kirkcaldy. He had visited the city, of course, to deliver trial sermons, to see old friends, to buy and borrow books. Still he had some acquaintance in the town, and he determined to live on some accumulated savings (although he had with characteristic generosity helped his father to set up a small farm, as a better alternative to the stonemason business). The city offered opportunities of employment as translator, teacher, tutor, and freelance literary writer.

First Carlyle tried again to see if he could make use of the University's resources. He enrolled in Professor Jameson's mineralogy and natural history classes, but with little enthusiasm.

The unsettlement of Kirkcaldy really operated against him, and he wrote to a friend of '. . . the small degree of attention I pay to the shadow rather than the su[bstance] of mineralogy', blaming it on his 'unsettled [con]dition and . . . indifferent state of health'. Health begins now to loom large in correspondence, and never fails to do so for the rest of Carlyle's life. The result of ill-health was at least partly the decline of interest in Jameson's lectures, and a testy dislike for Jameson himself, 'destitute of accurate science, without comprehension of mind,—he details a chaos of facts, [which] he accounts for in a manner as slovenly as he selects and arranges them'. The classes were soon dropped, and left little impression on Carlyle, though a dilettante interest in the subject shows through in *Wotton Reinfred*. One may conjecture that perhaps a more permanent fruit of this study lay in Carlyle's ambition to study German, for Carlyle was later to write to Goethe that his first stimulus to study the German language arose from a desire to read Werner in the original. Werner had been one of Jameson's teachers, and so one can credit this as a real possibility. Otherwise there is little to commend this half-hearted attempt on Carlyle's part.

Law also presented itself to Carlyle at this time as a possible source of income, and a possible career, but it raised even less interest. The drier aspects of the law interested him even less than they interested Scott's Alan Fairford. Professor Hume and his colleagues, though respected by fellow-lawyers, 'seemed to me mere denizens of the kingdom of Dulness, pointing towards nothing but money &c as wages for all that bog-pool of disgust; Hume's Lectures once done with, I flung the thing away for ever'. The lectures he was to describe on another occasion as a 'Babel of sounds and everlasting talk about nothing'. Other lecture-notes from the same classes survive, in Edinburgh University Library; certainly they are technical, but no more so than the subject might demand, and they indicate constant attendance. What seems to have happened with Law, as with Moral Philosophy and Logic, was that Carlyle's interest in the subject was never very strong, and the personality of the teacher an easy pretext for casting the study aside. With law this process took place for the last time;

Carlyle attended some lectures merely as a spectator in later years—for instance he attended some of 'John Wilson's volcanic lectures'—but he did not again enrol, nor hope to take a vocational training in the University of Edinburgh.

The absence of a regular form of study did little to help him in the unsettled years which followed his abandonment of school-teaching at the end of 1818. Till 1826, he was to be mostly unemployed, or at best a freelance tutor with no fixed address, and no incentive to settle down. His health has already been mentioned: these uncertain years seem to have been at the heart of his lifelong digestive weakness. It is easy to imagine that poor and cheap lodgings, indifferent food and habitual late study would aggravate an already nervous man to an unsteady frame of mind. Some writers have tried to go further than this: J. L. Halliday, in *Mr Carlyle My Patient* has all but psychoanalysed Carlyle from his childhood onwards, neatly pasting together titbits from early letters and late reminiscence, but never having the unfortunate patient to speak in his own defence. Carlyle's ill-health undoubtedly came and went. He complained endlessly of sleeplessness, yet had to be wakened by his hosts in the mornings. He complained incessantly of his digestion, yet refused advice on his diet, and ate willingly the foods which he knew and liked—even when this included a late-night bowl of porridge just before bed. There can be no doubt that Carlyle was a nervous man, and had a weak digestion, but his reputation has suffered in part through the very excellence of the letters in which he made his complaints, and through the vividness with which he spoke of his troubles. Frederick Harrison has an acid review of Carlyle where he sums up, very well for one so close to Carlyle in time, the effect which the digestive and other complaints were bound to have on the public.

'As we read these letters and diaries, these tales of Carlyle and his wife, on which art has thrown a light so dazzling, and a magnifying power so peculiar, we feel as if we were caught up again into the bewildering realm of Brobdingnag ... But though we know better than to take it all as literal, we are not raised or purified by it. We do not know our fine old master any better, we do not love him more, we do not feel him to be a greater, more creative spirit.'

What we do feel is that Carlyle not only saw offence through a magnifier, he also magnified it in the telling. City inconveniences in Edinburgh (never the most sanitary of cities) become in Carlyle's words the '. . . unsupportable abominations which human animals when crowded together in cities occasion to each other'. Edinburgh 'resembles a day on the shores of Acheron more than any Christian place'. The city was a place to love and to hate.

'Edinburgh looks beautiful in the imagination, because the heart, when we knew it of old, was as yet unwrung and ready to derive enjoyment from whatever came before it. Visit the *Alma Mater* now, and you are disgusted probably with the most feeble drivelling of the students—shocked by the unphilosophic spirit of the professors—dissatisfied with the smoke and the odour and every thing else in or about the city.'

So the perspective glass of ill-health and nervous excitement coloured the city of Edinburgh, and all the years spent in it. Significantly, Carlyle (who knew himself well) saw back to the origins of this failing in himself. His father's speech was of great power: 'Emphatic I have heard him beyond all men. In anger he had no need of oaths; his words were like sharp arrows that smote into the very heart.' So far he might have been describing himself. 'The fault was that he exaggerated (which tendency I also inherit); yet only in description and for the sake chiefly of *humorous* effect.' What was a humorous twitch in the father became a habit of mind with the son.

Ill-health and loneliness were compounded by a sense of frustration in his vocation. This was not teaching, it might perhaps best be described as self-improvement to the fullest extent of the abilities, books and teachers he had at his disposal. His nervous disposition forced him on to this, yet he seemed to receive no benefit from it. A passage has recently come to light, belonging to 1827, in which Carlyle writes a tribute to one of his student friends who had died in the course of his medical studies, infected with typhus fever by one of his patients. The funeral oration shows clearly the bitterness which Carlyle felt: he *knew* the frustrations he attributed to George Cron.

'His spring was indeed stormy—he had tasted in full measure the hardships of the scholar; sickness, disappointment, isolation, were familiar to him; and while he turned an unflinching front to the world, and abated no whit of his truth and stedfastness, hope many times grew faint, and his heart was in bitterness within him. For, though in the fair arena of academic life, he had advanced himself among the foremost, in the tortuous politics of the world he was surpassed by many. With the instinct of true worth, to sue for preferment was not given to him; and to the best, preferment, unsued for, is slow in coming. What though in general knowledge, in classical and sacred learning, he had in his own sphere scarce any equal, and no modern literature, not excepting Spanish and German, was unfamiliar to him; what though he was of walk and conversation unblameable, strong in faculty, true-hearted, at all points a sterling man? . . .'

These qualities did not seem to help George Cron, nor did they seem to help Carlyle. Many years later he was to say bitterly to Robert Herdman that '. . . I was nearly in despair, for I could not see any recognised path of life for me to follow, and yet when I looked about me, I didn't see that anyone was much better than myself or more fit for work; whether the work was ruling men or making shoes.'

With characteristic immodesty (Margaret Gordon's last letter seems close to its mark) Carlyle recalls in this passage the bitterness at having no stated position in society, no success following on hard work.

For he continued to study, very hard, even while abandoning classes at University. He read incessantly, and he kept up his undoubted abilities in mathematics and natural philosophy. The years spent in Edinburgh were partly spent in tutoring these subjects, and in translating early papers on crystallography and other technical subjects. Indeed he even offered a technical paper to the famous *Edinburgh Review*, an interesting insight into his thoroughness at this time. This paper has puzzled writers for many years. In the *Reminiscences* Carlyle wrote of '. . . a foolish enough, but new French Book, a mechanical *Theory of Gravitation*, elaborately worked out by a late foolish M. Pictet (I think that was the name) in Geneva'. A caustic review of this book was Carlyle's article: the book has, however, never been traced. In fact the mystery is illuminative of Carlyle's thoroughness, for the book did not exist (which explains why subsequent critics have sought it in vain), but was in fact a review article by Marc Auguste Pictet in his *Bibliothèque Universelle*, a Genevan periodical which concerned itself with the current European discoveries in sciences and the arts. M. Pictet was in the habit of writing long 'notices' of recent works of scholarship, and one of these notices concerns the work of a young Swiss scholar, Gautier, on interplanetary gravitation. This essay, entitled 'Le Problème des Trois Corps', must have sparked off Carlyle's anger, and his (lost) article: it indicates both that he read French technical articles for interest, and that he took the trouble to read the latest numbers as they arrived in the University Library, for the article was written in the same year that Pictet published his notice, and the book reached Edinburgh.

Carlyle's restless interests, in short, did not stop at keeping up to date with the latest Swiss periodicals on natural sciences. They also took him into the learning of German in which he made fast progress, and they were soon to take him into the heady fields of German transcendentalist literature and philosophy. In his Dumfriesshire home, he could be sure of quiet attentions on his holidays, and he recalled with pleasure his first reading of *Faust* in the fields of the family farm in Mainhill. German books were rare, and their import difficult: Provost Swan of Kirkcaldy had business connections, and helped Carlyle greatly in this respect. 'I well remember the arrival of *Schillers Werke* Sheets at Mainhill (and my impatience till the Annan Bookbinder got done with them): they had come from Lübeck, I perceived;—and except for my gratitude it was needless offering Swan any attempt at payment.' Payment was possible, for through Edward Irving's help Carlyle found two years' employment as tutor to Charles Buller, soon to become famous as a public figure and member of parliament. In the Bullers' aristocratic homes, in Edinburgh and in Perthshire, the solitary tutor was made kindly welcome: when he accompanied the family to Perthshire, he enjoyed country peace. When he was in Edinburgh, he retained lodgings, and visited his pupil daily. Increasing financial security gave him the means to buy more German books, to visit Irving (now a successful young minister in Glasgow), to have better rooms in the countryside just outside Edinburgh.

As the 1820s progressed, Carlyle's black cloud lifted. Slowly, he was becoming known. He had translated technical papers, and published (in the *New Edinburgh Review*) his first faltering critical papers on German writers. He had done hack-work, translating Legendre's *Elements of Geometry*, writing short articles for the *Edinburgh Encyclopaedia*. With the financial security the Bullers offered (from 1822 to 1824) he was able to undertake his first substantial literary projects, a life of Schiller, and a translation of Goethe's *Wilhelm Meisters Lehrjahre*.

The dark years were coming to a close: with Carlyle's first visit to London, in the summer of 1824, they were all but over. Ill-health ceased to dog him so closely, success seemed to be a more real possibility. Friends were more plentiful, and an acquaintance with Jane Welsh was deepening into romance. This, however, belongs to the next chapter. These years of uncertainty and doubt—and real suffering—culminated in the experience transformed, in *Sartor Resartus*, into the climactic experiences of the 'Everlasting NO', the 'Centre of Indifference', and the 'Everlasting YEA'.

Really there is only one point to make in this context: the progression through these chapters follows the progression of Carlyle's life as described in the years since leaving University, and the climax of the 'Everlasting NO' is a very partial one in its final effects. The memorable description of the machine universe, at the heart of the 'Everlasting NO', is justly famous.

'To me the Universe was all void of Life, of Purpose, of Volition, even of Hostility: it was one huge, dead, immeasurable Steam-engine, rolling on, in its dead indifference, to grind me limb from limb. O, the vast, gloomy, solitary Golgotha, and Mill of Death! Why was the Living banished thither companionless, conscious? . . .'

The loneliness is familiar, as the consciousness is of a world without a manifest design, when faith in a controlling God is lost. The surviving belief is merely in a mechanical process without Divine authority, without apparent purpose. Then Carlyle's native strength of mind rebels.

'All at once, there rose a Thought in me, and I asked myself: "What *art* thou afraid of? Wherefore, like a coward, dost thou for ever pip and whimper, and go cowering and trembling? Despicable biped! what is the sum-total of the worst that lies before thee? Death? Well, Death; and say the pangs of Tophet too, and all that the Devil and Man may, will or can do against thee! Hast thou not a heart; canst thou not suffer whatsoever it be; and, as a Child of Freedom, though outcast, trample Tophet itself under thy feet, while it consumes thee? Let it come, then; I will meet it and defy it!" And as I so thought, there rushed like a stream of fire over my whole soul; and I shook base Fear away from me for ever. I was strong, of unknown strength; a spirit, almost a god. Ever from that time the temper of my misery was changed: not Fear or whining Sorrow was it, but Indignation and grim fire-eyed Defiance.'

This is the crucial point for present consideration, and it will bear some examination. This is not spiritual rebirth, nor is it, indeed, wholly to be taken seriously. If Carlyle were to believe that at this moment in his life, which he was to identify later as a flash of self-insight experienced at Leith Walk in Edinburgh in 1821 or 1822, he ceased to whine about physical suffering, and merely faced up to it from that point on, he was grossly deceiving himself.

What this moment signifies in Carlyle's mind is a realisation that the world will not necessarily all be in his favour, and that in a potentially hostile, or at least unfavourable universe, he will have to fight for progress. In short, he is not looking for removal of suffering, he is facing up to the probability of having to live with it, and of having to accept the fact.

This is a brave stand, but it is not total spiritual new-birth, still less something which can be attributed (as the whole of *Sartor Resartus* too easily is) to the influence of the Germans. To read this passage from the 'Everlasting NO' is to hear, clearly, the echo of 'James Carlyle' from the *Reminiscences*. Carlyle's father faced up to the world, and he believed that he was in a potentially hostile universe, in which a man had to assert his manhood by buckling down to suffering, and working. His faith had given him this outlook, but he had also been conditioned to it by a youth and early manhood of actual want, hunger and physical brawling which had all been necessary to start him on his successful business career. Life had been hard, and James Carlyle had learned to be hard to face it. He believed 'That man was created to work, not to speculate, or feel, or dream. Accordingly he set his whole heart thitherwards: he did work wisely and unweariedly . . . and perhaps *performed* more . . . than any man I now know.' Such a man was obviously to be admired in Carlyle's eyes. Repeatedly James Carlyle's conduct is described as 'manly', and his willingness to ignore physical discomfort and suffering stressed. Verbal similarities to the passage in *Sartor Resartus* are notable, and they reinforce the similarity in tone. His whole world-philosophy is wistfully what his son seeks for.

'. . . He was among the last of the true men, which Scotland (on the old system) produced, or can produce; a man healthy in body and in mind; fearing God, and diligently working in God's Earth with contentment, hope and unwearied resolution. *He* was never visited with Doubt; the old Theorem of the Universe was sufficient for him, and he worked well in it, and in all senses *successfully* and wisely as few now can do . . .'

This is Carlyle's clear intention in the sudden squaring up to the problem which is the 'Everlasting NO': it *is* negative, but its refusal to buckle in the face of adversity can best be interpreted as the culmination of the years of uncertainty which have been the basis of this chapter. Seeming failure, shifting of place and position, doubt, family stress, loneliness, failure in love conspired to bend him: he would not break, and the force of will clearly belongs to the distant family in Ecclefechan. The 'Everlasting NO' shows the strength of the bond to Carlyle's earliest years. In the moment of supreme stress, he reverts to the family type. He imitates the example of the man he most admires, and although he does not—cannot—share his father's faith, he wishes to share the strength that faith gave. The 'Everlasting NO' is Carlyle's Heart of Darkness, its result the beginning of a return, very selectively, to some of the standards of his home. It is a personal choice, a re-assertion of a powerful will and self-control which years of indecision and doubt could not quench. From this time onwards, says Carlyle in *Sartor Resartus*, he became a man. Certainly from this time onwards, his fortune seemed to improve steadily. The brightest single star in his sky was now Jane Welsh, and increasingly his growing intimacy with her dispelled the darkness of the 'Everlasting NO'.

ROMANCE

IN THE sense that each needed the other, few people can have been more perfectly matched than Thomas Carlyle and Jane Baillie Welsh. Each was clever, sharp, to a large extent self-educated; each came from a home where the parents were strong characters, whose memory dominated their children even after the parents themselves were dead; each was driven by restless energy; each suffered fools badly, and satirised them wickedly. On the other side, they were both kind people, people whose friendship and help were valued by an enormous circle, people whom others liked to visit. Their conversation was brilliant, and an evening with the Carlyles was unforgettable. Their letter-writing skills were probably unparalleled in the nineteenth century. When Jane died in 1866 it was (as Carlyle wrote in her epitaph) as if the light of his life had gone out.

Jane's father was a doctor in Haddington, a three hours' ride east of Edinburgh. He worked hard, and was a man of ability, and at the time of his death in 1819 (of cholera, which he had caught in an epidemic) he was fast making his name and fortune. His wife was a good-looking but insecure person, possessive in personality, quick-tempered and obstinate. Mrs Welsh and Jane were left with memories of a fine husband and father, and with £200 a year on which to keep up appearances. Being the people they were, they entertained well, and were popular members of Haddington society, but in private they quarrelled frequently and violently.

What the world saw, however, was a widow and a charming daughter, not formally beautiful, but quick and vivacious. She had many admirers, especially Edward Irving, who had been her tutor while her father was still alive. He had lived in Haddington then, and it has been conjectured that he would have liked to marry his pretty pupil. But he was engaged to the minister's daughter of Kirkcaldy, and this engagement he honoured. It is a tribute to Irving that he continued to visit the Welshes in Haddington, and that he took with him, in 1821, perhaps not quite unintentionally his closest friend Thomas Carlyle. Carlyle fell helplessly in love with Jane: five years were to pass before they married, five years marked by occasional visits, and a remarkable correspondence (published by Alexander Carlyle as *The Love Letters of Thomas Carlyle and Jane Welsh*) in which the reader can trace, with extreme clarity, the deepening of passion to the point at which each impatient soul felt they could marry the other. The letters are an extraordinary blend of Platonic intellectual love (concerning themselves much with Jane's education, with Carlyle's developing interest in German literature), of human obstinacy, and of hesitantly expressed love. Jane was determined she was to be educated, however unfeminine this was regarded in Haddington; she coaxed her parents to teach her Latin, and in Carlyle she found a tutor in German, Spanish, Italian and English literatures. Initially she saw him as little more, for his social *gaucherie* made him almost impossible to take seriously. In February 1822, Jane wrote to one of her friends and confidantes, listing the young men who had visited her among them Mr Carlyle who '. . . was with us two days during the greater part of which I read German with him—It is a noble language!—I am getting on famously—He scratched the fenders dreadful[l]y—I must have a pair of carpet-shoes and hand-cuffs prepared for him nextime—His tongue only should be left at liberty his other members are most fantastically awkward—.'

This is the only mention of the unfortunate Mr Carlyle in a long letter; his own letters to Jane indicate how much more seriously he took their friendship, and indeed Jane had once or twice to show distinct coolness to him, for what seemed like a forward spirit. These letters were written just before the beginning of Carlyle's tutorship of Charles Buller, when his income, and his manners, both improved, and he must have become a more welcome guest with the Welshes. Still, Mrs Welsh was very slow to accept the idea of Carlyle even as a serious suitor, and for

years it looked as though Jane's friendship would be as interrupted as Margaret Gordon's.

The reader of Carlyle's letters can sense a distinct uplift in his
spirits from this time onwards. Jane's friendship, the security of
a good tutoring position, the growing awareness that he had an
almost unrivalled critical knowledge of German literature (though
tempered by a realisation of how few would be interested in this
knowledge), and a growing experience of the world all contributed to this well-being.

The summer of 1824 brought an important widening of
Carlyle's experience, in the form of a visit to London. He had
travelled quite extensively in Scotland, going on walking holidays
with Irving, and making his trips to and from the South-West to
the Lothians. He had been to England on visits from his native
Dumfriesshire, and on one occasion had gone as far as York for
an interview for a tutor's position. London, however, was
something new. Here Edward Irving was now becoming established as a very successful young minister, his commanding
presence and powers of oratory filling his chapel with not only a
devout Scottish congregation, but considerable numbers of the
great and famous city. Carlyle had a good friend, and a powerful
one, in London, and this tempered what might otherwise have
been an overwhelming experience.

The visit to London (followed by a pleasant week in Paris and
Northern France) presented Carlyle with the opportunity to
experience a much wider range of cultural activities than hitherto,
as well as giving him the chance to meet many famous names with
whose work he was familiar on the printed page.

Carlyle refused to be bowled over by the metropolis, although
plainly he was excited by the experience. What he enjoyed was
the pace of life, the proliferation of famous men, the sheer size
and bustle of the city streets. The narrow Old Town of Edinburgh,
and the leisurely New Town had nothing to compare with
London. They had, however, their famous literati, and in this
respect Carlyle found that Edinburgh easily bore comparison
with London. Thomas Campbell, a favourite since student years,
disappointed him cruelly. 'His talk is small, contemptuous and

shallow: the blue frock coat and trowsers, the eyeglass, the wig, the very fashion of his bow, proclaim the literary dandy.' Coleridge is 'a steam engine of a hundred horses power—with the boiler burst'. Southey and Wordsworth 'have retired far from the din of this monstrous city', De Quincey 'lives here in lodgings ... He carries a laudanum bottle in his pocket; and the venom of a wasp in his heart.' Hazlitt and Leigh Hunt are dismissed as dilettantes who live on the continent, and Theodore Hook, Darley and Maginn as mere 'spotted fry that "report" and "get up" for the "Public Press"; that earn money by writing calumnies, and spend it in punch and other viler objects of debauchery ... Filthiest and basest of the children of men! ... Such is the "Literary world" of London ...', writes Carlyle.

This cross-section shows how little Carlyle was captivated by the city writers he found in London. He was fascinated by Coleridge, and still remembered his fascination when he wrote his memorable sketch of the poet in the *Life of John Sterling* many years later. But he could not bear Coleridge's dreamy meanderings, his endless soliloquies when Carlyle wished for incisive answers to incisive questions about German metaphysics. He took refuge in less memorable, but more immediately useful, company: Henry Crabb Robinson, although he found Carlyle offputting, slowly warmed to the intolerant young man and from initially crediting him with only 'the appearance of a sensible man' came to enjoy his company. By February 1825, Robinson recorded spending his morning 'partly in a long gossip with Carlyle, who had sent me his *Life of Schiller* and was about to leave London'. The two exchanged ideas, and Carlyle, particularly, gained from his contact with Robinson knowledge of German books and writers. In Edinburgh there were few teachers, and fewer books; Robinson in London knew the literature better, and the minor authors' works, and after Carlyle returned to Scotland he was to write valuable letters of help.

The visit to Paris (23 October-6 November 1824) was similarly received with qualified pleasure: 'To live in Paris a fortnight is a treat; to live in it continually would be a martyrdom ... The idea of *studying* it is for me at present altogether out of the question; so I quietly surrender myself to the direction of guide books and *laquais de place*, and stroll about from sight to sight, as if I were assisting at a huge Bartholomew Fair.' Paris was beautiful enough, but frivolous and dirty, everything seeming 'gilding and fillagree, addressed to the eye and not to the touch'.

In sum, these impressions of Paris and London were stimulating, but did not give Carlyle any definite direction to his ambitions. He was also to travel round the industrial midlands of England, after leaving London, so he saw his fill of the new industrial cities, the conditions of urban life, splendid pomp as well as poverty. After a sheltered youth—sheltered from the worst deprivation of Edinburgh slums, sheltered from the worst of agrarian poverty—he must have awoken to the extremities of his society, and he must have been revolving in his mind from this time onwards the protest against the worst failings of the social systems of his time, which animate his writing from the early 1830s. The impression of this trip was of intellectual stimulus, but on a restricted social plane, and not from the 'literary lions' whom he had greatly looked forward to meeting. The 'fraction of true friendship which had been established' in some hearts in London he found gratifying after 'icy Edinburgh', but he still considers Scotland as his home. '*Athens* is dear to me as the centre of all that is best in Scotland; but in my former state of frightful solitude, I will never abide in it.' This meant not moving out of Edinburgh, but seeking to find congenial company in the city, for '. . . As I wish to live in Edinburgh, it were good that I attempted to form relations there, rather than elsewhere'. The relations, it is easy to surmise, with Jane Welsh must have been at the forefront of his mind, yet he was to be curiously undecided for the year which followed his return from London. For all his expressed wish to stay in Edinburgh, where he could find employment, literary friends, and the stimulus which literary company and conversation offered, he was still sufficiently at heart a countryman to consider setting up house in the countryside, and visiting the city only as often as his publishing projects demanded. But Jane refused to agree: insensibly she was coming to consider herself as the prospective wife of Thomas Carlyle, but she would not be this in a country retreat. She was too fond of the conveniences of city life, and of elegant society, to face a Dumfriesshire retirement.

While they considered what to do, Carlyle returned home and spent one of the happiest years of his life in the farm of Hoddam Hill, high above Ecclefechan and commanding a superb view of the south of Scotland. His father worked a nearby farm, but his mother lived with her favourite son, and the family split in two, and worked both farms, for the year 1825-1826. Carlyle was utterly content, as never before. The companionship he welcomed, the country air and food quietened his nerves and buoyed his health. The 'Centre of Indifference' of *Sartor Resartus* plainly owes much to this episode, described by Carlyle himself as a 'rustic idyll'. He 'lived very silent, diligent, had long solitary rides . . . my meditatings, musings and reflections were continual; thoughts went wandering (or travelling) through Eternity, through Time, and through Space, so far as poor I had scanned or known . . . This year I found that I had conquered all my scepticisms, agonising doubtings, fearful wrestlings with the foul and vile and soul-murdering Mud-gods of my Epoch . . . and was emerging, free in spirit, into the eternal blue of ether.' Again the note is one of self-assertion, of the successful battle against doubts. He has not embraced a system, rather he has emerged from a confused plethora of systems to a belief in himself, and his own freedom. This was not without regret, for high on his hill he could hear the nearby church bell of Hoddam, 'like the departing voice of eighteen hundred years'. His parents tolerated his scepticism, and respected his honest attempt to put himself in a calm frame of mind. The 'Centre of Indifference' *is* indifferent, but because it is self-centred. When the self is secure, it is able to contemplate the approach of the 'Everlasting YEA', a state where a new faith occupies the empty, but cleansed, self.

'With other eyes, too, could I now look upon my fellow man: with an infinite Love, an infinite Pity. Poor, wandering, wayward man! Art thou not tried, and beaten with stripes, even as I am? . . . Truly, the din of many-voiced Life, which, in this solitude, with the mind's organ, I could hear, was no longer a maddening

c

discord, but a melting one; like inarticulate cries, and sobbings of a dumb creature, which in the ear of Heaven are prayers. The poor Earth, with her poor joys, was now my needy Mother, not my cruel Stepdame; Man, with his so mad Wants and so mean Endeavours, had become the dearer to me; and even for his sufferings and his sins, I now first named him brother.'

That a change has taken place is clear; that a complete reformation has not followed is equally clear. 'The old inward Satanic School was not yet thrown out of doors.' The process which is seen in the 'Centre of Indifference', and which culminates in the 'Everlasting YEA', is the establishment of a self, a *persona* capable of surviving, and respecting itself. The initial feeling in the 'Everlasting NO' had been one of self-loathing, but one with the seeds of its own cure. For the self-loathing was not directed towards a mystical escape from the prison of the self, but to a stiffening of the moral fibre to make living with oneself (recognised as a fact which has to be suffered) possible, if not even fruitful. The feeling of selfhood accepted, the 'Centre of Indifference' makes possible a growing pride in selfhood, along with a realisation that the self has to live with its own imperfections, and not expect too much help from outside. 'Experience is the grand spiritual Doctor; and with him Teufelsdröckh has been long a patient, swallowing many a bitter bolus.' Bitter, yes, for Teufelsdröckh has not found happiness, not true self-knowledge. The latter is growing: 'Thou art still Nothing, Nobody: true; but who, then, is Something, Somebody? For thee the Family of Man has no use; it rejects thee; thou art wholly as a dissevered limb: so be it; perhaps it is better so!' The tone again resembles that of James Carlyle: it is a tone of proud willingness to suffer, unwillingness to suffer, unwillingness to be indebted to any one else.

Where James Carlyle fell short was in the final transition between the 'Centre of Indifference'—Carlyle repeatedly notes in the *Reminiscences* his father's indifference to public opinion, amounting almost to a smug feeling that only he is right, of the whole world—and an 'Everlasting YEA', pulsing with energy because of the joy in self-realisation which it brings. The power which animates the third section of the spiritual struggle in *Sartor*

Resartus comes from the joyful emergence from years of uncertainty, doubt, and guilt. It is an emergence fought for, achieved through hard study and self-discipline. Although it brings relief, it brings also the realisation that the relief is not so much a gift as something one has struggled to gain. And the achievement gives it its driving force.

The critic must beware of transferring the happy year of Hoddam Hill (1825-1826) literally to the pages of the 'Everlasting YEA' of *Sartor Resartus*. The triumphant assertion of a metaphysical belief, compounded of German transcendentalism and half-remembered and half-rejected childhood Christianity is well catalogued and traced in C. F. Harrold's *Carlyle and German Thought*: Harrold, and other critics (notably René Wellek and G. B. Tennyson) have stressed to what extent Carlyle's reading in German literature and philosophy in the late 1820s underlies the assertion (in 1831) of the 'Everlasting YEA'. In 1825 Carlyle was still tentatively feeling his way in Goethe and Schiller, and was almost entirely ignorant of Kant.

The Hoddam Hill 'rustic idyll' is an important contributory factor towards the 'Close thy Byron, Open thy Goethe!' of *Sartor Resartus*, but its importance lies in biographical rather than intellectual history. In this tranquil year, spent mostly in rural isolation, Carlyle made peace with himself, with Jane (after endless argument about where they should live), with his family, who welcomed Jane for an extended visit, with fellow-humanity. The serenity of this year gave him an inner calm, manifestly lacking in his relationships with other people up to this point. The few descriptions we have of his early manner and bearing suggest immaturity, insecurity, and abrasive and unpleasant stridency. The calm of Hoddam Hill did much to change this: the following year was to see the emergence of Carlyle as a genial host in Edinburgh, good company, prized by intelligent and witty men as no misanthrope would have been. Carlyle had secured his own centre, his own self-respect, and the advantage showed in his relations with other people. The difference from James Carlyle lay in this: James Carlyle had an unwavering faith, and could have been proud of a life which lived out his religious beliefs to the fullest extent, but 'We had all to complain that we *durst not* freely love him. His heart seemed as if walled in; he had not the free means to unbosom himself.' Only once (when Carlyle's mother was gravely ill, in 1817), did he allow his natural force of feeling to break through, and the contrast was genuinely alarming to the family. 'It was as if a rock of granite had melted, and was thawing into water. What unknown seas of feeling lie in man, and will from time to time break through!—'

The breaking through, in Carlyle's case, took place in Hoddam Hill: he saw himself clearly, he mastered himself, and he was able to re-enter the stress of city life in 1826 as a man who wrote well and fluently, who knew a modest measure of success, and who was to have two years in Edinburgh to enjoy the brilliancy of the last decade of Edinburgh's greatness as a golden city of literature.

Jane's mother solved the continual debate as to where her daughter and Thomas Carlyle were to live, by renting a pleasant house in suburban Comely Bank, at the foot of the steep hill of Stockbridge which led down, north, from the edge of the New Town. The new houses were creeping downhill into the countryside, but the road was still '. . . lined with hedges enclosing cornfields. The Water of Leith was a clear running stream, with plenty of roaches and eels.' The city was continuously being improved, particularly in the matter of communications: water supplies and cleaning facilities were better, and the living conditions which had made the older part intolerable in 1810 were quite unknown in the fresh air of Comely Bank. Some measure of country quiet and cleanliness seemed necessary to Carlyle all his life, and never more so than in the late summer of 1826, which had been the hottest in living memory. Even Sir Walter Scott, who loved the city, thought it this summer '. . . fit for nothing but wasps and flies and my lodgings are hot and stifling . . .'. Still the decision was made, and on 17 October 1826 Thomas and Jane were married in Templand, Dumfriesshire. The same day they drove north to Edinburgh, and settled in their new home. In his bleak student days, Carlyle had whiled away his time by scratching on the window of his lodgings the old rhyme:

Little did my mother think
That day she cradled me
What land I was to travel in
Or what death I should die.

Certainly he could hardly have guessed in those lonely days that
he would be returning so soon to a city he had so much cause to
hate, as well as to love, a married man, with an excellent future in
the Athens of the North.

MARRIAGE

THE ATHENS of the North had changed somewhat since Carlyle's student days. In his troubled years between school-teaching, and visiting London, Carlyle had lived as much as possible outside the city (principally in the suburb of Pilrig, between Edinburgh and Leith) so he had had little opportunity to see what was happening in the city proper. Even before then, as a student, he had spent most of his time in the University *quartier*, for he specifically mentions in the fragment of the *Reminiscences* entitled 'Christopher North' that the crowd of promenaders in Princes Street was very attractive, a crowd 'into which, if at leisure, and carefully enough dressed (as some of us seldom were) you might introduce yourself, and flow for a turn or two with the general flood'. He suggests that his appearance would have made him conspicuous, and adds that '... As for me, I never could afford to promenade or linger there; and only a few times, happened to float leisurely thro', on my way elsewhither'.

The New Town was, of course, an area where those people lived who could afford to escape from the noisomeness of the Old. Tourists remarked on its wide and spacious streets, but also on their ordered calm and serenity. Grass grew between the paving stones, and it was so quiet on Sundays that the city might have been plague-stricken. Princes Street was a gay promenade only on fine days, and the custom was passing as the 1820s progressed. When he revisited the city in 1832, Carlyle was to find even Princes Street relatively deserted. '... Already in 1832, you in vain sought and enquired Where the general promenade, then, was? The general promenade was, and continues, nowhere ....'

Part of the reason for this change lay in the migration of business premises into what had originally been splendidly isolated residential quarters. Princes Street, George Street and Queen Street were conceived of as elegant housing, architecturally superb, appreciated and maintained by those who could afford the privilege. When shops, bookstores, lawyers' offices and the other manifestations of a modern business city began to invade the eastern end of the New Town, the original residents responded by moving away to the west. Curiously, the Conference on the Preservation of Georgian Edinburgh in 1970 discovered the same difficulty in its planning as then affected the citizens of the New Town: if a city is to sustain a busy commercial centre, it has to accept a business community and the consequent high traffic levels. The New Town in 1974 is confronted with strangulation by motor traffic, whereas in 1826 it was faced with the encroachment of an unlovely business community on its classical streets and squares.

The original vision of Modern Athens was being modified, coming to terms with the realities of a new commercial world. The displaced citizens created new streets and crescents, perhaps even more magnificent: in the years under review, 1826 to 1828, Moray Place was being built, perhaps the most handsome street of all. Yet the original plan had gone, the cohesion of a new, self-consciously successful community in Modern Athens had faded.

More than the original vision had faded. The years which followed the end of the Continental wars had brought in time an upsurge of wealth, as the economy accelerated into a peacetime prosperity. Trade with overseas countries recovered, and Scotland's links with Europe were re-established. Loss was involved as well as gain; Henry Cockburn wryly noted in his *Memorials* that the war years had led to an artificial concentration of native talent remaining at home, and English talent visiting Edinburgh in place of making the Grand Tour of Europe. The war had led to the 'last purely Scotch age'; native talent left in alarming numbers with the coming of peace, and visitors poured into Europe, flocking not only to see the natural beauties denied to them for over a decade, but streaming to the battlefields made famous to them by newspaper despatches.

While the city was being altered in this way, there was sufficient material prosperity to ensure that building would go on and that there would be material prosperity on a spectacular scale in some fields. Literature was one of these; Scott earned close to £100,000 by his pen, and for single novels both Lockhart and Susan Ferrier were able to secure advances of £1,000. With only 1,000-1,500 titles published yearly, reviewing was important, and Francis Jeffrey headed the 'circle' of the *Edinburgh Review* on one side, while John Wilson and John Gibson Lockhart were the chief writers of the brilliant *Blackwood's* circle. Edinburgh polarised in several 'circles'; especially later in the 1820s, there was a very marked split between Whig and Tory circles, but literature was a uniting force in the discussions and social gatherings throughout the town.

The prosperity could not last, of course. Scott's financial ruin, which took place in 1826-1827, was the most spectacular, and involved him in debts which have been estimated as amounting to close to one million pounds in modern terms. Scott was fortunate—widely respected and admired, he was allowed time by his creditors to work in order to repay his debts, but many businesses were closed, and their owners ruined, in the catastrophic months which Eric Quayle describes in *The Ruin of Sir Walter Scott*. This was just at the time when Thomas and Jane Carlyle settled in the city. By 1828 the London publisher, Taylor, was offering Carlyle the 650 remaining copies of the *Life of Schiller* for one shilling and sixpence, a ridiculously low price, simply to rid his shelves of this useless stock. Carlyle was unfortunate to miss the golden age of prosperity for writers.

What he did not miss was the golden flow of conversation and intelligence which still characterised the New Town. The two main political groups included talented literary circles: the Tories had John Wilson and Lockhart, while the Whigs had Jeffrey and his followers. Carlyle was not deeply committed to either ideology, and he enjoyed the company of both. Wilson he had a grudging respect for (as the *Reminiscences* testify), and as a conversationalist he found him absorbing.

'Wordsworth, Coleridge, and the minor Lakers, he gave us at

great length, in this serio-comic or comico-serious vein; of De Quincey . . . he had much to say, in farce-tragedy style, wildly coruscating and caricaturing; Brougham, too, Dugald Stewart, at last even Jeffrey and his own Edinburgh rivals, all done with swift broad strokes, not insincere . . .'

It is difficult to resist a suspicion that nights of talk such as this must have helped mould Carlyle's own mature conversational style: in later years, in Chelsea, Carlyle was to hold his friends spellbound with just such talk, describing, criticising and caricaturing the literary men of his day. The other great talker of Edinburgh was Francis Jeffrey, and he was a close personal friend of both Carlyles. Clearly, he felt a close friendship for Jane, and gallantly admired her from a distance, much to Carlyle's annoyance. On the other hand, he was a good friend to Carlyle, introducing him to much of Edinburgh literary society, accepting contributions from him for the prestige-laden *Edinburgh Review*, even though, as editor, he considered them wrong-headed and badly written. The case of Carlyle's essay on Burns is the most celebrated—Jeffrey found it necessary as editor to tone down the language and the thoughts in proof, and Carlyle obstinately restored almost all the missing passages. Jeffrey meekly accepted the changes, and printed the essay, which has become one of the most well-known essays of his review. He was under no compulsion to, however. He tolerated this, as he tolerated Carlyle's occasional bursts of temper, and impatient arguments, from friendship, and let no opportunity pass to help Carlyle, to introduce him to useful friends, to recommend him for suitable positions, to visit him, to invite him to his country home, Craigcrook, outside the city, where both Carlyles were frequent and welcome guests. Jane was a brilliant talker, as was her husband: they were accepted at such literary gatherings, and they enjoyed them very much.

In their own home they wisely did not try to emulate the style of Craigcrook, or of the 'Blackwood's' literary dinners. With publishing in decline, Carlyle's income certainly did not permit generous entertainments, and they established a rule that with few exceptions (such as for Craigcrook) they neither gave, nor accepted dinner invitations. They paid more informal calls, and welcomed them, and once a week, on Wednesday evenings, they held open house for their friends. These were brilliant but economical gatherings, the entertainment lying in the talk and the flow of ideas. Carlyle described his powers in these years as akin to 'fencing', a sharp repartee of ideas in which he could take as well as give points. Certainly Jane was a captivating hostess, and it emerges clearly from the circle of correspondents which they amassed in these Comely Bank years that they had established themselves not only as a social success, in their own terms, but that they retained these friends in later years. Francis Jeffrey, for instance, was quite willing to take time off from a very busy life in Edinburgh to travel a hundred difficult miles to visit the Carlyles in the 1830s. The attractions of their personalities, and their conversation, were very considerable. The foundation of their success as the centre of a literary circle in Chelsea was being laid.

Carlyle found himself bored very easily with nothing to do. His letters indicate that he was emotionally very uneasy in the first months of his marriage, and the unease expressed itself in dyspeptic attacks, in bursts of ill temper, in general restlessness. A translation of *Wilhelm Meisters Lehrjahre* and a life of Schiller were published, and had gained him some fame. He had just completed his *Specimens of German Romance*, which were further to enhance his reputation as an authority on German literature.

Carlyle's letters reveal a growing dissatisfaction with the miscellaneous nature of his literary output. Translation, commissioned criticisms, commentaries could not satisfy his urge to write what he called 'a Book of my own'—a literary creation which would to some extent embody the spiritual experiences through which he had passed in the years immediately preceding his marriage. One unsuccessful attempt to perform this difficult task is the fragment which survives to-day as *Wotton Reinfred*, an unfinished semi-autobiographical novelette which occupied him in the first difficult months of his married life. Wotton, the hero, is very much the image of his creator: troubled, bodily and spiritually upset, unable to settle, carrying the memory of past disappointments in work and in romance, he seeks to travel to take his mind off his constricting troubles. His friends (based unmistakably on living originals, including Coleridge, Edward Irving and Jane Welsh) cannot help him, further than acting as sounding boards for his ideas. He has to travel, and in his travels he will perhaps learn the answer to his world-weariness. The scheme has obvious indebtedness to Goethe, and indeed Carlyle had translated *Meisters Wanderjahre* as part of the *Specimens of German Romance*, but it was an indication of his upset condition, and the imperfect state of his ideas at this time, that he was unable to finish Wotton's history, indeed abandoned it in mid-paragraph.

The letters of this time indicate emotional strain, some quarrels between husband and wife (although Jane was tactful and did her best to please) and a sense of aimlessness. Later writers, anxious to trace the causes for strain between husband and wife, gathered fragments of gossip which suggested a rapid breakdown of any deep relationship between Thomas and Jane in these early years. At their most extreme, these stories take the form of the after-dinner gossip of Sir Richard Quayne, whom Frank Harris quotes as repeating Jane's confidential story that Carlyle slept with her only once after their marriage, but found the experience disastrous and never repeated it. This makes good writing, of course, but it is very unlikely to be true. The emotional dependence of the two was to grow steadily, and their physical attraction for each other is inescapable to any student of the letters written after 1826. When Carlyle is absent, his wife bemoans the empty bed; when Jane is absent, Carlyle is helpless in the home till her return. The Carlyles were no Lammles, satirised by Dickens as good company in society, but murderous enemies in private life. They were highly strung and highly intelligent people who both made high demands on their fellows. The adjustment of each to the other's habits took time, and during this initial period quarrels did happen. Carlyle was hypersensitive to noise, and his moans on this subject, and on his digestion, are part of the folklore of Victorian studies. He had a morbid desire for fresh air, which caused draughts throughout the house. He had a more than usual passion for cleanliness, which somehow he reconciled with a desire to smoke continuously: he would eat very few dishes, and these had to be cooked in familiar and unchangeable ways. Jane in her turn was quick and jealous; she appreciated male attention (including Jeffrey's), and she was determined to keep up with her husband's intellectual pursuits. She was an excellent hostess, but inclined to dominate conversation. And she had a wicked temper. Together they evolved a relationship which was deep and inviolable: the collapse brought about by Jane's death is unmistakable in the *Reminiscences*. Their childless marriage was tense, and full of strain, but the tension must, like Carlyle's comments on his own health, be seen with allowance for the magnifying glass of exaggeration. Jane exaggerated as did her husband, and she had a quick, dramatic, epistolary style which often enlarged things for effect. The clouds over Comely Bank were not tempests. In 1839 Jane was to write to Carlyle's mother of her attempts to keep peace in the home:

'Now if you will please recollect that, at Comely Bank, I also wrote down an old maid's house-dog, and an only son's bantam-cock, you will admit, I think, that my writings have not been in vain.'

The disagreements in Comely Bank were over things as trivial as this, and Jane's 'writings'—her tactful notes to neighbours whose noisy pets might disturb Carlyle's sleep—dispelled many storms. 'The house is a perfect model of a house', Carlyle was to write to his mother soon after his marriage, 'furnished with every accommodation that heart could desire, and for my life I may say in my heart that she is far better than any other wife, and loves me with a devotedness, which it is a mystery to me how I have ever deserved.' To his mother, Carlyle admits that his wife has had to put up with his bad temper, '. . . for in truth I was very sullen yesterday, sick with sleeplessness, quite nervous, *billus* [bilious], splenetic, and all the rest of it . . .'. Jane, though, was resolutely cheerful, and determined to be a good wife. She found it easy to be economical, for her home in Haddington had been an excellent preparation. She wrote of being appalled by '. . . all the waste that goes on around me, when I am needing so much care and calculations to make ends meet. When we dine out, to see as much money expended on a dessert of fruit (for no use but to give people a colic) as would keep us in necessaries for two or three weeks!'

This face was not the face seen by their friends and their literary acquaintance: Carlyle was remembered for his conversational brilliance and power, a combination which Emerson aptly dubbed 'a trip-hammer with an aeolian attachment'. Carlyle, as Basil Willey has remarked, 'can never write urbanely; he is always on the stretch . . . [he] writes almost exclusively from the heart or the solar plexus, not from the head'; the same could have been said of his conversation, always eloquent, always superlative, always flowing irresistibly. Hartley Coleridge was in later years to complain that Carlyle was guilty of '. . . sometimes uttering gorgeous pieces of eloquence and deep and everlasting truths, at others spending equal strength in announcing the merest trivialities'. Perhaps so, but this power and energy was what captivated the hearers. Jane's was a more poised and witty style. She appeared to some men as '. . . one of the most natural, unaffected, fascinating women I ever encountered', but female listeners saw perhaps a different Jane. 'Clever, witty, calm, cool, unsmiling, unsparing, a *raconteuse* unparalleled, a manner inimitable, a behaviour scrupulous, and a power invincible—a combination rare and strange exists in that plain, keen, unattractive and yet unescapable woman.' Different audiences saw different Janes: one detached observer noted that she was witty and fascinating, yet '. . . sharp, brilliant, often extreme and unreasonable in her prejudices, and inclined to be sarcastic', so influencing her husband that when they were in company she tended to prepare a subject for conversation, then leave her husband's more massive conversational powers to bring the discussion (or, increasingly, the monologue) to a climax—as the same observer phrased it, '. . . she made the balls, and he fired them'. This apart, they were reckoned excellent company in Edinburgh, a talking town, a social clique noted for 'brilliant disquisition, . . . sharp word-catchings, ingenious thrusting and parrying of dialectics, and all the quips and quibblets of bar pleading'. Carlyle flung himself with delight into this style, practising energetically with Jeffrey whose powers were considered to be of the front rank. Carlyle possessed, according to David Masson, '. . . the most perfect command of temper in meeting objections', and was 'the pleasantest and heartiest fellow in the world', and certainly he and Jeffrey were the closest of friends, as well as the most adroit of conversationalists. Small wonder that Dickens was later to write that he 'would go at all times farther to see Carlyle than any man alive', and that 'No one who knew Mrs Carlyle could replace her loss when she passed away'. In Edinburgh, their success was remarkable. They had found a circle, in which they were appreciated, and they loved their two years in the city. Carlyle was to write after leaving Edinburgh, 'Alas for the Wednesday nights. Alas and alackaday . . . .' These years in Edinburgh were truly happy for both Carlyles.

Why, then, did they not settle down to enjoy this brilliant and thrifty existence? The answer is simple, and it has already been adumbrated in the description of the collapse of the prosperity in the publishing trade in 1826. Carlyle simply could not afford to stay in a city, or even on its outskirts, in these early years of his marriage. Had his applications for academic posts made in these years been successful, he would have lived in Edinburgh gladly. But each one failed. While he had been in Dumfries he had had many advantages, such as cheap food from the family farm, and cheap clothes made for him by his mother and sister. There had been little entertaining, and expenses had been few, except for judicious book-purchasing. Marriage in itself changed this, for now Carlyle had two to support. Although his parents still sent presents of food, or else sold him fresh produce, they could not now support him in his social position as they had before. Clothes had to be professionally made, and modest entertaining was necessary. The rent of Comely Bank was little, merely £32 per year, yet even this was a heavy drain on Carlyle. He was supporting his brother John, then a student doctor, and this cost him at least £50 over the two years spent at Comely Bank. Living expenses are difficult to calculate, although indications exist that prices were on the decline at this period. One indication lies in the various pamphlets published on how to budget for family expenses, and these suggest that prices in the 1820s were certainly not rising in many sectors. In 1829, for instance, pamphlets in the John Rylands Library, Manchester suggest that maidservants should note prices charged in 1822, and halve them for an accurate picture of costs at the end of the decade, for '. . . many of the articles would probably not greatly exceed half the price here stated'. Economic histories agree unanimously on the difficulty of accurate generalisations on the cost of living at any period, but literary historians are bolder. David Alec Wilson, in his life of Carlyle, estimates that the Carlyles must have had £200 a year to live in Edinburgh, and based this figure on very detailed calculations which he heard David Masson perform: David Masson, curiously, states in his *Edinburgh Sketches and Memories* that the figure must have been '. . . necessarily not less than about £300'. While Carlyle was in Comely Bank he received some £150 for articles written, so he must have drawn heavily on his savings, and on the income from *German Romance*, to support his own family, and his brother, in these years. An Aberdeenshire working family of six in these years might live on 13 shillings a week, and did, according to the historian L. J. Saunders, but Francis Jeffrey moved more in Carlyle's social class, and when he daydreamed of a pleasant rural existence he pronounced himself willing to live on £300 a year, '. . . only it is rather too little, and I should like to have the means of moving about a little'. Sir Walter Scott calculated that in town £500, well managed, 'will maintain a large family with all the necessaries and decencies of life, and enable them to support a very creditable rank in society'. Both daydreams were equally remote from the Carlyles, who could not raise even £200 a year: inescapably, they had to leave the city, in which they were enjoying a literary life and pleasant society.

Jane's father, before he died, had bought the farm of Craigen-puttoch in Dumfriesshire from a relative. His intention was to have it as a country home, and on his death its life-rent passed to his widow, and its ownership to his daughter. This arrangement was confirmed after Jane married, for both she and her husband were scrupulously anxious to be correct in their dealings with Mrs Welsh, even if they found her a nerve-wracking house guest. When Edinburgh proved too expensive, the natural choice for the Carlyles was to move to their property in Dumfriesshire. There was land, and there was a substantial house. A farm-house was built, and Carlyle's brother Alexander moved in to be farmer of Craigenputtoch, and tenant to Mrs Welsh: the large house adjoining was prepared to accept Thomas and Jane and, in May 1828, they left Modern Athens with feelings of genuine regret. 'I do not relish the name of your Country habitation,' wrote a friend from London. 'I have a strong notion that the Scottish people give not names in vain—and I fear there is something desolate in that name.' Carlyle confessed to 'doubts and misgivings', and Jane more positively wrote that 'Country air and country fare would hardly counterbalance country dulness for me. A little exciting talk is many times, for a person of my temperament, more advantageous to bodily health than either judicious physicking or nutritious diet or good air.' Yet finance was an irresistible argument, and with Whitsun of 1828 the Carlyles moved their belongings to Dumfriesshire, pausing to spend two nights with Jeffrey in his brand-new town house, splendid in the sandstone crescent of Moray Place. The gesture of offering this hospitality was a kind one, while chaos was cleared in Craigenputtoch, but it must merely have emphasised the city pleasures which they were leaving. The summer season was approaching, and the Carlyles were leaving for seclusion. In the sourness of old age and bereavement Carlyle might describe Edinburgh as '. . . a gloomy intricate abode to me; and, in retrospect, . . . nothing of pleasant but *Her*', but Jane's impetuous 'Dear Edinburgh! I was very happy there, and shall always love it . . .' comes closer to the truth. The two years in Modern Athens gave them a wonderful start in married life, social poise and experience, employment for Carlyle among the reviews, and a wide circle of friends; the latter was to stand them in good stead in the lonely years that lay ahead on the moors of Dumfriesshire.

CRAIGENPUTTOCH

DUMFRIES STANDS on the River Nith, a busy market town and regional centre, a financial and management centre now, as in Carlyle's time, for an excellent and prosperous agricultural region. The traveller who leaves the town and crosses the river finds himself in the twin city across the water, Maxwelltown; taking the Kilmarnock Road, he rapidly leaves all trace of habitation, and begins to mount towards the uplands which separate the South-West from the populous Lowlands of Scotland.

The main road is sparsely marked by small villages, but off the main road there is little settlement. The region is a historic one, and has a long history of ecclesiastical and civil settlement; to-day the spread of modern farming efficiency has produced scanty population, and long desolate, empty roads. None of these is longer or more desolate than the track which climbs from the Kilmarnock Road to Dunscore, and from Dunscore to Glenesslin; narrowing continually, the road is little more than a track at the head of the Glen, where a rough path strikes off it to a tree-shaded farm-house under a long, iron-grey ridge of hill. The hill is Craigenputtoch Hill, where Carlyle and Emerson walked and talked, and helped to change the course of literary history; the farm is Craigenputtoch.

All is not desolation, although the spot can be supremely silent and lonely. In winter the snows are heavy, and in spring the rains are often endless, accompanied by violent thunder. Yet in fine weather the stillness, the clarity of the air, the perfect freedom from industrial or urban pollution, above all the total silence have an impressive beauty. In Craigenputtoch it is possible to feel totally alone; only the trees, the hills, the sheep and cattle are visible, and human contact almost unimaginable.

Biographers, since Froude, have painted a black picture of life on these hilly moors. Like so much that is written about the Carlyles, it is true, but it needs qualification. Life was lonely, unendurably lonely and dull for a couple who had spent their first two years of married life in Comely Bank. For company they had Carlyle's brother Alexander, who was a poor conversationalist, and who in due course was married, and had his own life to lead; otherwise they had to go down the valley to visit neighbouring farmers (who seem all to have been dull), or to Dunscore village to call on the minister, Bryden. Bryden was later to sever the friendship, when he saw that neither Carlyle was an orthodox church-going Christian, and this emphasised the loneliness. Occasionally there would be relief; a shooting party would come, and use the moors; a local farmer or businessman would call; in one case a mentally ill young man was lodged in a nearby farm, and came to Carlyle for lessons. Otherwise, Thomas and Jane had each other, and the company of their books and letters.

When they could, they asked people to stay, although visitors (like some of the uninvited company) could be trying. The Jeffreys were welcome guests, who accommodated themselves to country life well, and expected little of urbane entertainment. Various minor Edinburgh friends came to see them, and in 1833 came Emerson, unannounced but exciting to a writer who thought himself little read, if not ignored, in the outside world. Carlyle thrived on visits; he tolerated his mother-in-law, he welcomed his own family, he repeatedly wrote to Edinburgh and London begging other people to come. In plain fact, the Carlyles needed companionship, and however devoted to each other they were, they could not satisfy the desire for social conversation. Jane wryly noted in her letters how she came increasingly to help her husband by providing a mute audience for his monologues. Certainly when they visited cities, whether London or Edinburgh, both Carlyle and his friends noted the change in his conversational style, from 'fencing' to violent monologue, not expecting the riposte, and willing to trample it down and push on by sheer force and volume. Jane, too, becomes more bitter in many of her Craigenputtoch letters; her initial notes to Edinburgh friends are gay and witty, much concerned with keeping up her domestic supplies of tea and coffee. Later, her letters are catalogues of complaints, or scribbled notes indicating she had not the will, or the health, to do more. Although her husband's health improved in the clean air, quiet and good food of Craigenputtoch, Jane became prone to colds and to repetitions of her earlier complaint of violent headaches: loneliness and ennui did little to help. She learned some Spanish and improved her German, with Thomas's help; she read, but she wrote little, and in boredom sometimes dabbled at housework, such as scrubbing floors and baking bread, when winter weather had kept the servant away.

Thomas had by now become fixed in his working methods. He began his working day early, and once fixed to his task grimly wrote it through. He set himself a daily quota, and was miserable until he had filled it, although like most writers he had days when he found it impossible to get under way, or when what he wrote pleased him so little that he destroyed it all. He was hypercritical of his own writing, and surrendered it to the press with reluctance. In proof-reading he was fussy and over-punctilious, changing frequently, to the anguish of the compositors, and to the alarm of publishers. Above all, he could not tolerate interruption to his thought. Later, in Chelsea, this was to be a major source of irritation for him, as London spread and city noises proliferated. In Craigenputtoch he did not suffer from his desire to be alone, although Jane did. The best help she could give him, while he was writing, was to be elsewhere, or silent. His relaxation from writing was talking (when she dutifully listened) or solitary walking: these pursuits offered little satisfaction or relief to someone as bored and as frustrated in her sociability as Jane.

Tensions thus were inevitable in Craigenputtoch, particularly in winter, when the relief of walking, or expecting visitors, was impossible. Tension was made worse through lack of money, for away from the city it became even more difficult to find employment in the reviews. Jeffrey was to go to London in 1831, and to become Lord Advocate in the first Reformed Parliament, and although he kindly did his best for Carlyle in London, his patronage in Edinburgh was missed. Carlyle's increasingly radical ideas, and his reluctance to submit his material to editorial change, made him less and less acceptable to many editors, although *Fraser's Magazine* gave him a platform, however inadequate, for his essays.

The essays are, along with *Sartor Resartus*, the great fruit of this period. The loneliness and frustrations of the six years on the moors led to an intense concentration, a steady tension of the mind which produced first a stream of shorter pieces in which ideas were formulated and examined, and then the masterpiece in which many of the ideas were linked in a 'clothes-philosophy'— for the world is all appearances, like our clothes: the truth lies underneath. In later years Carlyle was to write his major historical works of scholarship involving interruption, research visits to battlefields and major libraries, but here in Craigenputtoch he was to settle to his work, and without much interruption produce essays which reveal his thinking on important topics, social and religious and literary, rather than the fruits of his researches. Admittedly the absence of a major library was a great drawback, and the frustrations of the weekly post, and the difficulty of cajoling city friends to trust their books to this post, were considerable. Late in this period a local landowner heard of Carlyle's difficulties and gave him the keys to the substantial private library in the country house of Bargjarg in Dunscore parish. Carlyle went rejoicing, and left with boxes of books for consultation. Otherwise he was thrown back on the resources of his own private library, and this often hindered his work.

In circumstances like these, with a monotonous daily task and every unexpected interruption a pleasure, holidays and excursions become a major topic of conversation. The roads in winter were barely passable (even to-day this is true); when they were, it was a regular treat to celebrate the finishing of some essay, or piece of commissioned writing, by a visit. This might be to Templand, where Mrs Welsh lived, a comfortable day's drive away. Alternatively, they might visit the Carlyle family, who now occupied a number of farms in Dumfriesshire, as members of the family married and formed outposts of their own. These family excursions were a welcome break from monotony.

Inevitably, they derived more pleasure from excursions further afield. Edinburgh was the obvious choice, and they went to the city in the autumn of 1829 for a very happy reunion with old friends, particularly with the Jeffreys in Craigcrook.

The momentous excursions took place over two winters. In 1831-1832, they visited London, and in early 1833 they spent four months in Edinburgh. These were crucial holidays, because they were to dictate the Carlyles' choice of a residence when in 1834 they decided to leave Craigenputtoch, at whatever cost, and again live in a populous district.

The London trip was not Carlyle's first (he had enjoyed his holiday there, with Irving, in 1824), but it was Jane's first visit to the capital. They spent it in reading, meeting people, and talking. In Craigenputtoch a recurrent complaint had been fitful progress, '. . . waiting for Books, beginning again and again with fierce energy, and again & again obliged to make a dead halt'. There was no halt in London, merely the 'fierce energy', which manifested itself in an almost alarming desire to make friends, disciples, converts, men with whom to share the pent-up energy of his thoughts in the moorlands of Craigenputtoch.

His thoughts there had been increasingly turned towards the social state of the country: Carlyle's own personal plight was sometimes forgotten in this. 'Rain! Rain! Rain! The crops all lying tattered, scattered, and unripe; the winter's bread still under the soaking clouds. God pity the poor!' In this mood, described by his wife as 'Craigenputtoch gloom and acerbity', he saw less and less hope for the country, as it approached the convulsion of the Reform movement of the early 1830s. As his conviction and his anger grew, so did his nervous restlessness, which evidenced itself in more than the harsh monologues with which he astonished young Londoners who met him. 'I can be a guest, beyond two days or so, with no mortal known to me, without mutual grief,' wrote Carlyle, and this was proved uncomfortably true time and again. He had seen some evidence of the change working in him in 1829, as Jeffrey's guest at Craigcrook. Jeffrey was ill with over-work, and had not had his old sparkle in 'fencing' verbally, but Carlyle in a moment of clear self-analysis saw the deeper

cause. The verbal fencing '. . . could decide nothing for either of
us, except our radical incompatibility in respect of World-
Theory, and the incurable divergence of our opinions on the most
important matters'. Carlyle was no longer open to persuasion: he
was sure, and his bitter certainty was reinforced by his solitary
walks and self-musings in Craigenputtoch. 'You are so dreadfully
in earnest!' upbraided Jeffrey wittily, but Carlyle took it as a
compliment. He said, only half-penitently, of this same occasion
that he '. . . had not then, nor, alas, have ever acquired in my
solitary and mostly silent [sic] existence, the art of gently saying
strong things, or of insinuating my dissent, instead of uttering it
right out, at the risk of offence or otherwise . . .' These were
'stormy sittings', as Mrs Jeffrey laughingly called them, but they
not only drove a wedge between Carlyle and one of his most
valuable friends, they also showed the change working in
Carlyle, which made him unwelcome in Edinburgh, yet welcome
in London.

In the autumn of 1831, when Carlyle reached London, there
was a buzz throughout the city of discussion, argument, disagree-
ment about reform. Various measures had passed, or were passing,
through Parliament, but it was too early yet to see whether the
movement for reform would be successful, and what form the
eventual changes might take. The political parties were in
embattled positions, but among individuals there was heated
discussion—and Carlyle threw himself into this with vigour. His
letters home indicate how much he enjoyed the experience, the
complete antithesis of the years he had spent alone in Craigenputtoch. Sometimes a letter will be begun and interrupted five or
six times, so great is the press of company. London he finds
'engrossed with political questions': Sir Walter Scott, in London
at the same time, noted in his journal that the town was 'in a foam
with politics'. The result was both good and bad for Carlyle: bad
in the sense that '. . . the whole English world, I find, has ceased
to read Books of late', and while Carlyle sardonically remarked to
the booksellers that this was 'the wisest thing the English world
could do', considering the books it had to read, it certainly
harmed his chances of finding a publisher. He was hoping for em-

ployment in reviews, for commissions to write, above all for a publisher for a manuscript he had in his pocket, tentatively entitled *Sartor Resartus*. In the sense that Carlyle was hoping for a commercial return for the risk of a visit to London, he had little chance.

The good result, however, was the undoubted stimulus to his political thought, a stimulus which could be argued to have continued for the rest of his life.

'Meanwhile I am not without my comforts: one of the greatest of which is to have found various well-disposed men, most of them young men, who even feel a sort of scholarship towards me. My poor performances in the writing way are better known here than I expected: clearly enough also there *is* want of instruction and light in this mirk midnight of human affairs, such want as probably for eighteen hundred years there has not been: if *I* have any light to give, then let me give it . . .'

The discipleship was something, we notice, directly involved with *himself*, not with any preconceived political creed. Just as Carlyle had won his way to relief from religious doubt through a consistent loyalty to himself, as an individual, so he based his political thinking on his own convictions, rather than on adherence to political loyalties new or old. Whigs he could not support, although he plainly thought that the political system was ripe for the sort of reform which the Whigs supported. 'Whiggism, I believe, is all but forever *done*. Away with Dilettantism and Machiavellism, tho' we should get Atheism and Sansculottism in their room! The latter are at least substantial things, and do not build on a continued *wilful* falsehood.' A major change is involved here: the old Carlyle, closer to his Ecclefechan childhood, could never have written the last two sentences. Atheism was something so unthinkable as never to be preferred to political decay. Admittedly, the sentence is probably pitched strongly for rhetorical effect, yet it shows new trends of thought in Carlyle's mind. The necessity for change is in the foreground, the sweeping away of the old, the inevitability of struggle and suffering before the new can be found to replace the old. His description of the old effete forms as '*wilful* falsehood' indicates a conception of them not as generalised activities, indulged in by society at large, but as the acts of reasoning individuals, who know what they do to be wrong, but who will not make the necessary change. This change, in all London letters, is unmistakably at the forefront of Carlyle's mind. The Great Wen is ripe for change, as is society in its complex forms revealed in London: Carlyle, as an individual, is aware of the change in himself, and eager to persuade others to embark on the same process. When he had earlier appeared in the *Edinburgh Review*, in 'Characteristics', with an early embodiment of this conviction, Jeffrey's successor had described the piece as 'inscrutable'. Carlyle's opinion to his brother John was that it was '... too *scrutable*; for it indicates decisively enough that society (in my view) is utterly condemned to destruction, and even now beginning its long travail-throes of Newbirth'. With the powerful imagery which dominates *Sartor Resartus*, of fiery death and rebirth, imagery which was to pattern *The French Revolution*, Carlyle clearly makes his *credo*.

Older friends were still glad to see him, though in this new mood he was less willing to receive them. Edward Irving, for instance, now past his peak of popularity, was still at the heart of contention with a large congregation which had followed him into exile from his original charge. Irving's popularity as an orator had always filled his church, and he tended to exploit his large audience for quasi-theatrical effect. He was a tall, handsome man and a powerful speaker, and nerves tended to break with the strain of long sermons. Almost hysterical outbursts by women in the course of his sermons he interpreted as 'The Gift of Tongues', a divine manifestation on earth, and instead of slackening the tension of his services, and shortening the sermons, he did his best to encourage these outbursts, in the sincere belief that they were authentic messages from Heaven. A large part of the congregation left, and the Church authorities expressed grave displeasure, which was in its turn heightened by certain heretical beliefs Irving held about the human fallibility of Christ during the Incarnation on Earth. The result was that Irving formed a separate Church (which gave birth to the present-day Catholic Apostolic Church), and continued to be famous. Carlyle could not be reconciled to the 'tongues':

'Edward Irving I meet with very often. He is kinder, stiller than usual; a very good man, and not at all what I can name an unwide one, tho' surely but ill-informed, with such a crowd of crackbrained zealots and "silly women" about him, shrieking out at his prayer-meetings, and *clavering* downright jargon, which they name Gift of the Holy Ghost, and Speaking with Tongues!'

Not only was there the hostility to the manifestations which marred Irving's preaching, but there was the divergence which had been noted in Kirkcaldy, and which now came between both men in a more final way. Irving was first and foremost a minister of the Church, and when he spoke about contemporary conditions, as he often did, he saw things from the point of view of the Church. In Glasgow, as in London, he had seen at close quarters the industrial revolution's effects, the destitution and fearful living conditions endured by the urban poor. He had as much cause as Carlyle, if not more, to call for a social reconstruction which would sweep away this human suffering. Yet he saw things in a theocentric way, which was bound to separate him from Carlyle.

'What matter though "the abstract principles of justice" be better understood, as they are always prosing to you? What matter though "the principles of free trade" are the more acted upon? What matter though "the rights of the people" be more clearly defined, and more rightly acknowledged? What matter though intelligence of any kind be more widely diffused, inasmuch as God's authority is not in it at all . . . ?'

The voice of James Carlyle is heard in this passage, a voice which abrogates 'progress', in a simple-minded conception, in favour of a consistency to a world-view which completely submits itself to the authority of God. Edward Irving was to accept ruin, and expulsion from the ministry of the Church of Scotland, for the sake of this belief; he accepted that the 'Gift of Tongues', which disrupted his services, was a manifestation of the Will of God, and so not to be resisted. Yet the finality of the break between Irving and Carlyle in these early 1830s, underlined sharply at the end of the *Reminiscences* of Edward Irving, shows what a distance separated the two men. Indeed, as the years were to show, Carlyle was to adopt an attitude to society, to 'progress' and to the 'rights of the people' which astonishingly resembled the opinions expressed by Irving in the paragraph quoted above. Yet the fundamental validity of the individual, and his interpretation of what constituted 'God's Will', which emerged clearly from the struggles of *Sartor*, stood in the way of Carlyle's accepting Irving and his message. Irving stood for the earthly manifestation of God's will, it is true, but the selfhood is abrogated in the face of a divine presence and omnipotence: this Carlyle could never accept. Also to accept Irving's view would have involved Carlyle in agreeing with Irving's interpretation of the role of the Church, and the function of the 'tongues', which Carlyle (a hard-headed realist, with little faith in divine manifestation) could in no way do. Carlyle was to preach a similar message, hardly surprisingly for one so close to Irving in his birth and education. Yet he was to arrive at it in a different way, and Irving's way was decisively rejected in this 1831-32 London visit.

The two men met, they were quiet and kind to each other; indeed Carlyle had a long talk with Irving, trying earnestly to dissuade him from what Carlyle took to be theological error. The situation was curiously reversed, for some ten years before Irving had been father confessor to Carlyle's theological difficulties, as admitted by Carlyle in the *Reminiscences*. Irving, like Carlyle, was too strongly involved in his principles to be moved, and he preferred to lose Carlyle's friendship. And so the two men parted. From this time the Carlyles 'heard of Irving and his catastrophes only from a distance'. Yet in his memorial essay, *Death of the Rev. Edward Irving*, Carlyle publicly paid the most eloquent of tributes to his wayward countryman. He had been the first to give him true companionship, he had sustained and helped him when he most needed comfort and support. For this Carlyle was to be grateful all his life.

In fact Carlyle needed less and less help. As he found himself widely listened to, and to some extent lionised, in London, his insecurities and doubts fell away, to be replaced by a consciousness of the freshness and vitality of his message to a generation very consciously on the brink of change. The tone of his remarks on Francis Jeffrey, also in London at the time, show how he was becoming more self-reliant, less inclined to have much time for outside assistance. He was 'kindly received' in the Jeffrey home, but found Jeffrey (now Lord Advocate) 'very ill', with 'greyish face', very concerned with the cholera threat which was then hanging over the whole country. Despite their 'hurried assiduous talk', there was less in common between the two. 'In the afternoon, Jeffrey, as he is often wont, called in on us: very lively, quick and—light.' In fact Jeffrey's older remark to Carlyle, 'you are so dreadfully in earnest!' may throw some light on the divergence between the two men. Jeffrey was not willing to be so terribly in earnest about the state of society, for he had had his public quarrels over the reform agitation, and now was fully engaged not in discussing the rebirth of a new society, but in helping administer it as a high government official. A sentence in one of Carlyle's diaries shows how this changed the relationship between Jeffrey and himself. 'It sometimes rather surprises me that his Lordship does not think it would be kind to show me to the faces of those [London] people: Something discourages or hinders him; what it is I know not, and indeed care not . . . .' Perhaps he did not consciously care, but this passage (intended for the privacy of his diary) shows that he had noticed it. His years of isolation and self-examination in Craigenputtoch had not only sapped his powers of verbal fencing (an art in which Jeffrey still excelled), they had made him more extreme in his opinions, and therefore less gladly received among the political figures among whom Jeffrey moved. To the diary also was confided the remark that 'Whiggism is, I believe, all but for-ever *done*', and this would not have made him a welcome guest in Jeffrey's Whig circles. Irving, we know indirectly from a letter written by Carlyle's brother John, approved of Carlyle's radical views, but Jeffrey could not wholeheartedly. Opinion in the press in the years following successful reform is specifically pitched against too severe, too early reform: this is what Carlyle must have been seeming to advocate. '*La classe la plus pauvre*', Carlyle wrote in his diary, 'is evidently in the way of rising from its present abasement', and clearly he awaited the rise with keen anticipation, which would not have been shared by the established classes of his day. He read the new radical *Examiner* eagerly, and shared it with his family in Dumfriesshire. He made friends where he could, including Lockhart and Hogg, now met for the first time. He knew a formidable circle, Galt, Lardner, Detrosier, Mill, Hunt, Lamb, Maginn, Procter, Crabb Robinson, the Bullers—his pleasure in good society was all the more intense for the shortage he had known in Craigenputtoch. Yet London did not captivate him entirely.

'On the whole', he wrote to his brother John, 'this London is the most *twilight* intellectual city you could meet with: a meaner more utterly despicable view of man and his interests than stands pictured even in the better heads you could nowhere fall in with.' The city, too, although it excited him by its size and business at the first contact, began to appal him. London he described as 'a true all-ruining anarchy . . . It is a huge Aggregate of little systems, each of which is again a small Anarchy, the members of which do not *work* together but scramble against each other.' Yet he admitted he did not regret his visit, for '. . . [I] already feel my mind much stimulated, and as it were filled with new matter to elaborate. It will be very useful for me to come back from time to time: tho' I think I have hardly found a single man that has give[n] me a new idea.'

The exaggeration of the last sentence can be discounted: the excitement in this description shows he was fascinated by the intellectual stir of the city. Yet several other factors intervened to send them home. James Carlyle died in far-off Scotsbrig, the family farm in Dumfriesshire, and Carlyle (although he wrote the *Reminiscences* of his father as a distant act of piety) deeply regretted his distance from his mother, and the rest of his family, at this time. Cholera was rife, too, and the Carlyles both guessed they would escape it better in the countryside than in the city, which in any case presented them with many of the problems they had known in Dumfriesshire. 'We are both . . . considerably hurt in health, and longing to be home; which we expect soon. The climate of this place is among the most detestable on Earth: otherwise, the place has been wholly agreeable to us.' London was a place to be enjoyed for a change, and a pleasant one, but Craigen-puttoch was the permanent home. And yet the contrast was frightful: to return to Craigenputtoch after a holiday elsewhere was to be most conscious of all of isolation. 'Well do I remember our return to Craigenputtoch, after nightfall amid the clammy yellow leaves, and desolate rains, with the clink of Alick's *stithy* alone audible of human . . .'

The other major excursion from Craigenputtoch was to Edinburgh, in the spring of 1833. Winters were intolerable, and the Carlyles, cut off and miserable high in their glen, felt early in 1833 that they required city life again. They had been in regular correspondence with friends in the capital, and had of course enjoyed their return to Edinburgh in 1829, so it was with pleasure that they took lodgings in the New Town, not far from Comely Bank, and settled in. The visit was not a success, and this lack of success (and its causes) was crucial in Carlyle's important choice between London and Edinburgh as his eventual home.

Perhaps it is Froude, Carlyle's official biographer, who is responsible for the impression that Carlyle was cold-shouldered by Edinburgh on this visit. 'London treated him, in 1831, as a person of importance', writes Froude, 'when he spent the winter following [that is, the Spring of 1833] in Edinburgh he was coldly received there—received with a dislike which was only not contempt because it was qualified with fear.' This is quite extraordinarily wide of the mark as criticism.

The Carlyles spent a very agreeable season in Edinburgh, in respectable lodgings, living a respectable middle-class existence punctuated by much visiting, and meeting of friends. They knew many people: Carlyle remarked in a letter to Mill how village-like was the impression given by Edinburgh, where one met so many familiar faces on the streets. Hamilton the philosopher, McRie the biographer of Knox, John Wilson and many others met him and treated him kindly: the coldness came from Carlyle himself. Thomas Murray, his close student friend, he described as 'withered up into a poor sapless creature': John Wilson he met, but 'whether we meet a second time or not is of little or no moment'. McRie is 'dull, heavy, but intelligent and honest':

another friend is liked because 'there are no bounds to his regard for me', yet 'otherwise he is a wearisome man'. Carlyle veered away from his old friends. His new London acquaintance, their memory still fresh, seemed more vital and more exciting. To John Stuart Mill he complained by letter of 'much that is spiritually *Kleinstädtisch*' in Edinburgh, adding that '. . . no John Mill will come in on the Wednesday evenings here; but a much fainter sort of spiritual worth must suffice'. The letters to Mill, in these years, become increasingly important. Mill was young, alert, in London, at the heart of the nation. 'On the whole I predict that in this country, as in France, the movement, political and other, will proceed from the Capital,' wrote Carlyle. To Mill, as to others, Carlyle admitted that he tried to use in Edinburgh the style of speaking and rhetoric which he had found effective in London— and that the experiment was no success. Edinburgh's political composition was too unexciting:

'No Benthamite, or Islamite, or other false Believer, exists here that I see: innumerable respectable Whigs, that know not the right hand from the left, and desire of all things to eat their pudding in peace; numerous distressed, partially distracted Conservatives (they too are *numerous* in the *washed* classes); a small forlorn hope of half-rabid Cobbett Radicals . . . this is our condition in respect of Politics, whereby you may judge of us in others'.

In this atmosphere, Carlyle was regarded as a dangerous fellow. Napier, editor of the *Edinburgh Review*, 'dislikes my Radicalism, worse than I do his Toryism'. Indeed on Edinburgh as a whole, 'My utterances fall like red-hot aërolithes [*sic*] or bursting bombs into the peaceful tea-garden of their existence, and they look upon me with astonishment, and an incipient shudder'. So when the professor of Rhetoric at Edinburgh University, an old friend of Carlyle's, invited him to visit, he turned out to be in Carlyle's description '. . . *settled* in every way into a *Dilettante* . . . dry, civil, and seems rather to feel *unheimlich* in my company'. When a close student friend, Robert Mitchell, asked him out to a family dinner, he '. . . astonished them, I fear, with my exposition of Belief and Radicalism, as compared with Opinion and Whiggism'. Wilson drew back from him: '. . . he cannot look at me, as I look at him, with *free* regard; but eyes me from behind veils, doubtful of some mischance from me, political or other'. The inference is clear: Carlyle alienated himself from a friendly Edinburgh society, by crude political rhetoric and what seems to have been ill-mannered attempts to shock. 'The talent of conversation, tho' I generally *talk* enough and to spare, has as it were quite forsaken me. In place of skilful adroit fencing and parrying, as were fit and usual, I appear like a wild monstrous bison among the people, and (especially if *bilious*) smash everything to pieces.' One last but interesting piece of indirect evidence may lie in a diary entry of 1834, in London, to the effect that he was '. . . surprised occasionally and grieved to find myself not only so disliked—suspected—but so known' and uncomfortably received 'in all Whig circles'. Whig circles in Edinburgh may well have closed their ranks against Carlyle's excesses, and the reputation thus gathered may have been transmitted to London.

The point, however, is surely that Carlyle chose to reject the familiar pleasures of Edinburgh society and 'circles', which had sustained his creative and social powers up to this time. The new attractions of a politically hyperconscious London outweighed the more cautious approach of Edinburgh; new friends seemed more glamorous than old—and it was true that by the 1830s many literary figures had left Edinburgh to settle in London, thus making the Southern city a much more pleasing alternative to an Edinburgh-bred writer.

One other point requires to be made. This concerns the equivalence which Carlyle makes in his letters between the level of political consciousness and activity in London, as compared with Edinburgh, at this time. In London, in the winter of 1831-1832, Reform was a live issue, Bills of Parliament being passed and vital decisions being taken. Publishing was affected—Carlyle found it quite impossible to find anyone willing to take the risk of publishing *Sartor Resartus* in these troubled months—and politics were quite the dominant topic. In early 1833, on the other hand, Reform was a *fait accompli* both in London and in Edinburgh, after the passage of the legislation which effected Reform in Scotland in 1832. Perhaps because of the very violence of the feeling which had been aroused, the voters and citizens generally were glad to let political agitation drop, and life resume its even tenour. Carlyle spent this period in Craigenputtoch, and when he returned to city life it was to Edinburgh, to continue a debate with full vigour, when other people had been glad to let the subject drop. To accuse them of political apathy, of small-town indifference to world politics, which is what Carlyle did in Edinburgh, is grossly unfair. Indifference is hardly an apt term to use of the political climate of Edinburgh during the Reform period, as any reader of Henry Cockburn's *Journal* will testify. When the Scottish Reform Bill became law on 17 July 1832 the city was convulsed: 'The bitterness of the hostility felt at that time by the young men of the two opposite political creeds cannot easily be understood by those in the same stage of life at the present day.' The words are John Hill Burton's, written a whole generation later. 'We used to make faces at each other as we passed; and if a few words were exchanged, they were hostile and threatening.' The reviews carried savage articles on either side, and hostile demonstrations followed the Town Council's rejection of Francis Jeffrey (who had a petition with 17,000 signatures to back him up) as the town's Member of Parliament, in favour of one Dundas, 'a respectable young man and a keen anti-Reformer'. The situation was an outrageous one, and the Town Council was itself shortly reformed, and Jeffrey made Member of Parliament. Yet riots followed the rejection, riots which made elderly citizens write in their diaries that 'Such conduct is giving up every thing to the mob'. Perhaps it was, but the mobs which celebrated the success of the Reform agitation amounted to 55,000 in Edinburgh alone, and were distinguished by peaceful demonstrations of 'orderly joy', records Cockburn.

In short, the Carlyles left Edinburgh restless and dissatisfied, but very largely because they had grown away from the friends and the interests which had made Edinburgh so pleasant to them less than a decade earlier. Solitude, more radical political convictions, and a greater knowledge of the world had made them both very different people from what they had been in 1826. They still craved companionship and stimulus, but their eyes turned

South. Another winter of loneliness in Craigenputtoch was the last straw: in the spring of 1834 they resolved to take the risk of settling again in a city, and with little hesitation chose London. Jane wittily spoke of it as burning their boats, and with their slender savings, and poor prospects of earning, this was no joke. Yet as Carlyle pointed out in family letters, even cheapness had ceased to be an advantage in Craigenputtoch, for he was never so poor, as then.

And so in the spring of 1834 Carlyle set off for London to search for a home. In May he was in the city, and in June he was followed by Jane, who confirmed his choice of a quietish house in Chelsea, which like Comely Bank offered proximity both to city and to country, ease of access to the bustle of the centre, but a measure of cleanliness and quiet. In many ways the move of 1834 was like the move of 1826, a fresh start. But this was to be the last such move. The Sage of Ecclefechan was preparing to become the Sage of Chelsea.

LONDON

CARLYLE'S LIFE in London began with much of the sense of confusion which was to characterise it. He left his Craigenputtoch home precipitately in May, in order to be in London for Whitsunday, 1834, when houses would change hands. Expecting the English house market to follow Scottish practice, he was eager to be in the city for the great exchange of leases on that day. In this he was disappointed; the custom in London was to change houses at any convenient time, and so his hurry in leaving Scotland had been to a great extent unnecessary.

One of the results of this haste had been to leave Jane behind to settle their affairs in Scotland, and (more difficult) to pack some of their scanty belongings, and sell the rest to friends and neighbours in Dumfriesshire. The letters to and from London were long and detailed: he wrote home of footsore days spent inspecting houses in Kensington, Hampstead, Chelsea and other districts which might fulfil the two main conditions—quietness, to which he had grown accustomed (almost addicted) in Craigenputtoch, and cheapness, for the finances of this early period in London were to be very meagre indeed. Carlyle was too poor, and too inexperienced, to take short-cuts in his inspection of houses. He travelled by foot, and he visited each house repeatedly, with friends, without them, now favouring the cheapest, now the smallest, now the most seemingly convenient. His own letters most eloquently convey the impressions of Chelsea which made it his final choice.

'As to Houses, I continue wandering like the Shoemaker of Jerusalem, and realise for a day of wearied bones, wonderfully little. This place is among the worst for me in point of position; but so comfortable otherwise I will not dream of changing it.'

Here he is referring to his London lodgings off Gray's Inn Road, where he had been hospitably received on several occasions, and where he had spent, with Jane, a happy holiday over the winter of 1832-1833. 'Yesterday', he continues, 'I examined all the East side of the Regent's Park, with Park Village, Camden Town &c, and came home sniftering and blubbering (with a cold I had, which tonight is nearly gone), as wearied as Hercules after his labours. I found nothing, or next to nothing. One smart little Cottage only, close by the Park itself, very compact, tidy, well-situated; but so small, so inconceivably small! Rent 45 guineas. A Garden which in my spleen I likened to something between a bedquilt and a pancake: unjustly; for it was bigger than either. In the course of my travel, however, I met with adventurekins: saw a pitched battle a-fighting; dined (for 7^d and had 2^d more for drink) in a chophouse; talked a long time, and rested, in Regent Street with Fraser, &c &c. On the previous day (Monday) I went down to Brompton a second time, and made a most minute re-inspection of the cottage. I found myself mistaken in several things, particularly the size and the pavilion-roof; but on the whole, I still consider it nearly the likeliest thing we can expect to get; tho' that same day as you shall hear there started up a kind of rival to it in Chelsea. I also waited on the Proprietress, a very decent woman, of prepossessing physiognomy (as I saw her in the dusk, in a Court of the Strand); a Wine-Merchant's Widow, who built the House himself, and resided in it for years, as she till these very weeks did after him. Both the front rooms are smaller than ours, the big Bed may stand in the back-room (Library) but will have little height to spare; the 4 upper rooms 8f 6 inches high; the dressing-room, alas, is but a box to ours; on the other hand the stairhead press is what you wanted ours to be, a kind of closet with shelves. There is a pump in the kitchen (with clear hard water, which I tasted); a *tank* (worked by another handle of the same pump) under the kitchen for rain-water which "never fails". There are Larders cellars &c adjoining; and you have access to the kitchen by a back-door also, or rather side-door (for coals &c; rather a rarer convenience than I expected): the whole house has an air of tightness, cleanliness, modesty and sufficiency, much according to our humour. As built for the owner's use I fancy it may be the *best*-built house in Brompton, and have most of a *cosy* character. The back-garden has gooseberries and apple-trees; a space is *flagged* between the house and it; a door issues direct upon this from the lobby (if you should wish to avoid the kitchen in going out); a green painted nick-nacky kind of porch (with mat and two *seats* in it) defends this: the front garden is in two section*lets* divided by railing and a flagged passage; looks really, or might very easily look, modest and snug. A high wall, as I said surrounds us all; the gables of the House are *part* of this wall. Now do you understand it? (There are Bells, in both stories, *only* in the front rooms).—Finally Brompton boasts of being a "genteel neighbourhood", but except that it would look better on a Card, I see no symptoms of superior gentility: there is a large Public House at small distance, yet invisible from the House; Baker, Butcher and all Etceteras are close enough at hand: the ground generally is laid out in nurseries, and looks tolerable enough, in good wholesome order, nowise affected neat. You are a good half mile from Mrs A. a little nearer Mill, about the same from Hunt: the Cunninghams are also within reach; but hardly on any of our routes. To Mrs A. you go thro' Kensington Gardens.

'After surveying all this on Monday I went down to Chelsea; found Hunt, avoided all Huntesses and Huntlets, indeed never asked after them, but smoked a pipe with Hunt, and then went out again for Houses,—tho' with comparatively little care about them. Not a gunshot from Hunt's I came upon another house, greatly the best in quality and quantity I had yet seen. I went down again today (by a new route from Buller's and Westminster bridge: Millbank, Vauxhall, and confused causeways of shot rubbish, a dusty, sultry, squalid, detestable road, but not *ours* in general), and took the minutest survey. It is notable how at every new visit, your opinion gets a little hitch the *contrary* way from its former tendency; imagination has outgone the reality. I nevertheless still feel a great liking for this excellent old House, and it almost balances the Brompton one. Chelsea is unfashionable; it was once the resort of the Court and great, however; hence numerous old houses in it, at once cheap and excellent.—But behold the end of my sheet; the clocks all striking eleven, and Eliza coming up with a gruel for me!—Good night my dearest own Jeannie! Sleep well, and dream of me. God be with all of you!

'*Thursday morning.—Sey mir gegrüsst, mein Herzchen!* Hast thou slept, and breakfasted; art strong for the toils before thee? O that I were there to take thee on my knee, in my arms, and rest thee one five minutes;—or even "to be scolded" a little! It would "do me *so* much good". But it will not be long: by Heaven's blessing, my little Dame will be here in few days; and Heaven already knows how precious she is to me; that I would not think of exchanging her with the Best in London,—not even with "the celebrated Mrs Jamieson"! *Himmel und Erde!* In fact, Goody, it seems to me I have been especially lucky in marriage, and wedded simply the best Wife of this age (considering all things), which is a great comfort to me.

'I proceed with a description of the Chelsea House. It is within a gunshot of Hunt's; but tho' tinkerish-nomadic, I find the Hunts are not intrusive; the sick old woman would perhaps of her own accord steer clear of us. The street makes a right-angle with Hunt's, and runs down upon the River, which I suppose you might see, by stretching out your neck from our front windows, at a distance of 50 yards on the left. We are called "Cheyne Row" proper (pronounced, *Chainie Row*), and are a "genteel neighbour-hood", two old Ladies on the one side, unknown character on the other but with "pianos" as Hunt said. The street is flag-pathed, sunk-storied, iron-railed, all old-fashioned and tightly done up; looks out on a rank of sturdy old *pollarded* (that is *beheaded*) Lime-trees, standing there like giants in *tawtie* wigs (for the new boughs are still young) beyond this a high brick-wall, on the inside of which, from our upper stories, appear a garden surrounded with rather dim houses and questionable miscellanea, among other things, clothes drying. Backwards, a Garden (the size of our back one at Comely Bank) with trees &c, in bad culture; beyond this green hayfields and tree-avenues (once a Bishop's pleasure-grounds) an unpicturesque, yet rather cheerful outlook. The House itself is eminent, antique; wainscotted to the very ceiling, and has been all new-painted and repaired; broadish stair, with massive balustrade (in the old style) corniced and as thick as one's thigh; floors firm as a rock, wood of them here and there worm-eaten, yet capable of cleanness, and still with thrice the strength of a modern floor. And then as to room, Goody! There is room for a Mrs Dr Maxwell. Three stories besides the sunk story; in every one of them *three* apartments in depth (something like 40 feet in all; for it was 13 of my steps!): Thus there is a front dining-room (marble chimneypiece &c); then a back dining-room (or breakfast-room) a little narrower (by reason of the kitchen stair); then out from this, and narrower still (to allow a back-window, you consider), a china-room, or pantry, or I know not what, all shelved, and fit to hold crockery for the whole street. Such is the ground-area, which of course continues to the top, and furnishes *every* Bedroom with a dressing room, or even with a *second* bedroom. Red Bed will stand behind the drawing room; might have the shower-bath beyond it: the height of this story is 10 feet; of the ground floor 9 but some inches; of the topmost floor 8 feet 6; of the kitchen (where is a Pump and room forever) about the same. Neither this nor the Brompton house have a kitchen-*range* (that is, Grate like the Miles's), but only a grate with move-able niggards &c. In Chelsea is, or lies ready for being, a kitchen-jack; from the boiler-house the boiler ("*Coppa*") is taken out, but "would be replaced". No back-door (communicating with the street); bells in disorder but would be rectified; new locks, some of which threatened to act *a la Puttoch*, but seemed very oilless. On the whole a most massive, roomy, sufficient old house; with places, for example, to hang say three dozen hats or cloaks on; and as many crevices, and queer old presses and shelved closets (all tight and new painted in their way) as would gratify the most covetous Goody. Rent £35! I confess I am strongly tempted; yet again incline rather towards the Brompton place (for what *use* have we for so much room?), and so go wavering between the two. Chelsea is a singular, heterogeneous kind of spot; very dirty and confused in some places, quite beautiful in others; abounding with antiquities and the traces of great men: Sir T. More, Steele, Smollett, &c &c. Our Row (which for the last three doors or so is a *street*, and none of the noblest) runs out upon a beautiful

"Parade" (perhaps they call it) running along the shore of the River: shops &c, a broad highway, with huge shady trees; boats lying moored, and a smell of shipping and tar; Battersea Bridge (of wood) a few yards off; the broad River, with white-trowsered, white-shirted Cockneys dashing by like arrows in their long Canoes of Boats; beyond, the green beautiful knolls of Surr[e]y with their villages: on the whole a most artificial, green-painted, yet lively, fresh, almost opera-looking business, such as you can fancy. We are not a mile from the Cunninghams, above a mile from all the rest; and, alas, the Cunninghams I dread are hardly worth being near. I found them as I came up the first time from Chelsea; had a loud guffawing reception, was more struck than ever with the Wife's *unerfreuliches Wesen*. Allan himself is a good fellow on the whole. They said tea would be ready before long; but, alas, I had to walk farther on some mile and half to seek a chop for *dinner*.—Finally, Chelsea abounds more than any place in *Omnibii* (Bayswater least), and they take you to Coventry-street (within a mile of this) for sixpence. Revolve all this in thy fancy and judgement, my child; and see what thou canst make of it. Some amusement, on the journey, at worst.—

'No Newspaper has come this morning. *Was* there none at hand; or did you think it superfluous having already sent one; or has something gone wrong? I will not think *that*.'

The letter to Jane was written on 21 May 1834: his mind was fairly plainly set on the Chelsea home, with its tight wainscotting, its peaceful setting, and the questionable benefit of the proximity of the Hunt family. He waited only for Jane's confirmation: she reached London on 4 June, and after some debate she confirmed his choice. The bargain was struck on Saturday, 7 June, and they took possession of the house on Tuesday, 10 June 1834. Carlyle vividly remembered the journey to Chelsea in a cab with Jane, their servant and their canary which sang as it approached its new home, a favourable omen they thought. The house looked promising, 'and *here* we spent out two and thirty years of battle against Fate; hard but not quite unvictorious, when she left me as in her car of heaven's fire'. In fact when he died, in 1881, he had been resident in the same house for nearly fifty years, and he had earned the nickname 'The Sage of Chelsea', so firmly had he become identified with the district.

The Chelsea of to-day, exclusive and rich or popular and avant-garde, is at the furthest remove from the pleasant retreat Carlyle found himself so attracted to in 1834. Thea Holme's history of the village of Chelsea sufficiently records the story of a district rich in historical associations, which both the Carlyles (who were fond of walking, and found the exercise beneficial to their precarious health) were to explore thoroughly, and come to love. The district offered Jane a sense of community which she appreciated on her first lengthy experience of big-city life. She had her own grocer and her own particular tradesmen who, if they could not provide the food of country freshness to which she had been accustomed, could at least give her an insight into the community life, and a sense of 'belonging' which she had missed desperately in Craigenputtoch. To the over-neighbourly Hunts she was cool: an excellent housekeeper herself on a frugal budget, she was upset at the disorder and waste of the house round the corner where children ran barefoot, where china was broken and stores ran short, and whence servants came steadily to the Carlyles' to borrow.

But if Jane found a sense of involvement, and a release from the gloomy isolation of Craigenputtoch, so doubly did her husband. One noteworthy observation about Carlyle is the extent to which he found himself stimulated by travel. While he made a difficult, frequently an impossible travelling companion, complaining of beds, noise, dirt, food, stuffiness, indigestion, even complaining because foreign people did things in an unaccountably foreign way, Carlyle's imagination was unfailingly stimulated by the act of travelling, and exposure to new conditions and surroundings. His descriptions of his journeys to France, to the Low Countries, Germany and Ireland are fascinating and very well written. They were 'flung on paper' immediately on his return while the memory was vivid, and they carry the freshness of an awakened interest and a stimulated imagination which reflected in a sharper style and a more penetrating gift for description even than Carlyle's usual level. It is easy to think of the move to Chelsea as

one in which Carlyle threw aside loneliness in favour of new
companions, and the stimulus of metropolitan life, but the
reality must include the new surroundings, quite apart from the
Londoners with whom he mixed. From his earliest years in
Chelsea Carlyle walked and rode miles every day: very frequently
he did it alone, or if in company, he walked or rode in silence. The
aim of the ride was to see new surroundings, explore new roads.
Like Dickens, he loved especially to walk the streets at night,
alone, when the mighty heart was beating stiller, and when he
could listen to sounds and analyse them more precisely, could
look at the detail surrounding him without the obscuring traffic
which was already heavy enough to be a real danger during the
hours of business. Carlyle walked miles, every night, to 'purchase
a sleep', as he put it. Perhaps it was less than judicious to follow
the walk with a bowl of porridge before retiring, then to complain
of difficulty in sleep. Yet the porridge, as much as the walk, was
an inviolable routine.

The Carlyle home in London, for all its evolutions and
domestic 'earthquakes', when Jane decreed there would be
reconstruction or repainting, was very much a place of routine.
Thea Holme again provides us with the most detailed picture of
life at 5 Cheyne Row in *The Carlyles at Home*: nevertheless some
detail here is necessary to convey the life in Chelsea into which
both Carlyles settled so happily.

Throughout their London life the Carlyles had at least one
servant: to her the dark basement of the house was consigned, and
it was her kingdom. Carlyle himself might descend the steep
stairs to the basement to smoke his pipe late at night (for he
considerately never smoked where Jane might be irritated by the
smell) but Jane herself rarely went down. The two kitchens
downstairs are even to-day dark, and without electric light they
must have been cheerless in the extreme. Food, fuel and other
supplies had to be taken down, and stored. With all the good will
in the world (and most of the Carlyles' innumerable servants seem
to have worked with good will) cleanliness, a rigorous part of the
Carlyles' routine, must have been difficult to maintain. All water
had to be drawn hot from a boiler which formed part of the range

in the basement, or heated in kettles. In the dark of winter cleaning was trying, and we know that beetles and cockroaches were found in the kitchen. The maid worked there, and slept there at nights after Carlyle had ceased to smoke and gone to his own bed. In many ways a gently courteous and thoughtful man, he seems to have shown little regard for his maids, who must have waited shivering while he smoked in meditative silence by the fire, before retiring to his bed.

Up the steep staircase is the entrance-hall of the Carlyle home. From the street the visitors entered this hall, and could walk straight through to the narrow garden if they wished. More likely they would be ushered into the two inter-connecting rooms on this storey which were at various times reception-rooms and dining-rooms. Robert Tait's famous painting of a 'Chelsea Interior', which dates from 1857 to 1858, shows the pair of rooms with folding doors thrown back, Carlyle placidly smoking by the fire-place (for he would blow the smoke up the chimney) and Jane sitting rather tensely in a corner, all too aware that she herself, as well as her house, is the subject of close and permanent scrutiny. The detail, right down to the lapdog, is precise: the room to-day contains much of the same furniture, and the visitor can recreate the scene with almost uncanny accuracy. The rooms are sunny and the Carlyles (who slept ill) used to breakfast there in the cheerful light of the morning, perhaps lessening the gloom of a sleepless night or a morning headache.

On the first floor were the two large front rooms (which the Carlyles were to amalgamate into one) in which most of their entertainment was done in afternoon and evening. There were also a bedroom and dressing-room, where Jane slept. The front rooms, or later single room, were bright and spacious, and a steady stream of 'notables' and bright spirits passed through in the years during which the Sage lived in Chelsea. When either Carlyle was sick, and particularly in Carlyle's infirm old age, it was useful to have a bedroom close to a public room, for the stairs throughout the house are perilously steep.

On the second floor, again one finds bedrooms and dressing-rooms. Quite early on, the sleepless nights (and the short-

tempered mornings which followed) forced the Carlyles to sleep
in separate rooms. Jane's nerves were sensitive, and if she felt that
Carlyle was sleeping badly, her own sleep was ruined. Carlyle, for
his part, tossed and turned when he could not sleep, and frequently
walked about the room, or leaned out of the window to smoke, or
(if the night was fine) would leave the house and smoke in the
garden. Jane, lying alone in her bedroom, would dread this last
development, for it indicated a bad night, and a testy breakfast.
Her own temper, however, could be sharp if she had slept ill, and
when either was upset—which certainly was not always the case
—the separation of the night before was a wise precaution.

On the top storey, the most remarkable feature of the Chelsea
house. When they moved in 1834 this was mere attic space, useful
perhaps for storage or a maid's bedroom, but as Carlyle's income
was to grow, and the city noises to grow proportionately, this top
storey was to become the famous 'soundproof study' at the top of
the house. Chelsea had much about it of the country village in the
1830s, but London housing spread remorselessly out towards it
as the century progressed. The main road was a merciful distance
away, but the rumble of increasing traffic grew steadily. Worse
than either of these was the development of the network of
railways, suburban and main-line, near Carlyle's new home.
Carlyle used railways freely when it suited him, indeed he
invested wisely in railway stocks, yet he never lost an opportunity
to inveigh against the invasion of privacy which came from the
noise of the cars and—worst of all—the devil's shrieking of the
steam whistle. Carlyle hated it, and with repeated exposure the
hate grew to monstrous proportions. A steam whistle carries far
in distance—not unreasonably—and wherever Carlyle went, even
in the heart of the country, he would find his ears assailed from
afar by the unmelodious sound. On a sunny afternoon it would
move him to rage: on a still evening, in a strange house when he
was trying desperately to sleep, it would move him to paroxysms
of fury. In Chelsea, at least, he could do something about this
phobia. In August 1853 he put in hand the work which culminated
in the conversion of the top storey into a theoretically 'soundproof' room: double walls, double windows and patent ventilators

cut down the noise, so that even to-day, in the approaches of London Airport, it is one of London's quieter rooms. Unfortunately, Carlyle's wish for peace was allied to a passionate wish for fresh air: patent ventilators were not enough, and to open a window undid most of the good of the double walls. It was an insoluble problem, but the soundproof room was an expensive, if only partial, answer.

Before the construction of the soundproof room, Carlyle did his writing in a variety of locations in the house, both front and rear, where interruptions might be most easily avoided, and the sounds from neighbouring gardens least obtrusive. Cats and dogs were an annoyance, but far more serious was the habit of many of the residents of Cheyne Row of keeping hens in their gardens, to assure themselves of eggs fresher than the shops could supply. These crowed or clucked from the dawn, and at intervals during the day, and the nervous inhabitants of no. 5 waged continual war with their neighbours to put a stop to this nuisance.

The orderly daily routine of the Carlyle household was quite simple. The morning, after breakfast, was given over to work. Carlyle worked alone, and in a state of restless concentration; visitors who interrupted him at his desk were received with little courtesy, for he felt it necessary to put in a daily 'task' of writing. After this came a walk, and early dinner. The rest of the afternoon and evening might be devoted to walking and riding, or to entertaining. Although the Carlyles did little entertaining in a formal sense, and accepted few invitations to dinner-parties, they loved to have friends visit, with warning or without. The last visitor of the day would be accompanied part of his way home on foot, by Carlyle, who would then return to his porridge, and to bed.

Economy was the keystone of Jane's household management. Furniture was simple, and had often seen long service before coming into the Carlyles' hands. Carpets moved with them from house to house, and were re-tailored to fit their new home. Curtains and bed hangings were dyed and cleaned regularly, and frequently re-hung and moved. Jane believed in systematic cleaning, but also in 'earthquakes', in which everything was changed, thoroughly cleaned and perhaps repainted, and a complete overhaul performed. At such times she did her best to send Thomas as far as possible into the countryside, and have everything done before he returned. He disliked the bustle of a cleaning, and he loathed the smell of fresh paint. Yet paint, and thorough cleanliness, were essential parts of their life-style. Both insisted on scrupulous personal cleanliness, and shopped where they might be reasonably sure of clean fresh food. In an age when bed-bugs seem to have been very common in London, they took the utmost care to exclude them from their own home, and noted their traces with sheer dismay when sleeping in a strange home. Each of them took a cold shower, often at daily intervals, and apparently thought their frequent colds and occasional neuralgia a small price to pay.

In her ideas of catering, Jane was no more modern than her contemporaries. Her husband's tastes did little to help here: with a frail digestive system, Thomas knew which foods suited him, and which did not. He was reluctant to experiment outside the familiar list, and tended to insist on a diet which seems disastrously repetitive. Old potatoes he loved: boiled greens and grilled mutton were also frequent favourites. A boiled or steamed pudding, and scalding hot tea or coffee completed his main meal. Breakfast would be very hot coffee and toast. He was fussy that the meal should be properly cooked and presented, yet its content was a matter of strange indifference to him. Jane readily complied with his simple wishes. The absence of fresh fruit or vegetables, and dairy products, did not disturb her, for to her fruit was good 'only to give people a colic', and desserts an expensive extravagance.

Again the letters form one of the best introductions to domestic life in Cheyne Row. A letter of 1858 has recently come into the possession of Edinburgh University Library, written from Scotland by Jane (who was on holiday) to her servant Charlotte (who was in Chelsea, looking after the house). Carlyle was on the Continent, researching for his monumental life of Frederick the Great, and the letter shows the tension Jane must have felt at the prospect of his return, yet her confidence in the domestic arrangements which she left behind her.

Thornhill, Dumfries
Thursday

Dear Charlotte,

Your own letter hit me to-day in the most beautiful manner just in the transit from the Place where I have been these three weeks to this Place where I shall stay some days at least. I have only a few minutes as usual for writing in; but if I wait till tomorrow the Sunday intervenes and you will not be able to get any letter till Monday.

The winter stock of coals had best not be ordered till I return and can see about the price &c, but if you are in danger of running out altogether, you must order a ton from Alden to be brought in on Monday morning—that the oil cloth may be put down in time for Mr Carlyle. I have no further news from him; indeed ever since he went abroad, my knowledge of his movements has been gained chiefly from the newspapers—he has been too hurried and flurried for writing.

If he keep to the intentions he expressed in his last letter to me he will be home to you next Monday—that is, the 20th but I hope you will receive some direct instructions from himself, thro' Dr Carlyle.

I should like that he had stayed away a week or two longer that I might have been home to receive him; but not expecting him so soon, I have staid all my time at one place and have several friends and relations to visit still before I leave this country, and it would be a pity to have incurred so much expence for less than a months stay. Besides *hurry-scurrying* back in time for *him* would probably undo any good I have got by coming. So I must just trust to your making him comfortable for a week or so; and the week after next I will return and relieve you of your responsibility at latest.

You know his ways and what he needs pretty well by this time. Trouble him with as few questions as possible. You can ask him what he will take tea or coffee to breakfast?—and whether he would broth, or a pudding to dinner? You must always give him one or other with his meat and either an egg to breakfast or a slice of bacon. I think you can now cook most of the things he takes oftenest boiled fowl, mutton broth, chops and bread and ground rice puddings—If you take pains to please him I have no doubt you will. And if he look fussed and *cross*, never mind, so long as you are doing your best; travelling always puts him in a fever, and nobody can look and speak *amiably* with sick nerves . . .

If you *can* catch Mr Edwards the gardener it would be well to have the garden done up. Only tell him to be careful of all my little pot-plants. You need not order in anything till Mr C arrives—or till he tell you he is positively coming—then get what is needed at your own discretion, without troubling *him*.

Heaven help you and him well thro it!

Take care your kitchen be in order—when he goes to light his pipe.—He will see.

Yours truly, Jane Carlyle.

These are the trivia which made up the rich comic texture of life in the home of the Sage of Chelsea.

8

THE THIRTIES

ROBERT TAIT'S picture of a Chelsea interior shows a placid, domestic scene, the morning sunlight streaming in on a quiet homely room with peaceful occupants. The description of their life might make this scene seem more like a thinly disguised inferno. To take this view would be extremely unjust to both Carlyles: the truth was complicated and large-scale, just as were the characters of the Carlyles. For despite their shattered nerves and short tempers, their acute hearing which rendered noise outside a torture and noise inside unbearable, the Carlyles were very fond of each other, excellent hosts, and warm and true friends to a remarkable number of people, Londoners and visitors to the city alike. It is exactly this, apart from their high intrinsic literary qualities, which makes the collection of the Carlyle letters such an important and worthwhile project. The Carlyles touched literary London at a great number of points, and their home was a focus for a literary circle of great intelligence and brilliance. People knew the Carlyles as 'literary people' of rare merit, as talented conversationalists, and also as quite sincere friends who were responsible for much unassuming, anonymous benevolence and charity. When they were famous, many people sought their acquaintance as literary lions: many like William Allingham, Charles Gavan Duffy and Francis Espinasse came back again and again to visit a family which welcomed them as friends, and which was one of the focuses of their life. Allingham's *Diary*, Duffy's *Conversations with Carlyle* and Espinasse's *Literary Recollections and Sketches* are perhaps the best known, but are only a sample of the great variety of reminiscence which was produced following visits to Cheyne Row; many visitors rushed home to take notes of the *bons mots* of the Sage, and the quieter

Carlyle's study in Craigenputtoch, where *Sartor Resartus* was written, along with many important essays

The Carlyles' Chelsea home

Jane Carlyle. Drawing by Samuel Laurence

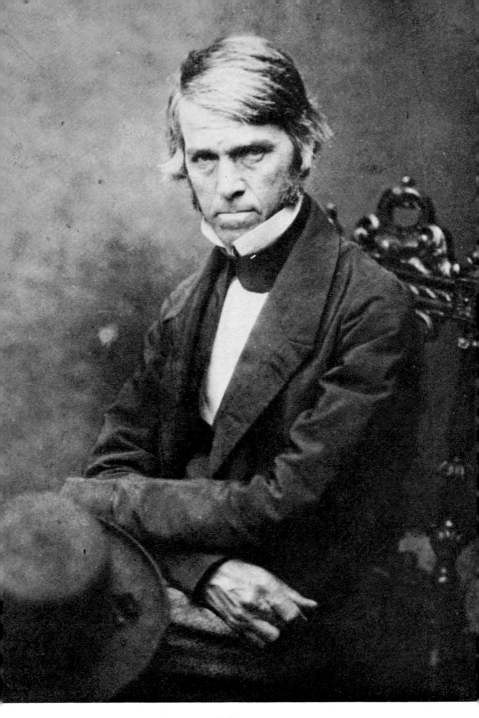

Thomas Carlyle, 1854

John Carlyle

Jane Carlyle, 1854

yet equally penetrating sayings of Jane. A night with the Carlyles was something to be remembered. Jane welcomed guests kindly, and steered the conversation wisely when it seemed to be becoming too controversial or personal. Carlyle himself held aloof to begin with, then took over the conversational role more and more from Jane: he spoke with emphasis, his strong Scottish accent (which he did not lose throughout his London years) thickening under the stress of emotion. He talked copiously and well, though intolerantly: people were amazed by the flood of his imagery, the profusion of his illustration, though they realised uneasily that they were listening to an inspired monologue rather than to inspired argument. Carlyle simply prevented opposition, either by dismissing argument contemptuously, or by raising his voice and bearing them down.

Consciously or unconsciously, there was much about his talk that was performance contrived for serious or for comic ends. Often the most shattering denunciation would end in a loud laugh, and a 'poor fellow, after all!' apostrophising some political figure or literary person whose character had been assassinated. Yet people came back, fascinated. Jane steered the conversation, indeed often judiciously fed it so as to prepare topics for Carlyle to speak on.

As with so much else in Carlyle, the question resolves itself into one of scale. Froude, who knew Carlyle very well, admitted that 'Carlyle was wilful, and impatient of contradiction. When his will was crossed or resisted, his displeasure rushed into expressions not easily forgotten.' Whether you forgot them, or remembered them with admiration, depended on your attitude to Carlyle's political thought, and his personality. Thus Grant Duff, who was unsympathetic to Carlyle, wrote in his diary of one encounter: 'Met and walked with Carlyle, who raved about the general anarchy he imagined he saw around him, and praised Bismarck to the skies'. This was all Duff recollected of what was no doubt several hours' emphatic rhetoric. Carlyle was very alert to other people's feelings, and he found himself quite aware of the effect he could produce, even if he could do nothing to stop himself.

This is the negative side. Positively, there is much to admire in the Carlylean conversation, which we can trace back (if we wish) very easily to the example of his own parents, particularly his father:

'None of us will ever forget that bold glowing style of his, flowing free from the untutored Soul; full of metaphors (though he knew not what a metaphor was), with all manner of potent words (which he appropriated and applied with a *surprising* accuracy, you often could not guess whence); brief, energetic; and which I should say conveyed the most perfect picture, definite, clear, not in ambitious *colours* but in full *white* sunlight, of all the dialects I have ever listened to'.

Carlyle clearly saw his indebtedness to his parents' example, and he voiced it in a comment to an early biographer, who had attributed the Carlylean 'style' to the influence of Jean Paul Richter.

'Edward Irving and his admiration of the Old Puritans & Elizabethans . . . played a much more important part than Jean Paul on my poor "style"; and the most important part by far was that of Nature, you would perhaps say, had you ever heard my Father speak, or very often heard my Mother and her inborn melodies of heart and of voice!'

Early on, his student friends attributed to Carlyle a vivid gift of speech, 'copious and bizarre': as we have seen, he was described as possessing 'a strong tendency to undervalue others, combined, however, with great kindness of heart and great simplicity of manner'. The kindness of heart did much to counteract the exaggeration and the undervaluing of others: so, too, did his realisation of his faults. Speaking of his father, Carlyle was to admit that '. . . he exaggerated (which tendency I also inherit); yet only in description and for the sake chiefly of *humorous* effect'.

To assign the Carlylean style of speech to his early home background is no exaggeration, for many hearers did this spontaneously. An early visitor spoke of him as '. . . very homely, the air so rustic and peasant-like, not to say uncouth . . . Carlyle was a thorough Scot . . . Those who enjoyed the privilege of visiting Carlyle, especially if they were fellow-countrymen, can testify how vivid were his reminiscences of his early days at Ecclefechan and Annan, and how he liked nothing better than to hear of the old companions of his boyhood.' His appearance tallied with this. Another writer recorded that 'His face had not yet lost the country bronze which he brought up with him from Dumfriesshire . . . His long residence in London had not touched his Annandale look, nor had it—as we soon learned—touched his Annandale accent.' 'Had I seen him by the fireside of a Scotch farm', admitted William Robertson Nicoll, 'I should have taken him for a remarkably intelligent farmer, the grandfather of the family.'

Impressed by his appearance, the hearers would be equally impressed by his style. His speech was '. . . never for an instant commonplace. The whole diction was always original and intensely vivid, and it was more saturated and interlaced with metaphor than any other conversation I have ever heard.' Yet another wrote, 'On religious matters his language had a sublimity and an air of inspiration which always reminded me (and many others) of what a Hebrew prophet must have been; and sometimes when very earnest he had a strangely solemn way of turning and looking full in the hearer's face for a second before speaking, which added extraordinarily to the impressiveness of what he said.' Clearly an evening with the Carlyles was an experience to be remembered: clearly, too, the effect was calculated and imitated from memories of home, yet the habit grew on him, and as his father had been renowned in his circle for a gift of speech, so Carlyle enjoyed his reputation for his own accomplishment. He was no show. People came not just to marvel at the words, but to enjoy the companionship and the conversation which took place around these oratorical displays. Dickens valued the Carlyles above any other guests for companionship at table, and round a fireside, and many other gifted people, themselves outstanding speakers, added to this opinion. Undoubtedly the modest house in Chelsea attracted its brilliant circle of friends by offering good talk, and excellent conversation tending occasionally to monologue. Any library of nineteenth-century books will contain many memoirs and biographies which testify to the eagerness with which people went to Cheyne Row, and the impression they carried away, to be recorded in their diaries.

Economy and thrift were characteristics of Jane's housekeeping, we have seen, and the entertainment at these parties was modest: tea or coffee and light refreshment. Carlyle drank little except diluted brandy, though he enjoyed smoking in companionship with his friends. To both Carlyles companionship and social intercourse were essential parts of their lives. To each other they gave a lot of attention, and the company of others was a necessary release.

Economy and thrift were not mere habits carried over from early Scottish days: they were vital in the first years of the Carlyles' Chelsea home. Thomas had some money saved up from the publication of *Sartor Resartus* in *Fraser's Magazine*, though it brought in very little: he had earned more by the publication of essays, and by the repayments which his brother John (now a prosperous doctor) had made on loans which had supported him through College. They calculated they had enough for at least one year's residence in London, and Carlyle set about writing the 'Book' which he had for years promised his mother, in letters, that he would write—an original book, his own, untampered with by editors, and freely expressing his own preoccupations. *Sartor Resartus* had only partly fulfilled this urge, for it had been modified for serial publication (it was not published in book form till 1836, in North America, and 1838 in Great Britain). *The French Revolution* was to be Carlyle's own work, uninterfered with, and was to bring to a head his developing interests in history, in social reform, and in the example of decaying society in the late eighteenth century in France which had all been preoccupations in the later years at Craigenputtoch.

Carlyle set to work in Chelsea with a will. At an early stage, the work habits which were to characterise his London years became very obvious. He worked in the mornings, hard, and he felt miserable if he had not accomplished several pages by noon. He was quite liable to burn them at noon, and indeed much of his writing perished in this way, but at least he felt he was making some progress. Carlyle wrote with pain: he drafted out ideas, then refined them, and he kept no, or few, notes. His expression seems to pour out in a volcanic stream, but in fact it was carefully constructed, and changed often. He altered his manuscripts to the extent that some printers refused to set them into type. One hoary old story is that a typesetter moved from Edinburgh to London in 1834, partly to get away from having to set type from Carlyle's messy handwritten scripts: on his arrival in London, he was aghast to find more of the same waiting for him.

Carlyle's writing habits were in keeping with the quality of the results: as Basil Willey has remarked, Carlyle writes on the stretch, and his writing seems to come more from the solar plexus than from the heart. It was composed at this fever-pitch, and once done was a source of constant worry. Carlyle's irritability came and went with the progress of his writing: if he was about to start something, he was unbearable, but once started he settled down. At the end of a long project (such as *Cromwell*, or *Frederick*) he was worn out and his nerves badly shattered: at such times Jane wisely sent him away for long holidays. He never wrote easily, though sometimes (as with the *Reminiscences*) he wrote fast. Every book was written with pain.

The blow which struck him in March of 1835, after his first London winter, was all the more severe for these reasons. Edward Irving was dead, but otherwise the winter had been a pleasant one: the first volume of *The French Revolution* had been wrung out of his mind, and he was working well on the second. The finances of the family were precarious, but survival seemed possible. At this juncture the loss of the manuscript of the whole of the first volume of his history was a terrible blow. The story is a familiar one. John Stuart Mill had borrowed it to read and criticise, and in his turn had lent it to Harriet Taylor, the intimate friend with whom he spent the greater part of his adult life, only marrying her after the death of her husband. They shared their closest thoughts, and it was natural that Mill should lend her the manuscript of a work he so admired as Carlyle's history. Harriet Taylor, not being a writer, was less careful with the manuscript than Mill might have been, and left it lying out overnight. The piles of loose paper, written and re-written, altered times without number and with frequent pasted-on additions looked for all the world like scrap paper, and it is not surprising that the maid should have torn them up and used them to light the fire. Only a few scraps (preserved in the Chelsea Museum) survive; otherwise the whole labour of the winter of 1834 was lost, and as no notes survived it seemed a final blow.

Mill was deeply upset, and the labour of soothing him occupied the Carlyles much more than the contemplation of their own loss. It is typical of their warm friendship for others that this should have been so, for the position was really serious. Even with notes, it would have been difficult for Carlyle to re-create what he had written, but without notes he had really to go back to the beginning, and read anew the painful and dusty research, which he did punctiliously for all his historical writing, though he plainly loathed it. The writing took time: 'My will is not conquered; but my *vacuum* of element to swim in seems complete.'

Writing, of course, did not occupy all his time, and the flow of company did much to comfort him. Mill remained an intimate friend of the family, and forced Carlyle to accept £100 (he offered £200) to support him while he re-wrote the lost volume. Jane's mother visited the house, as she was to do at intervals throughout the rest of her life, and many new acquaintances were made, as well as old ones visited. Among the new friends was John Sterling, for whom Carlyle early conceived a warm affection.

The remainder of 1835 and the whole of 1836 were spent on the French Revolution and its affairs: minor articles written and published allowed them some financial respite, and in January 1837 the final pages were written. This was a decisive moment. With the publication of *Sartor Resartus* in the U.S.A. accomplished, and with a major historical work written, Carlyle stood ready to convert a considerable reputation as essayist and translator into a major reputation as historian. The book was printed by April, and published on 1 June 1837. Reviews were at first slow, then a rush of enthusiastic ones ensured the success of the book. Carlyle was a prominent figure, and having attained this eminence he was to retain it for the rest of his career.

Simultaneously he embarked on a new and unlikely career in London, namely that of public lecturer. Literary figures frequently appeared to give lectures, particularly when they needed the financial support which was available from lecturing. Coleridge was a well-known case, though his frequent 'indispositions' made his appearance a dubious event, and the public finally lost their taste for him. Carlyle, on the other hand, appeared punctiliously to his advertised schedule, and his lectures were on balance a distinct success in that they added to his reputation in the city, and in the sense that they brought in a good deal of money—six lectures on German literature (in May 1837) earned him £135. In all, Carlyle lectured on German literature (1837), the History of Literature (1838), Revolutions of Modern Europe (1839), and most memorably on Heroes and Hero-Worship (1840). Notes survive of most of these occasions: the audiences were captivated by Carlyle's unusual manner (a graver version of his Annandale drawing-room appearance) and his obvious earnestness, and when he warmed to his subject he had the ability to hold the audience easily for an hour.

Carlyle seems to have lectured from copious notes, but not to have written out his script *verbatim*: his last public lecture of any significance, his inaugural address as rector to the University of Edinburgh, was delivered in 1866 without recourse to the notes which he had in front of him. When the Heroes lectures were published, they had to be 'written' for the press. Thus, Carlyle seems to have had the ability, under pressure, to yield orally the connected stream of thoughts which he achieved in private conversation, but which he could not achieve in the study. His books were conceived with labour, his lectures prepared for and delivered with damage to the nerves for himself and those around him—the result was splendid, but the process of gestation horrendous.

At the end of the 1830s, Carlyle was a famous man on a moderate scale. Instead of a Scottish translator and essayist, he was now an established part of the London scene, well known for public appearance on the lecture platform, and for published historical works. His fame had spread to America, where Emerson popularised him tirelessly, and arranged for a much-needed and appreciated steady flow of income from American editions of his works. 'This year for the first time', he wrote at the end of 1839, 'I am not at all poor.' It was a fine end to the most momentous decade of his life.

9

THE FORTIES

THE 1840s were to see a steady development of the advances which Carlyle had made in the 1830s. He had made his name as historian, and his history had opened out whole new horizons to British readers—particularly in the discussion of social change, for Carlyle's view of history kept society and its evolution very much in the foreground. December of 1839 had seen the publication of *Chartism*, in which Carlyle directly addressed his countrymen and contemporaries following on from the sardonic and oblique references towards the end of *Sartor Resartus*, calling for a thorough overhaul of the social system of Great Britain. With the terrible example of the French Revolution before them, the people of Britain should see (Carlyle argued) that a bankrupt society produces not only human suffering—which was plainly visible to anyone who looked around the cities of Victorian Britain at the end of the 1830s—but the possibility of catastrophic social revolution reminiscent of 1789. The ruling classes of Britain were sufficiently aware of the implications of the French Revolution for the British social system, and Carlyle tells us in the *Reminiscences* how he had witnessed, along with other friends, the raising of volunteer regiments in Edinburgh to counter the threat of revolt and compulsory reform. Peterloo and the troubles of 1819 were vivid memories to Carlyle who had been poor at the time himself, and acutely aware of the social inequalities which lay behind the violence of the day. Yet with the increasing maturity of the 1830s behind him, Carlyle saw that the possibilities of change and improvement lay not in violence of this sort, but in the more rhetorical arguments of the magazines. Unlike Dickens, he did not choose to involve his audience in the world of fiction, and through this means try to convey to them some of the reality of suffering which lay behind the fantasy and the humour of the novel. Carlyle's method was much closer to his father's and mother's—able, vivid 'preaching' which would hold the reader's attention without recourse to fiction, and perhaps persuade the reader to acquiesce. The tone of apostrophe to the audience grows in *The French Revolution*, and comes to prominence in *Cromwell*. For the rest of his career as historian and social critic, Carlyle held a dialogue with his audience, treating them in part as any writer would his audience, but for the rest placing them in the position of his guests at the fireside of Cheyne Row, and captivating them with the power of his rhetoric.

To be successful, such rhetoric plainly had to be involved, and to believe sincerely in the message it tried to convey. Carlyle believed completely. In the writing of *Sartor Resartus* he had lived through personal poverty, but also a succession of poor harvests, and he noted at the time in his journals that 'la classe la plus pauvre' seemed to be set to rise out of its present abasement: the ridicule of the parasitical landlord in *Sartor Resartus* was clearly aimed at helping on that process. As the 1830s progressed Carlyle learned about poverty and hard work. Although he kept up the outward appearances of a comfortably off writer, his exchequer was often very near to being empty, and he complained (as in his 1839 essay 'Petition on the Copyright Bill') about the meagre returns which society offered him for the work he did. Carlyle was serious, and his seriousness added to the immediacy of his message to Britain, calling for social reform throughout the 1840s and 1850s.

The 1840s saw a great deal of development in Carlyle's thought. With *Chartism*, published at the very beginning of the decade, he had made a major public pronouncement on his private belief that society badly needed total overhaul. The discontent of the working classes was obvious, in a time of Chartist riots; 'To say that it is mad, incendiary, nefarious, is no answer'. So Carlyle looks more deeply, to the causes behind the discontent, very notably the Poor Law legislation on which he poured scorn for the simple reason that it was not working. 'Any law, however well meant as a law, which has become a bounty on unthrift, idleness, bastardry and beer-drinking, must be put an end to.' People were willing to work, but in disordered times there was no work for them, no chance of human dignity—which Carlyle regarded as very important.

To restore dignity to society Carlyle looks in *Chartism* to a new Aristocracy, capable of governing and capable of putting right what looks like an impossible mess. They will not take part in the meaningless mumbo-jumbo of parliamentary routine, nor will they let things slip—the doctrine of 'laissez-faire' which became one of Carlyle's *bêtes noires*. These leaders once found, 'Obedience, little as many may consider that side of the matter, is the primary duty of man'. Rights and mights are freely discussed in this book, but the overall emphasis is, frighteningly, on disorder and bloodstained revolt, in the shadow of the French Revolution. In such circumstances, Carlyle urgently advocates order, proper management, and submission to capable rulers to put Britain to rights again. It may seem fanciful, as may seem his serious suggestions that education and emigration are the two best services which the ruling classes can provide for the workers. Yet the suggestions are seriously made and seriously meant. Carlyle, acutely conscious of the dignity of each individual (and the indignity of the suffering which had brought about Chartist unrest) was advocating education to raise the dignity of each man, and the means of easy emigration if this was to be the only way to make a new life possible.

Many of the ideas were expanded in the more elaborate *Past and Present* of 1843. Here Carlyle adopted a four-fold form for considering the present. In part one he looks at the chaos of the present, in part two at order emerging from the chaos of St Edmundsbury when strong Abbot Samson was appointed. In the third, the modern worker is compared with his mediaeval predecessor, and in the fourth Carlyle looks to the future, to see what lessons can be applied to it from the study of the past. Many of the points made in *Chartism* can be seen in more vivid form. There are the same attacks on 'laissez-faire', on the mechanical measurement of everything by the 'cash nexus' which leads to an inhuman society working for money, measuring every obligation by money and profitability. Abbot Samson is compared very favourably with modern parliamentarians, and the settled order he made out of his decayed monastery put beside the chaos of Britain in 1843, crippled by misapplied Corn Laws, over-production in the cotton industries, stagnant agriculture and wide-spread unemployment and poverty. Abbot Samson, the central character, is no more than a historical person who took Carlyle's fancy when he read a book about him published by the Camden Society in 1840: yet he emerges in time as one of the Aristocrats of the book—the finest rulers—whom it is a duty to recognise and to work for, in the best traditions of *Heroes and Hero-Worship*. Carlyle does not pin down any of his contemporaries as a hero fit to be worked for, but he does stress enormously the importance of work. It is this which makes possible the triumphant ending to *Past and Present*, after painful description of the rottenness of life in Britain. What remains is the individual, his dignity and his future if he works for it. 'Subdue mutiny, discord, wide-spread despair, by manfulness, justice, mercy and wisdom.' In this way society would avert chaos, and find order—'the grand sole miracle of Man'.

There appears in the 1840s, then, an ideal of a ruler in Carlyle's mind—not a despot, but a strong man who emerges in response to an insistent demand of his times, and who will rule strongly because he is right—the powers that order the universe see to it that the right are also the mighty. It led him almost inevitably to Oliver Cromwell, the subject of the principal work of the 1840s. His research occupied the first half of the decade, and publication of the *Letters and Speeches of Oliver Cromwell* came in November 1845. As the title suggests, the method is distinctly new after *The French Revolution*. Carlyle painstakingly assembled surviving documents from Cromwell's time, and selected from them Cromwell's letters and relevant supporting documents from which to piece together a contemporary account of England. It is not a connected history, neither is it an imaginative re-experience of the events such as Carlyle had achieved in *The French Revolution*. Very large portions of the volumes are devoted to transcriptions of the documents themselves, with Carlyle's introductions and commentaries interspersed irregularly. The documents were carefully sifted and annotated, though Carlyle with human fallibility missed many (some he included in later editions), and was taken in by some forgeries, particularly the famous 'Squire Papers'.

The most striking feature of Carlyle's method in *Cromwell* is his attitude to his hero. Frequently he interjects into Cromwell's own prose some encouragement, or an emphatic agreement from the author, which leaves the reader in no doubt that Carlyle admired Cromwell a great deal, and was wholeheartedly behind him in his operations. Carlyle could accept much of what Cromwell stood for: Cromwell's strong Christian belief and motivation in his military affairs, his desire to bring order out of chaos, and to impose a strong, well-working monarchy on an exploited England were obviously ideas which Carlyle would applaud, and *Cromwell* is a curious congratulatory dialogue between author and subject. It is not uncritical, nor is it hasty. It is the work of a man who very thoroughly approved of what Cromwell was doing, and wished to infect the reading public with his enthusiasm.

Certainly *Cromwell* was a successful work, and though few would share Carlyle's ideological enthusiasm for his hero, they could only admire Carlyle's industry and his ability to bring history forcefully to life. He still surrounded himself with papers and pictures relating to his period, and he read very widely in others' work—frequently pencil in hand, annotating margins with 'fool', 'dolt', 'idiot', and other unflattering notes. He travelled, too, to country houses where he frequently had access to papers in family collections (such as the Kimbolton papers)— and sometimes left behind an essay on the papers he had consulted, as a gesture of gratitude.

Travel meant a great deal to Carlyle at this time. It was in travelling in preparation for *Cromwell* that he had crossed the ground near St Edmundsbury, and the idea of *Past and Present* had grown. He needed the stimulus after much writing, and he needed his vivid imagination to be disciplined by memory of the actual contours of the countryside. Travel was now much easier, for more than one reason. Increasing prosperity meant that he could travel wherever and whenever he felt like it. The hated railways made the journeys rapid and relatively painless. Once in his compartment Carlyle would fight for air, pulling the window right down and ignoring protests from the other passengers as he smoked placidly in the ample supply of fresh air which rushed in.

To Scotland he went as often as he could, usually every summer. No longer bound by Annan steam-boat schedules, he could go to Ecclefechan station by train and be met by his relatives who would drive him off to the Carlyle family farms to which various sons and nephews had moved. In Dumfriesshire he ceased to be a noted historian (although tourists covertly followed him about) and became 'Oor Tam'. The years, and the success, had not dimmed the fierce family loyalty, and their joy in reunion was mutual and sincere. He went North with enthusiasm, and left with regret. At other times correspondence flowed regularly: although Jane's highly strung mother was temperamental and visited or wrote relatively rarely, the Carlyle family were close, and their reunions were happy.

Throughout the 1840s Carlyle's health, apart from his nerves, seems to have been sufficiently robust rarely to interfere with his work. Occasionally he would complain of a heavy cold, but otherwise people remarked on his sturdy countryman's constitution. When in 1842 Jane's mother suddenly died in a bitter February, Carlyle departed immediately to see to funeral arrangements in Liverpool, then in Scotland. In the same year he was in the Netherlands. Certainly he was mobile, and enjoyed the journeys, although his complaints of accommodation en route were frequent and wildly exaggerated.

In short, Carlyle now enjoyed a very considerable success. In conversation, in letters and in published writing he had become confident in tone, losing his tentativeness as he moved into the peak of his career as interpreter and prophet. Alone, he had made the decision to move to London, risking his happiness—and Jane's—to achieve success. This achieved, he was convinced he had a 'message' for his age; the old, captivating conversational style gave way not (as hostile critics imagined) to a brutal self-assertiveness, but to a prophetic 'message' which he felt he had to some extent earned the right to preach, both by his personal struggle, and his success as essayist, translator and historian. Hence a radical change in Carlyle: in private he remained charming and a valued friend, in public he became a prophetic figure who believed he had a point to make of the first importance. Writing in confidence to his friend Emerson in 1835 he showed how much this change was troubling him:

'The truth is, I believe Literature to be as good as dead and gone in all parts of Europe at this moment, and nothing but hungry Revolt and Radicalism appointed us for perhaps three generations; I do not see how a man can honestly live by writing, in another dialect than that, in England at least; so that if you determine on not living dishonestly, it will behove you to look several things full in the face, and ascertain what is with some distinctiveness. I suffer also terribly from the solitary existence I have all along had; it is becoming a kind of passion with me, to feel myself among my brothers. And then, How? Alas, I care not a doit for Radicalism, nay I feel it to be a wretched necessity, unfit for me; Conservatism being not unfit only but false for me: yet these too are the grand Categories under which all English spiritual activity that so much as thinks remuneration possible must range itself.'

The distressing examination of the self continues, from the time of *Sartor Resartus*: no more than Teufelsdröckh has Carlyle adjusted to his own society. Yet his outsider's stance is painfully adopted, and honestly thought out.

Otherwise the 1840s showed much pleasure. The public success of *Cromwell* and the lectures on Heroes, the private tranquillity of Cheyne Row delighted Carlyle. Friends continued to visit, either for a night's literary talk, or for a longer holiday. In October of 1847, for instance, Emerson called and stayed with them for several days. He had been, for over a decade, warmly propagandising for Carlyle in North America, and more practically arranging for publication there of Carlyle's works, and sending over welcome remittances of royalties to London.

Emerson visited from time to time over the winter of 1847-1848, and his presence obviously gave Carlyle great inspiration and pleasure. Indeed to look at the list of Carlyle's friends, and how it increases in the 1840s, is to see how much Carlyle continued to impress people with his genial humanity. In 1841 Carlyle began a friendship (by correspondence initially) with Browning, in 1842 he visited Dr Arnold at Rugby. In 1842 he visited the Continent, and especially the Netherlands, and spent a good deal of time riding round the sites of various Cromwellian battles. In December of that year Tennyson came to Cheyne Row. In 1844 he visited the Grange, the hospitable home of Lord and Lady Ashburton, who were to be loyal friends to Carlyle. The first Lady Ashburton frequently welcomed both Carlyles into her home, and after she died, so did the second Lady Ashburton. Jane, not without some jealousy, joined her husband in these country-house visits to the aristocracy: she acquitted herself with credit, but was never at her ease in such society. Carlyle seems to have been very little affected by the experience; he plainly enjoyed the companionship and frequently visited that home. In 1847 we see Dr Chalmers and George Gilfillan calling at Chelsea, and in June of that year the Grand Duke of Weimar came. But perhaps most important of all, in the long term, was Froude's first meeting with Carlyle in 1849. He was to fall under the spell of his personality and his magnetic conversation, and find a Hero.

If Carlyle made friends in the 1840s, he also lost them. Charles Buller, whom he had tutored in Edinburgh in the 1820s, and seen go on and prosper as a Member of Parliament and notable public figure, died in November 1849, prematurely. Carlyle's obituary is brief, but sincerely regretful. Earlier, in September 1844, John Sterling had died. Sterling, a gentle and meditatively religious man, had been a very close friend of Carlyle: almost a decade later Carlyle was to pay tribute in a *Life of John Sterling* which remains one of his most attractive and readable works.

Steady progress seems to have been made in terms of material success. Publication of new works, and republication of existing successes brought in substantial cash sums to the Carlyle household. In 1847 republication of *The French Revolution* brought him

£700, and in the earlier part of the decade Carlyle earned several hundred pounds for essays, lectures and miscellanies. A similar amount came from Emerson. Jane sensibly invested some of the money in improvements to the house in Cheyne Row, in brightening up the decoration and in small ways adding to the comforts. It is notable, however, that despite the growing success of the Carlyle finances as the nineteenth century progressed, their life-style at no time became extravagant: Carlyle retained his cautious attitude towards expenses on household matters, and Jane even had playfully to write him begging letters to induce him to increase her housekeeping allowances as prices went up in the 1840s and 1850s.

At the end of the decade, this more direct involvement in contemporary affairs and politics crystallised in two momentous publications, a periodical article entitled 'Occasional Discourse on the Negro Question', which appeared in the last month of 1849, and the eight *Latter-Day Pamphlets*, written at the end of 1849 and in 1850. To have shown Carlyle growing more fixed in his ideas, and more willing to participate in contentious political debate concerning his own times in the 1840s, is to explain to some extent the extraordinary unpopularity which he courted by publishing *The Nigger Question*, as his essay has come to be called. Some explanation is still called for.

With the emancipation of Negro slaves in the British Empire, the British people had partially succeeded in expunging one of the more disgraceful means by which they had achieved commercial success, and the extraordinary expansion of trade and export in the late eighteenth and earlier nineteenth century. Their prosperity had been founded to a certain extent on human suffering abroad, and all through the 1820s and 1830s the newspapers were agitated by public debate on the rights and wrongs of emancipation. Wilberforce died in 1833, the year of the passage through Parliament of the Emancipation Act, which went far towards curing the abuse: the problem remained, of course, in the practice of other countries, and in the slow spread of the effectiveness of the legislation to existing slaves, and to those remoter parts of the British Empire where laws were difficult to enforce when they

E

conflicted with human—or commercial interest. The relationship between workers—often ex-slaves—and their employers in
the British dominions continued to be a matter for concern, and
anxiety was at its strongest in Great Britain, far from the scene
of the actual confrontations. Carlyle was extremely concerned,
but with characteristic decision and abruptness his involvement
focussed itself unexpectedly in a very different direction from
that of most of his contemporaries. Carlyle felt deeply the plight
of suffering people—his writings since *Sartor Resartus*, and
before that his private entries and letters amply illustrate this—
but in the case of far-off slaves or ex-slaves—'Quashee Niggers',
as he contemptuously called them—his concern showed itself
in a very qualified way. *The Nigger Question* looked at the
phenomenon of unrest among the coloured workers in West
Indian sugar farms, and it looked not at the abuses of labour, nor
at the need for reform in the system, but at the inefficiency of the
farms as working units.

Since the *Reminiscences* of James Carlyle, Thomas had been
insistent on *work* as a basic part of men's life; in writing of his
father, Carlyle had been very eager to demonstrate that his
memory was one of a man who feared God, and got on with his
work. The theme is repeated as the basis of the 'Everlasting YEA'
of *Sartor Resartus*, 'Work while it is called day, for the night
cometh when no man can work'. The admonition is a Biblical one,
and indeed the attitude to work is a direct inheritance from the
Calvinist admonitions of Carlyle's boyhood Church. In the
Seceder Church of Ecclefechan—James Carlyle's Church—work
was put before the worshippers as the ultimate end of life, work
in the consciousness of the responsibility of the working individual
to an all-seeing and all-controlling God. *The Nigger Question*
assumes this attitude, and the analysis of the problem in the
West Indies is carried out in the full consciousness that the world
was losing sugar because work was not being carried out. The
position Carlyle took seemed to most of his countrymen, who
lacked his own particular religious background, incomprehensible.
If the Negroes will not work, says Carlyle, compel them to work.
It was, to him, as simple as that. The climate was fantastically

productive, the soil fruitful, and life could be easy for the workers; they had their 'oceans of pumpkin' and could live with very little exertion on the fruit of the land. But the rest of the world lacked the sugar they might produce by working in the fields. So whip them in! Like Carlyle himself, these workers had a Divine obligation to work in his view, and so they must be forced to it.

The question is really not one of Carlyle's inhumanity, nor of his 'fascist' tendencies, although particularly in the 1940s it was fashionable for critics to speak of Carlyle in these terms. It is much more to the point to look to Carlyle's own upbringing, which left him with this rigid and unalterable view of man's obligation to work. The rights and wrongs of the position of the Negro workers by comparison seemed to Carlyle quite insignificant: that they had earned the right to live easily, after generations of slavery, never entered his mind. That they should work hard, in a hot climate, to produce sugar for the rest of world was natural, for this was their inheritance, and they had a clear duty to honour it. That, in clear cut-and-dried terms, was Carlyle's view of The Nigger Question. He wrote of it uncompromisingly, to many people offensively. As the 1840s ended, he established himself in a new public image: the opponent of liberalism, the propagandist of a forcefully administered society where a religious obligation to work (incomprehensible, doubtless, to many of his contemporaries) replaced more immediate humanitarian concerns. It was not an immediately attractive, nor even credible, position; yet a reading of Carlyle's early work (which will be reinforced in a later chapter) will illustrate amply how Carlyle took his position. His analysis of his own times in his essays, and of the relationship of Past and Present, had convinced him of two things, that his own age was in a state of moral decline, and that similar decline in the past had led to violent, sometimes catastrophic convulsion—as in the French Revolution. For the Victorian age, such violence would be disastrous, as more and more people crowded into Britain, and as transportation improved and drew the country closer and closer together. It was in order to arrest the decline, and avert the convulsion, that Carlyle preached consistently in his writing career an adherence to a strict morality, a dedication to a working life. *The Nigger Question* was of a piece with this, but it introduced a new note of compulsion—if they will not work, *make* them work! It was an ominous note on which to enter a new decade.

THE FIFTIES

As the 1840s ended with a hardening of attitude on Carlyle's part, a determination to make a public pronouncement on moral issues to stop a decline in standards which he considered potentially disastrous, so the 1850s began with the publication of the work which more than any other gave Carlyle public stature as such a figure, namely the *Latter-Day Pamphlets*. Carlyle made a stand: it was an unpopular one to many (he wryly reported his friends as thinking he had taken to whisky) but it showed how far he had come from the early self-questionings of his Craigenputtoch days. A passage at the end of *The French Revolution* is revealing in explaining the attitude Carlyle took:

'Meanwhile we will hate Anarchy as Death, which it is; and the things worse than Anarchy shall be hated *more*. Surely Peace alone is fruitful. Anarchy is destruction; a burning up, say, of Shame and Insupportabilities; but which leaves Vacancy behind. Know this also, that out of a world of Unwise nothing but an Unwisdom can be made. Arrange it, constitution-build it, sift it through ballot-boxes as thou wilt, it is and remains an Unwisdom,—the new prey of new quacks and unclean things, the latter end of it slightly better than the beginning. Who can bring a wise thing out of men unwise? Not one. And so Vacancy and general Abolition having come for this France, what can Anarchy do more? Let there be Order, were it under the Soldier's Sword; let there be Peace, that the bounty of the Heavens be not spilt; that what of Wisdom they do send us bring fruit in its season!'

'Let there be Order, were it under the Soldier's Sword': the historian of Cromwell speaks out here, but he turns his attention from the seventeenth to the nineteenth century. The tone is the tone of the *Latter-Day Pamphlets*, a work which surveys its time, and sees everywhere disorder. Not only is disorder rampant, but there is a near-total failure to try to put things properly right. The ruling classes do not rule, nor the working-classes work: democracy is a sham, and the 'ballot-boxes' rule of testing the validity of a plan seems to Carlyle to be idiocy. Certainly the *Latter-Day Pamphlets* were violent abuse of the Victorian age, and to many justified the suspicion that Carlyle had taken to whisky.

Yet they are written in earnest. The difficulty in comprehending them calmly lies in the pressure of Carlyle's writing. One recent editor can write of the '. . . latent sadism [which] underlies much of his comment', a remark which emphasises the extent to which an age like the present is out of touch with the urgency Carlyle felt in recommending to his own times a return to the moral standards of his own youth. Far from sadism, Carlyle tries in his work to portray the *urgency* of the problem in these latter days: the country is sick, and there seems no immediate prospect of a cure. In the circumstances, he sees any kind of rhetoric, an extreme (and often overstated) case, as valid, if it helps to make his point to the reader.

Perhaps among the most unpopular of his writing, Carlyle's *Model Prisons*, number 2 of the *Latter-Day Pamphlets*, is a good illustration of why he may seem at first sight illiberal and fascist, yet on a more sensitive reading he may be seen to adhere to a different logic.

Model Prisons arose from a visit to a London jail which had been 'improved' on the best humanitarian principles, with proper provision for feeding and sheltering the occupants, and perhaps more importantly, proper provision for keeping them active, and if possible educating them to prepare for their return to society. That such reform was necessary no one would have denied, and many admired Elizabeth Fry and the other Victorian philanthropists who laboured for the reform of prison conditions which were often scandalous. Carlyle will have known about this: he will also have had an acute and morbid interest in jails, one may conjecture, as a result of his close friendship with

Dickens, to whom jails held an unhealthy fascination, and who knew from bitter personal experience the misery of incarceration, and the miasmal effects of such an experience on the whole quality of life; not just of the person imprisoned, but his family and friends. The nightmare vision of this is what gives a novel like *Bleak House* or *Little Dorrit* a great part of its power.

Carlyle, then, knew about prisons, and went prepared to see the worst kind of human suffering. What he saw was remarkable: clean well-run cells, healthy prisoners, excellent food, industrious occupation. The commandant was 'A man of real worth, challenging at once love and respect': he was 'A true *"aristos"*', and commander of men'. On the surface, we would have expected Carlyle to applaud happily. Here was a work of reformation in the catalogue of abuses of his age, and a strong hero-figure at the helm. Yet Carlyle reports that he looked 'with considerable astonishment, the reverse of admiration, on the work he had here been set upon'. The reason is worth quoting at length:

'For all round this beautiful Establishment, or Oasis of Purity, intended for the Devil's regiments of the line, lay continents of dingy poor and dirty dwellings, where the unfortunate not *yet* enlisted into that Force were struggling manifoldly,—in their workshops, in their marble-yards, and timber-yards and tan-yards, in their close cellars, cobbler-stalls, hungry garrets, and poor dark trade-shops with red-herrings and tobacco-pipes crossed in the window,—to keep the Devil out-doors, and *not* enlist with him. And it was by a tax on these that the Barracks for the regiments of the line were kept up.'

This was Carlyle's urgent message to his benevolent comtemporaries: 'Yonder, in those dingy habitations, and shops of red-herring and tobacco-pipes, . . . there, I say, is land: here is mere sea-beach. Thither go with your benevolence, thither to those dingy caverns of the poor.'

So far it seems, very reasonable: what jars, however, is the violence of the rhetoric. To dismiss the inhabitants of the prisons as 'thriftless sweepings of Creation', let alone 'Devil's regiments' is not the most constructive of attitudes, nor is the intention to '. . . lay leather on the backs of you, collars round the necks of you: and will teach you, after the examples of the Gods, that this world is *not* your inheritance, or glad to see you in it'. Control, perhaps harsh ruthless control is the theme of his approach: in the third *Latter-Day Pamphlet* Carlyle calls for '. . . not a Reformed Parliament, . . . but a Reformed Executive or Sovereign Body of Rulers and Administrators'. The task of ruling Britain in the nineteenth century is a task for heroes—'it is heavy and appalling work', Carlyle admits, and it has to be approached with the greatest preparation and willingness to work exhaustingly. In exchange, the ruler is to expect obedience, for (as Carlyle points out in the last pamphlet) the ruler, or King, or Hero should listen to public opinion, but he should also be able to decide for himself whether to pay attention to it or not. 'If the weight be in favour of the Governor, let him in general proceed . . . often enough, in pressing cases, flatly disregarding that, and walking through the heart of it; for in general it is but frothy folly and loud-blustering rant and wind.' This is Carlyle's answer to the troubles of his age, as he saw them early in the 1850s. To find a ruler, and to obey him is what is wanted. This is not, in Carlyle's view, voluntarily to accept slavery.

'The free man is he who is *loyal* to the Laws of this Universe; who in his heart sees and knows, across all contradictions, that injustice *cannot* befall him here; that except by sloth and cowardly falsity evil is not possible. The first symptom of such a man is not that he resists and rebels, but that he obeys.'

It was an extraordinary message to a free country: the country could not wholeheartedly accept it, but the *Latter-Day Pamphlets* predictably stirred up a great deal of controversy (they alienated many permanently from Carlyle) and turned attention to sources of public dismay which might otherwise have been overlooked. There is no doubt that Carlyle's declarations were, to a considerable extent, justified. The slums of London and the other Victorian cities were scandalous, and while his friend Dickens might be content to achieve similar public re-awakening with the complexities of plot in a novel such as *Hard Times*, where benevolence and the ill-judged attempts to help others while ignoring suffering near home are vividly satirised, Carlyle chose the more direct way. His pamphlets loudly decried 'weak' benevolence, and called for a tightening of moral fibre and discipline, a more rigid structure of control and rule than the existing parliament—and at the same time they called for the alleviation of a great deal of human suffering which was all too easy to ignore, on the doorsteps of many of those in Victorian London who were most active in the work of philanthropy.

Carlyle was thus catapulted into controversy in the 1850s. He threw himself into the verbal debate with gusto, for he loved nothing more than to embroider the points he had made in print, over the fireside in his own home. People left Cheyne Row occasionally appalled by the illiberality of what they had heard. Carlyle advocated stern measures for the times, corporal punishment not only for those who were criminal, but for those who were lazy. His attacks on the Irish as an incurably lazy and superstitious race offended many gravely, and Carlyle seemed curiously insensitive to their feelings. It took a real devotion, such as that of Charles Gavan Duffy, to endure nights of vilification of his own Irish nature and Irish countrymen, and still to become one of Carlyle's closest friends and most valuable diarists. Some earlier friends took grave offence: John Stuart Mill found it very difficult to accept Carlyle's intolerance, and some diarists recorded real shock and disgust. Most, however, recall the playful humour which was always there to relieve Carlyle's most violent attacks: his booming laugh softened the offence of what he had said, and his transparent friendliness served to convince the hearer that they were in the company not of an ogre, but a human being with strong feelings and an unusual gift of speech, particularly in invective. The reaction was exactly the same as that recorded by visitors to the humbler cottage in Ecclefechan, who had been dismayed by the family's gift of denunciation of those they did not like. Carlyle, true to his family's custom, used this gift to the full. He noted (we have seen) that he shared his father's defect of *exaggeration*—'for humorous effect'—and this is what people remembered him for. His denunciations, in the privacy of his own home, were staggering in their all embracing fervour. When he attacked a political figure, or writer, the destruction was total. It became impossible to take the man seriously afterwards. And then the booming laugh, and Carlyle would have 'performed' again—but there was more to it than a performing instinct. In writing or in speech, Carlyle believed in the urgency of his message. Poverty is a reality, just outside the walls of the model prison; and anarchy, religious weakness and realities, are near every home.

While Carlyle plunged publicly into this dispute, his own home life was secure and well-run; Jane made sure that Carlyle's nerves, worn thin by the tension of writing and by the undeniable strain which his oratorical habits of conversation placed on him, received no further strain from household events if possible. The letter she wrote to their maid Charlotte, already quoted at length, is an interesting example of this. She finds it necessary to explain to her own maid that Carlyle may have moods—since Carlyle's moods were a very frequent occurrence, Jane must somehow have steered them into safe conversational channels, or in some way concealed them even from the maid. When the house was being cleaned or painted, she made sure Carlyle was on holiday, out of London. When he returned from a journey, tired and out of spirits, she always took care that he should be undisturbed and quiet till he was back to normal. Jane (a fact which emerges clearly between the lines of Thea Holme's *The Carlyles at Home*) to a large extent sheltered her husband. She made sure that he had his own way as much as possible, and shielded him as much as she could from the irritations of day-to-day life. Heroically, she even appeared before an income-tax tribunal to plead for her husband, realising that he would not be able to keep his temper.

In this peaceful home atmosphere, Carlyle was able to continue to work well throughout the 1850s. In public he might have the reputation of being willing to talk at length, and publish unpopular controversial articles, but still every day required to be in part set aside to quiet work and study, or Carlyle felt miserable. His historical researches temporarily exhausted by *Cromwell*, Carlyle turned to a field he had neglected since the 1820s—biography.

The Life of John Sterling has always been, along with the *Reminiscences*, one of Carlyle's most popular works. Its style is easy and informal, its argument affectionate, and clearly Carlyle admired Sterling as a person, while envying the security of his faith, and the calm which he found in his beliefs. Carlyle was far from agreeing with him in religious ideas, but he did clearly admire one man's answer to the spiritual dilemma of the age, an answer which had made Sterling a close and intimate friend of the Sage of Chelsea, who was more usually given to scorning Churchmen, and people who openly advocated a conventional Christianity. Much as Carlyle advocated himself a return to Christian values, he could not respect most of the Churches of his day. He was openly contemptuous of the Church of England, he felt the Church of Scotland had declined from the high values it held in his own lifetime, and he could not bring himself to conquer the strong anti-Roman Catholic feelings which were natural to his religious background. But John Sterling's life was so openly pure and calm, that Carlyle overcame this distaste: the biography he produced was a tribute to a man who had given Carlyle a fine example.

Even so, the *Life of John Sterling* is remembered just as much for the portrait it contains, incidentally, of a man who had not given Carlyle a fine example—Coleridge. In 1824, when Carlyle was a raw young writer paying his first visit to London, he had gone more than once (Irving and he had shared the ambition) to visit the poet and thinker in his home in Highgate Hill. Carlyle's letters home had been savage in their denunciations of Coleridge as a fat, lazy, ill-regulated thinker, never finishing his sentences nor knowing where to stop, aptly summed up by the young Carlyle as 'a steam-engine of a hundred horses' power—with the boiler burst'. Carlyle clearly was aware of the power which Coleridge had, yet he could not respect such power in a ruinous state. The feeling emerges clearly in the 1850s, when he writes reminiscently of these visits in the *Life of John Sterling*.

'To sit as a passive bucket and be pumped into, whether you consent or not, can in the long-run be exhilerating to no creature; how eloquent soever the flood of utterance that is descending. But if it be withal a confused unintelligible flood of utterance, threatening to submerge all known landmarks of thought, and drown the world and you!—I have heard Coleridge talk, with eager musical energy, two stricken hours, his face radiant and moist, and communicate no meaning whatsoever to any individual of his hearers,—certain of whom, I for one, still kept eagerly listening in hope; the most had long before given up, and formed (if the room were large enough) secondary humming groups of their own ... Glorious islets, too, I have seen rise out of the haze; but they were few, and soon swallowed in the general element again ... The truth is, I now see, Coleridge's talk and speculation was the emblem of himself: in it as in him, a ray of heavenly inspiration struggled, in a tragically ineffectual degree, with the weakness of flesh and blood. He says once, he 'had skirted the howling deserts of Infidelity;' this was evident enough: but he had not had the courage, in defiance of pain and terror, to press resolutely across said deserts to the new firm lands of Faith beyond; he preferred to create logical fatamorganas for himself on this hither side, and laboriously solace himself with these.'

Coleridge, in short, had not suffered the 'Everlasting NO': Carlyle studied him anxiously (he had hoped, he noted, to find something about 'Kant and Co', from the venerable sage) and Sterling treated him with friendliness, but there was no firm hope there for either man. The *Life of John Sterling* shows that Carlyle respected the memory of Sterling's friendliness, more than he could respect his example as a survivor of an old school of religious certitude. The 1850s were not to see a return on Carlyle's part to the religious institutions he had laboriously escaped from earlier.

A new direction was becoming obvious in Carlyle's thought, even so, as the decade advanced. Carlyle in late 1851 began to read with interest and energy about the military history of Prussia, a strong state whose military government and strong royalty came more and more to represent in Carlyle's mind a sort of shining ideal in a world which seemed to be convulsed by social change, social reform, and the decay of long-held institutions. Strong precise Prussian institutions seemed to suffer from no such decay. Further, Carlyle was no stranger to the sort of firm government which was implicit in the Prussian system: the *Reminiscences* (of his father particularly) show that it was natural to the young Carlyle to think of life as a systematic experience where men's destinies were controlled for them, their obligations clearly marked out, and their obedience enforced if necessary by a strong authoritarian régime which believed in the long-term correctness of its strategy—even if in the short term the methods seemed brutal. The quasi-military life-style of the Prussian Court as it existed under Frederick the Great matched this picture: it is partly reflected in the extremely authoritarian world-view of Ecclefechan in the *Reminiscences*: to a large extent it lies behind the argument of the sixth and vital chapter of *Chartism*, where Carlyle argues whether Right is Might.

The authoritarian aspect of life in Prussian times interested Carlyle in the light both of his own early life, and because of his conviction that such a strong government was necessary in his own upset times. As a historian Carlyle was drawn to the Seven Years' War, and he read upon the subject with zeal, following his usual work-pattern of immersing himself in the maps, pictures and accounts of a battle, or area, before deciding whether to write on it. Jane helped by collecting prints, cutting out pictures. In June 1852 Carlyle recorded he was 'reading about the Seven Years' War, with 10 maps spread out before me'. In August of the same year he paid his first visit to Germany, to survey some of the ground which would be involved in a history of Frederick the Great. Ironically, the man who had done perhaps more than any other to bring German literature and thought to the attention of the British people, in the 1820s, was paying his first visit to Germany in the 1850s. His German was halting, his enjoyment of the country very limited. Always a poor traveller, he concentrated on covering the country he wished to, then bolted for home. The experience was not a pleasant one physically, but it seems mentally to have convinced him that he was to write on Frederick. As the 1850s progressed, so did the history, laboriously, slowly, in a series of false starts. In 1853 Frederick was begun, but Carlyle was very dissatisfied. In 1856 a considerable part was done, and considered satisfactory. In June 1858, the first two volumes of *Frederick the Great* were finished, and Carlyle was committed irrevocably to a huge publishing project.

Frederick the Great grew longer and longer, and the end seemed more and more unattainable. Carlyle discovered more and more material, and decided he must incorporate more to make the history a fair one. The story of Voltaire, one of Carlyle's literary heroes (for Carlyle always admired this French writer, although he detested the French eighteenth century in general, and most of Voltaire's contemporaries) grew to occupy an increasingly large part of the story of Frederick's court. Voltaire spent many years there as Frederick's guest, and Carlyle delighted to counterpoint the characters of the enlightened French intellectual, and the stolid but powerful Prussian autocrat. Yet this added to the bulk of the book, and to the labour required. Another visit to Germany seemed necessary, and was reluctantly undertaken, in August and September of 1858. In October 1858, on Carlyle's return, volumes one and two of *Frederick the Great* were published. In financial terms they were extremely successful—Carlyle was paid at once almost £3,000 for them—and slowly the public grew to admire the work, although appalled by the length, and although some disliked Carlyle's plain and growing admiration for someone whom many regarded as an unpleasant autocrat.

Frederick the Great hangs over the 1850s, and the first half of the 1860s, as a huge black cloud. The journal entries, the letters to friends and relatives betray Carlyle's exasperation at the way in which the project grew, and the completion date (by which time Carlyle would be seventy) receded. Financial necessity was now a memory: he was impelled to write not by hunger or uncertainty, but by his own strong motivations to finish what he had begun, and to meet his own exacting standards. But in doing so he frequently exhausted himself, and exhausted the patience of his friends.

The decade saw many journeys undertaken by the Carlyles, often as intervals to periods of hard work. They paid almost annual visits to Scotland, to hospitable homes at Addiscombe (the Barings) or the Grange (the Ashburtons). In 1857 Carlyle lost a valued friend, Harriet, the first Lady Ashburton: Jane's jealousies had embittered this friendship, but Carlyle was clearly very attracted by the aristocratic friendliness of Lady Ashburton, who seems on her side to have been drawn to him. The second Lady Ashburton was to be a warm friend to both Carlyles: in neither case was there matter for scandal, but with hindsight one can see that Carlyle found pleasure in human companionship which Jane alone could not satisfy. It is an interesting comment on the later scandal that he was a man without interest in women, whose marriage failed because of his impotence.

Jane's jealousy over the Ashburton complication to their marriage was strong, but it has to be seen in the context of the decline in Jane's health over the 1850s. Always a sufferer from neuralgia and migraine headaches, Jane became more and more prone to severe pain which made it impossible for her to be as active socially as she had been at the beginning of her life in London. Photographs of her at this time—the art of commercial photography having made available pictures of both Carlyles from the mid-1850s onwards—show her face as becoming dreadfully thin, the skin drawn tight over the cheeks, the hair drawn severely back from an unsmiling sharp-drawn face in which the huge dark eyes stood out strangely. Her photographs are stiff, an unnatural and self-conscious pose. His photographs are stiff too, yet not so unsmiling: one superb pose survives from the earlier years of the decade, a fine upright seated profile, the dress neat and obviously well-cared for, the nose as always slightly curled in quasi-disdain, the mouth out-thrust in determination. Even in black-and-white photographs, the extraordinary faded quality of the light blue eyes is obvious. As the 1850s progress the beard (which Carlyle grew in keeping with a fashion, and never shaved after) becomes thicker, and the face at once ages. Lines of fatigue appear round the eyes, and the pose which Carlyle habitually adopted for the camera, sad and contemplative, emphasises the ageing of the face from the fierce and youthful beardless profile. Both Carlyles were growing into late middle-age. Carlyle carried into it apparently undiminished vigour, and an enormous intensity of will; Jane was physically failing, though her will too was still strong.

In 1853 came the last of the 'earthquakes' in Cheyne Row, this time the building of the soundproof room. The success of this was, as we know, a very partial one, but it was a room forever associated with *Frederick*. In its muffled (and stifling) walls Carlyle wrestled with the notes, the maps, the extracts, the heavy tomes which other historians had produced and which Carlyle either bought or borrowed for his use while working with Frederick. After the book was finished, the room was abandoned and later turned into a maid's bedroom. To-day its fading walls are hung with testimony to the years of intensive effort which went into the history. Over the desk, hangs a photograph of Carlyle sitting at the same desk, surrounded with papers, wrestling with the manuscript of *Frederick*. He looks supremely miserable.

Lady Ashburton's was not the only death in the Carlyles' acquaintance during this decade: a much more serious break with the past was the death of old Mrs Carlyle, his mother, who had been living quietly in Scotland on the family farm since her son's departure for London in 1834, regularly writing to him and receiving letters from him, and living patiently the long-suffering and hard-working life-style in which she had trained her children. Carlyle's emotional attachment to her was very great: he feared his father, while he respected him, yet to his mother he could be more open, and even in his student days the two of them had looked forward to his return for long vacation so that they could lock themselves in a quiet room of the house, and smoke pipes and drink tea together. Their intimacy was a rare one, and Carlyle valued it: he lost it on Christmas Day, 1853, and it was a link with the past cut for him. There was no spontaneous outburst of *Reminiscences*, as there had been twenty years before when his father had died. His literary energies were channelled elsewhere, and perhaps his emotional responses under better control. But there was a real sense of bereavement.

The 1850s ended with a summer in Scotland, to recover from the exertion of finishing the published portion of *Frederick*, and in Jane's case to try desperately to recover some normal health. The decade had been a productive one in terms of published work, it had seen friends made and lost: throughout it, visitors continued to make the Chelsea house the object of their attention, visitors like Charles Kingsley and Erasmus Darwin. The intellectual stimulus of these visits to both Carlyles was enormous, and it gave them the energy to go on with apparently hopelessly great work, to endure headache and physical misery. The placidity of Chelsea was still important to Carlyle in finding peace in which to work, but the silent street concealed an astonishing record of industry on his part, suffering on Jane's, and stimulating friendship and conversational ability on the part of both.

THE SIXTIES

THE HARD work and the perseverance of the preceding decade were rewarded triumphantly in the 1860s: the reward was a short one. The first half of the decade could be summed up in one word: *Frederick*. The letters and journals grow almost boring on the theme—when will Carlyle ever be done with the interminable history. Volume 3 was concluded in 1861, and published in 1862. Volume 4 followed in 1864, and the writing finally completed on 16 January 1865. In March volumes 5 and 6 were published, and Carlyle's life-work as a historian substantially complete.

It had been an enormous labour, and the price had been high for both Carlyles. Jane's health declined steadily, and a fall from a carriage accident aggravated a nervous condition. In pain, and in a confused nervous state, she moved constantly, to the seaside, to friends' houses, always with pleasure to her own room in Chelsea, but she found peace and freedom from pain very rarely. Carlyle paid her what attention he could, but he was obsessed with the unfinished *Frederick*, indeed Jane's letters indicate that she preferred not to have him pay her too much attention when she was ill, but to leave her to suffer. The accident in which she hurt herself (she had to step violently aside to avoid a speeding horse-cab) happened in 1863, in October, and the suffering which followed lasted for over two years. In 1864 the Carlyles engaged Mrs Warren, a housekeeper who was to be a faithful member of the family for over ten years, and who immediately took over some of the duties of running the household which Jane was too ill to keep up. Jane was slowly losing her hold on the Chelsea home which she had run with superb efficiency since arriving in 1834; the story of her dealings with a succession of unsatisfactory maids alone (wittily told by Thea Holme in *The Carlyles at Home*) sufficiently entitled her to a place in Carlyle's canon of heroes. In ill-health she could not cope, and Mrs Warren moved into some of her supervisory capacities with tact. Jane was to remain a formidable hostess, a drawn suffering face in an invalid's chair, but the day-to-day running of the house she surrendered. Carlyle worked on.

In 1865, the need for work was over. With *Frederick* published, Carlyle's reputation as a considerable historian was established beyond doubt. The book has never been among his most popular. Its promilitaristic tone, its adulation of a powerful monarch make it sufficiently out of tune with modern times, indeed with many of Carlyle's own generation, but perhaps one need look no further than the six heavy volumes, with their close type and their tight footnotes, to see a greater reason still for their unpopularity. Unlike Gibbon's *Decline and Fall* they do not lead the reader irresistibly by a calm but hypnotic style: they are of a piece with Carlyle's other historical work, declamatory, ejaculatory, apparently wayward and time-wasting. They were received with respect, but not with adulation. Carlyle's victory was a tempered one, but at least it was the victory of having survived the incredible, and finished the impossible. He was free of *Frederick*.

An honour which could not fail to please him came in November of the same year, 1865: Carlyle was elected by the students of his own University, Edinburgh, to be Lord Rector. The position is a largely honorary one, in Carlyle's time usually being conferred on a famous man for the prestige of having his name connected with the student body. The Lord Rector represented the student body, he accepted nomination in a public lecture which always attracted considerable attention, and in extreme cases he might chair meetings or plead for students in disciplinary measures. Carlyle's letter of acceptance made it clear that he deeply appreciated the compliment, but that while accepting he would do no more than deliver the address.

On 2 April 1866 Carlyle stood up in the Music Hall, George Street, and delivered his address, *On the Choice of Books*. It was an extraordinary occasion: the most distinguished man for many years to have passed through the University, world-famous as historian, social writer and ethical thinker, was to return to his *alma mater*. He was offered an honorary degree, but declined it. He was offered the customary robes, but soon shrugged them off. He took the customary prepared speech, but soon abandoned it. He stood before a packed audience, full to the doors, and spoke apparently extempore to a hushed house on his experience as a student, his life since leaving Edinburgh, and the conclusions he had drawn from the experience of a lifetime as writer and thinker. To the students he recommended a rigorous course of reading and self-cultivation as he himself had achieved; he commended them to keep up their standards in studies and in their lives, and to fight the decay of standards and of ethics which he himself had always fought. In retracing for them the steps by which he had emerged from the nightmares which had haunted his youth and student days, he ended with a message of hope, quoted from his early idol, Goethe—*Wir heissen euch Hoffen!* We bid you hope—after a lifetime of struggle and a good deal of suffering, of strenuous work and unceasing attempts to live up to an ideal which had been imprinted on him at the end of the eighteenth century, it was a remarkable message for the young generation of 1866.

As an address, it was sensationally successful. The affection and admiration felt for Carlyle in Edinburgh were unmistakable, and the applause was wild. Carlyle had survived, there was hope.

Less than three weeks later, the hope was extinguished. Jane's nerves had been too poor to share her husband's triumph: she had stayed in London, and waited anxiously for the telegram which John Tyndall sent after the address, 'A perfect triumph!'—indicating that all had gone well in the Music Hall. She was delighted—Dickens found her in her best and most cheerful mood shortly afterwards. She even went out for a drive, with a tame dog which she was looking after for a neighbour. Their carriage stopped in Hyde Park, and Jane allowed the dog to run out for exercise. Again the villain of the scene was a hard-driven carriage, which galloped past and slightly injured the dog. Jane rushed out and, having rescued the hurt and weeping animal, dropped back into her seat to rest. The driver went on, and it was some time before he stopped the carriage to see why there had been no movement, no directions given from inside. He drove to a hospital as fast as he could, but it was too late. Jane, apparently quite peacefully, had leaned back in the carriage seat and died.

Four hundred miles away, Carlyle was holidaying in Dumfries with his relatives. He had slightly twisted an ankle, and this delayed his return to London. Meantime he thoroughly enjoyed the country air and the company of his family, and when two telegrams were handed in to their home he tossed them, unopened, to his sister. In the family atmosphere there were no secrets, and no suspicion of bad news. His sister read them horrified, then handed them to Thomas. It was, as he was shortly to write on his wife's tombstone, as if the light of his life had gone out. He spent some time in solitude, then came back into the family life and quietly prepared to return to London. He was mentally in agony at the unexpectedness of the loss; the journey to London was an unbearable experience, and the preparations for a funeral (and the avoiding of an autopsy, which kindly friends managed to arrange, in consideration for Carlyle's feelings) drove him almost to the limits of his patience.

As Carlyle had loved Jane deeply before they were married, so he loved her memory deeply when she was taken from him. While they were married and lived together, their relationship was a tense one, yet they were clearly indispensible to each other. Both lived at high pressure, each needed the stimulus of the other to keep up this pressure and to find the impetus to work or to converse. The writing of *Frederick* had made a recluse of Carlyle, and very probably he looked forward to the years following 1865 as a time when he would have the leisure to devote to Jane, to enjoy her company and look after her in what was obviously very poor health. To have this prospect dashed was sufficiently painful.

What was more painful, was that Carlyle felt himself impelled to go through Jane's letters and papers, and set them in order. To begin with, it was a perfectly natural interest to see that her life was left in order, and her last requests would be carried out, but the project grew and grew until it provided Carlyle with an obsessive interest as great as that in Frederick which he had just recently discarded. Jane was buried on 26 April 1866; for the whole succeeding month Carlyle read letters, looked at souvenirs and relics, and brooded. Geraldine Jewsbury, a bright young novelist who had been a close friend of Jane's, indeed almost a worshipper of her, wrote a little notebook of reminiscences of Jane, and sent them to Carlyle.

Reminiscences came easily to a man like Carlyle who talked a lot, and (as we have seen) in his talking liked to characterise people, especially he had known in his youth. When visitors from Scotland called, Carlyle was bound to re-create in vivid speech some scene from the past: when Jane passed away, Carlyle had to find some vivid way to re-create her presence. In the house there was material enough: both of them squirrels, the Carlyles had never thrown away letters, and although Jane had torn up some of her most intimate diaries, she left behind an enormous quantity of letters and documents, which occupied many lonely hours for Carlyle. Everything was there, from the earliest (almost illegible) notes which had passed between them, in Haddington and London, to the letters which had most recently been posted, while he was in Scotland and she in London. The record of forty years of married life was there, and for several reasons, quite apart from the loss of Jane, Carlyle found it painful reading. In the first place, Jane's letters to her friends gave details which her own to Carlyle would not have—details about her health, which she had shielded from him to save his feelings while he was working on *Frederick*, and her inner feelings of testiness, or jealousy, or impatience which she naturally confided more easily to some correspondents than to others. To his pain, Carlyle would have come across letters written about him when he barely knew Jane, wittily satirising him for his clumsiness and lack of social grace. He might have come across stray details which revealed that they had had a quarrel, or he had in some hasty word (and his hasty words found powerful expression) wounded her feelings.

But there was another source of pain: Jane, like her husband, had been skilled in the gift of comic exaggeration, and when she was describing things in letters she could use this to devastating effect. The exaggeration is as effective when she is being critical of Thomas, as when she is praising him. To read letters and no more, might be to suspect that the relations between the two had been stormier by far than they were, and to find this in her papers must have wounded Carlyle. Certainly his reactions are powerful ones, eloquent tributes scribbled on the outsides of letters to the noble patience of his Jeannie, her suffering and his thoughtlessness.

Initially, it was perhaps a good and valuable idea to live in the past in this way. It took his mind off the immediacy of his loss, and it gave him occupation which was still very necessary to his day. A day on which he did nothing, which he wasted, left him feeling very miserable. By degrees he passed from merely sorting and annotating letters, to creating whole paragraphs of explanation to illuminate a paragraph which might have been a private joke, or an allusion to a family event so obscure as to be unintelligible without some further reference. At this stage there was no suggestion that this was prepared for publication—Carlyle was merely giving vent to his feelings by writing them down.

With Geraldine Jewsbury's notebook, however, the idea of communicating his feelings to paper grew strong, and from this came the collection of essays now known as the *Reminiscences*, and regarded by many as among the most immediately attractive of Carlyle's works. The volume we know to-day as the *Reminiscences* contains the 1832 section in praise of James Carlyle, as well as fragments written later in the 1860s, but essentially it is a continuous stream of narrative which Carlyle committed to paper between late May 1866 and March 1867. He did not spend time continuously on the project, indeed at times he felt that it was quite in abeyance. Kind friends took him to Mentone in the South of France for the sake of his health over the winter of 1866-1867, and he enjoyed the sunshine and took long walks, but the manuscript travelled with him and he worked at it when the mood took him.

Slowly there took shape an extraordinary work of literature. The *Reminiscences* were written with pain, obviously; they are interlarded with impatient comments by the author, by expressions of regret and indeed by admissions of the futility of writing them at all. But they were a relief. He regarded them not as his 'task', but as a 'quasi-task': something to keep his mind occupied, till he should return to his desk to his proper work.

The germ came from Jane's friend Geraldine Jewsbury, and her recollections of Jane's youth and early experiences (as Jane had told them). Carlyle read them with interest, though he was not interested enough to finish them. He found them mostly incorrect in details, in no way completely true, and it must have been this realisation which made him turn to producing some similar account of his own, based on his intimate knowledge of Jane's youth. And so he sat down to write everything he knew of Jane's early life, reminiscence and preserved letter, and the confirmations of family history which he made careful notes to follow up at a future date. In writing the *Reminiscences* he re-lived their first meeting, their tentative courtship and their whole married life. He vividly recalled their moments of high experience, like the removal to Chelsea, and their first meeting in Mrs Welsh's Haddington home:

'Mrs Welsh, though beautiful, a tall *acquiline* figure, of elegant carriage and air, was not of intellectual or specially distinguished physiognomy; and, in her severe costume and air, rather repelled me than otherwise at that time. A day or so after, next evening perhaps, both Irving and I were in her Drawing-room, with her Daughter and her, both very humane to me, especially the former, which I noticed with true joy for the moment. I was miserably ill in health; miserable every way more than enough, in my lonely imprisonment, *such* it was, which lasted many years. The Drawing-room seemed to me the finest apartment I had ever sat or stood in . . . Clean, all of it, as spring water; solid and correct as well as pertinently ornamented: in the Drawing-room, on the tables there, perhaps rather a superfluity of elegant whimwhams. The summer twilight, I remember, was pouring in rich and soft; I felt as one walking transiently in upper spheres, which I had little right even to make transit.'

Carlyle was writing from his own elegant drawing-room in Chelsea as he remembered these scenes, and the contrast must have seemed doubly wounding. Now the elegant whimwhams would have seemed normal, the elegant life-style the everyday surroundings of a successful London author. But their enlivening hostess was gone, and Carlyle left lonely in the Chelsea home. The *Reminiscences* temporarily brought the missing spirit back to life: like Tennyson in *In Memoriam*, Carlyle would briefly summon up a desperately missed friend by evoking the memory concisely but poignantly. But the difference is in the literary mode. Tennyson wrote in stanza 75 that:

> I leave thy praises unexpress'd
> In verse that brings myself relief,
> And by the measure of my grief
> I leave thy greatness to be guess'd.

Carlyle left very little to be guessed, as he lacked the controlling genius with which Tennyson manipulated the sense of loss in *In Memoriam* to lead to a final climax of faith that the living and the dead would be reunited. Tennyson worked sixteen years to ensure the climax, endlessly re-shaping and polishing the account of his grief at the loss of Hallam. Carlyle simply wrote, copiously and compulsively. He asked himself why, from time to time, but he did not, could not stop.

'I will write of this no further: the beauty of it is so steeped to me in pain. Why do I *write* it at all, for that matter? Can *I* ever forget? And is not all this appointed by me rigorously to the fire? Somehow it solaces me to *have* written it;—and to-morrow, probably, I shall fill out these two remaining pages. Ah me . . .'

Jane had herself written some *Reminiscences*, but burned them before her death. Carlyle, who plainly (from the passage quoted) intended to burn his own reminiscences, 'steeped in pain', wistfully would have liked to have seen Jane's, but she had refused '. . . all sight of them even to me'. What he had left were her letters (surely a richer vein than any number of her reminiscences would have been) and his memories.

Initially, the memories sustained him through a long-drawn bout of writing which produced 'Jane Welsh Carlyle' in the summer of 1866, 'Edward Irving' and 'Francis Jeffrey' over the autumn and winter, and various fragments on Southey, Wordsworth and other literary figures who dominated his memories in the Spring of 1867. These later *Reminiscences* focus more closely on the person named in the title: they are in a more literal sense Reminiscences of Wordsworth or Southey, whereas the earlier ones, on Jane Welsh, Irving and Jeffrey were wide-ranging autobiographical exercises built around the central idea of the friendship Carlyle had had with the main figure named. In non-chronological order they provide an amazingly detailed picture of life as remembered by Carlyle, always in painful conjunction with the memory of Jane at the period of his life he is writing of. To write of Jeffrey reminds him of the Comely Bank years, spent with Jane, and the Craigenputtoch period: to write of Irving reminds him of the first meeting with Jane, and the early trips to London which prepared for their married life there.

The *Reminiscences* are remarkable not only for the width of the material which is recalled in them, but for the immediacy with which Carlyle was able to present it sometimes half-a-century after the event. In 'Edward Irving' he can write:

'Those old three days at Roseneath are all very vivid to me, and marked in white: the great blue mountain masses, giant "Cobler" overhanging, bright seas, bright skies; Roseneath new Mansion (still unfinished, and standing as it did, the present Duke of Argyll has told me), the grand old oaks,—and a certain handfast, middle-aged, practical and most polite "Mr. Campbell" (the Argyll Factor there), with his two Sisters, excellent lean old ladies, with their wild Highland accent, wiredrawn but genuine good-manners and good principles . . . They are all dead, these good souls . . .'

The scene is set almost exactly fifty years before, yet Carlyle is recalling it with photographic accuracy. And it is not the accuracy of a finished picture, recalled exactly as it happened as if no intervening time had intruded, for Carlyle has updated his information, and interpolated the comments as he writes it all down together. Scenes and people alike spring vividly to his memory. Riding with John Badams he remembers going to Kenilworth, 'one Saturday afternoon, by the "Wood of Arden" and its monstrous old Oaks, on to the famous Ruin itself (*fresh* in the Scott Novels then), and a big jolly Farmer friend of

Badams's, who lodged us, nice polite Wife and he, in a finely human way, till Monday morning'. Sometimes it was actual physical conditions of life which impressed him most, as they did when he remembered the occasion on which Francis Jeffrey and his family visited Craigenputtoch in September 1830. The two families met on a similar occasion, 'and passed a night with them in the King's Arms Inn there, which I well enough recollect: huge ill-kept "Head-Inn"; bed opulent in *bugs*; waiter, a monstrous baggy unwieldy old figure, hebetated, dreary, as if parboiled; upon whom Jeffrey quizzed his Daughter at breakfast, "Comes all of eating eggs, Sharlie; poor man as good as owned it to me!" '
These happy moments are vivid to Carlyle, as vivid as the pancakes which Jane cooked for the Jeffreys in Craigenputtoch. The domestic happiness is most vivid: the contrast when the Jeffreys have to leave Craigenputtoch is severe, when they went and ' "carried off our little temporary paradise", as I sorrowfully expressed it to them, while shutting their Coach door in our back yard,—to which bit of pathos Jeffrey answered by a friendly little sniff of quasi-mockery, or laughter through the nose; and rolled prosperously away.'
To live in these moments of recollected happiness may have helped ease the pain of separation at first, but the relief by writing was offset by the absence of a controlling intention (like Tennyson's in *In Memoriam*) and by the exhaustion, after living for days and months in a remembered world, which contrasted all the more cruelly with the reality at the end of each day's writing. A firm journal note at the end of the last of the *Reminiscences*, that of Wordsworth, emphasises this:
'Finished the rag on Wordsworth to the last tatter; won't begin another: *Cui bono*, it is wearisome and naught even to myself . . . I live mostly alone, with vanished Shadows of the Past, —many of them rise for a moment, inexpressibly tender; One is never long absent from me. Gone, gone, but very . . .' Yet dear! 'ETERNITY, which cannot be far off, is my one strong city. I look into it fixedly now and then; all terrors about it seem to me superfluous; all knowledge about it, any the least glimmer of certain knowledge, impossible to living mortal. The universe is

full of love, and also of inexorable sternness and severity: and it remains for ever true that "GOD reigns." Patience, silence, hope!'

To reach a conclusion such as this gave Carlyle relief from the immediate impact of the loss of Jane: its long-term effects to readers of Carlyle were incalculable, for they gained in the *Reminiscences* an unvarnished account of Carlyle's earlier years which offered a remarkable insight into his developing mind. They were written under stress, and that fact must remain in the forefront of any interpretation of them. Against this, the immediacy of their picture guarantees the immediacy of the emotional response which they attempt to reproduce. When he wrote them Carlyle relived, with pain, the happier scenes of his life. When he finished 'Jane Welsh Carlyle', he was so conscious of the spontaneity with which he had written that he added a solemn note to posterity. 'I still mainly mean to *burn* this Book before my own departure; but feel that I shall always have a kind of grudge to do it, and in indolent excuse . . . In which event, I solemnly forbid them, each and all, to *publish* this Bit of Writing *as it stands here*; and warn them that *without fit editing* no *part* of it should be printed (nor so far as I can order, *shall* ever be);—and that the '*fit* editing' of perhaps nine-tenths of it will, after I am gone, have become *impossible*.'

If writing the *Reminiscences* gave Carlyle relief, so too did travel. He visited friends' houses, but more particularly he was taken by kind friends to the South of France for the darkest part of the winter, which he spent in Mentone. John Tyndall, a scientist who was to become a famous writer, travelled with Carlyle and found him a testy, but fascinating companion, interested in everything, and when he broke out of his increasingly habitual gloom, an interested and lively amateur scientist. 'His questions on scientific matters showed wonderful penetration', recalled Tyndall, which is an interesting commentary on how much must have remained of Carlyle's early Edinburgh scientific training. Science was not now his solace. Occasional company, the opportunity to write the *Reminiscences*, and a slow re-establishment of the pattern of visiting at Cheyne Row seemed to be the things best calculated to alleviate Carlyle's gloom.

Certainly he did not altogether withdraw from the circle of friends which he and Jane had built up, and indeed they rallied round him vigorously to protect him at this crucial time. Some younger ones, like William Allingham and Francis Espinasse, grew intimate with Carlyle and he relieved his mind by telling them of his youth and earlier experiences—experiences which they were quick to record in their diaries and preserve for posterity. Some acquaintances, like James Anthony Froude, became very close confidants indeed: in *My Relations with Carlyle* Froude was later to describe a friendship which developed from a young man's hero-worship of an established literary figure, to a protective relationship where Froude took some of the burden of guilt (real or imaginary) from Carlyle by sharing in his editorial labours.

For Carlyle deliberately set out to prepare a memorial of his wife in the shape of her letters and papers. Both the Carlyles were, as we know, outstanding letter-writers, and both preserved their papers with unusual tenacity. Carlyle had available, in the home in Cheyne Row, the materials for an extensive collection of his wife's letters, and the replies which he had sent her, as well as those she had received from others. After the *Reminiscences* were written Carlyle turned to the selection and editing of the letters with enthusiasm, and by December of 1868, he was involved in the task.

'Involved' is a good word to describe Carlyle's work with Jane's letters, for he was deeply emotionally involved in the preparation of the manuscripts. He read them and tentatively dated them: his emotional state can be guessed from his extreme attitude of caution in this dating and identification process. Even when the date is quite obvious, from postmark or internal evidence, Carlyle is quick to qualify his annotation by a question mark. He commits himself rarely, and frequently uses a sentence in the letter to form the core of a quite separate autobiographical section of reminiscence which is safely distanced from the letter which inspired it. These notes are of the greatest value to the historian, in that they offer explanations for persons, places and things in the letters which would otherwise quite baffle a modern editor; for the biographer, they are also immensely valuable in adding to the body of Carlyle's autobiographical writings those things which had not immediately suggested themselves to his mind when he was involved in writing the *Reminiscences*. These fragments were in their turn supplemented by the stories he told Espinasse, Froude and the other people who came to visit him, and slowly the story of his life emerged, under the influence of his loss of Jane.

Everything was not loss, although the mood of heavy grief hung over Carlyle for many years. The companionship of his youthful admirers was soon supplemented, in September 1868, by the arrival of his niece, Mary, who was soon to settle into Cheyne Row and be housekeeper, amanuensis and friend to her Uncle Tom for the rest of his life. A woman of strong character but retiring disposition, Mary was a good manager and with the aid of good servants (particularly Mrs Warren, the housekeeper) made the declining years of Carlyle's life comfortable as Jane had done when she was alive. Mary was quiet, but willing to work for hours sorting through letters with her uncle, writing to his dictation, and arranging books and papers for eventual publication. She learned a good deal about her uncle's affairs, and soon came to be invaluable.

Quiet though she was, she had a personality which occasionally showed itself to visitors; when Robert Herdman painted his fine portrait of Carlyle in 1875 he repeated some of the Sage's conversation to Mary, and she neatly punctured some of the more exaggerated accounts of Carlyle's minor ailments. She was a good influence in many ways, for the settled melancholy which followed Jane's death could easily have been hypochondriac, and Carlyle (never a good sufferer) complained very frequently about indigestion and sleeplessness. More seriously he complained about a shaking right hand which made writing very difficult. 'You perceive I am reduced to write with a pencil', he wrote in 1870 to Charles Eliot Norton in Harvard, '—disagreeably to myself and others; but with pen it is still worse. For the rest, a perpetual reminiscence to me how excell*t* is *Brevity*, the soul of wit!' Like Scott he found that another person's writing hand was a poor substitute for his own, and although Mary wrote letters for him frequently (he would sign them), she did not have much dictation of actual works of literature to cope with. Rather she annotated and arranged, and occasionally copied out things fit for the printer to read.

The abrupt withdrawal from public life at Jane's death did not continue permanently, partly because of Carlyle's desire for human contact and if possible stimulating, public controversy, partly also because he had become too famous to be a recluse. Unlike Tennyson he did not live in a remote district, where visitors would have to stand in wait to catch a glimpse of him. Visitors, it is true, did haunt the end of Cheyne Row for the privilege of seeing the great man, and bus conductors pointed him out proudly to their passengers. But Carlyle lived on in Chelsea, becoming more and more frequently seen as the 1860s ended, his habit of late-night walks firmly re-established, wandering far and wide into the city streets which more and more linked once-quiet Chelsea to London, and stretched out into what had been open country. His home was quiet and well-run, his major historical work was done. He craved human contact, and he received public recognition.

Perhaps the most notable instance of this latter fact was his interview on 4 March 1869 with Queen Victoria. Carlyle refused to be overawed by the Queen, who in her turn made commonplace conversation with the Great Man whose works were obviously strange to her. Carlyle enjoyed telling the story to his friends, and writing about it, as he increasingly enjoyed his re-emergence into society. Certainly he still had a taste for controversy. In 1867 he had published *Shooting Niagara—And After?*, one of the most violent of his statements about the decadence of his century, and its eventual political downfall. Earlier, in the autumn of 1866, he had been active in the Eyre controversy, in a manner as violent as in *Shooting Niagara*.

October 1865 had seen serious rioting in Jamaica, and equally serious concerns was expressed when the Governor, E. J. Eyre, suppressed the rioting with what many took to be quite excessive violence. The report of the investigating committee, published in April 1866, was unfavourable to Eyre, who was recalled, and who became the subject of fierce public debate. The two sides briefly took the following views. One was that the force, however severe, was justified by the necessity of keeping the colony in order so as to prevent further bloodshed, and preserve the economy. The other, liberal view was one of horror and dismay at the treatment of the native Jamaicans by the British administration. The latter party tried hard, though unsuccessfully, to have Eyre tried and punished for his actions, while the former party campaigned energetically in his defence. Carlyle was, predictably, on the defensive side, for his whole viewpoint was one in which force was justified if its long-term intention was a good one, and it was necessary to preserve the fabric of society. Cromwell, after all, had been a notable case of this principle in action. Unfortunately the principal figure on the other side was John Stuart Mill, and the bitterness which the Governor Eyre controversy stirred up between the two, a bitterness which expressed itself publicly in print, was to be the end of an enriching friendship. Carlyle was on the same side as Tennyson and Ruskin, and eventually it was the successful side, for Eyre was never punished.

In the Governor Eyre controversy, as in *Shooting Niagara*, Carlyle revealed himself more and more opposed to the liberal cause, and increasingly advocating a use of force, well directed, to maintain the balance of power in the world, and keep people to their 'work' which Carlyle conceived as the sacred duty common to every one. There was much in this position he adopted which was repulsive to his contemporaries, particularly his attitude to the coloured races in the West Indies, whom he clearly saw as there to work, and to produce the materials for trade and commerce which were necessary. Civil commotion in Jamaica could only interrupt this commerce, and so the natives had to be driven back to work. From the distance of London, it was easy for Carlyle to make this analysis; if he had had to see the problem at closer quarters, he would probably have taken a very different approach, but in his role as 'Sage' he found it necessary to state his position firmly—in *Shooting Niagara* particularly with his gift of comic emphasis well developed. The

comedy may have worked as a rhetorical device, but its humour
was lost on many readers.

The end of the 1860s, then, saw Carlyle approaching old age in
a frame of mind which was strongly overcast by the loss of Jane:
he felt that he had reached the end of his life and ambition, having
lost his wife and completed much of what he had set out to do as
historian and prophet. His health was failing, his trembling right
hand making work more and more difficult. From time to time
he abandoned the pen and employed a blunt blue pencil with
which he found it easier to write legibly (although later scholars
were to find it faded alarmingly quickly) while at other times he
simply dictated to Mary, or gave up writing altogether and
merely read. He was still enormously respected by many of his
countrymen, and the volume of help and sympathy which the
death of Jane had brought forward testified to the huge circle of
his friends, and their true regard for him. At the same time, his
rigid views on society were alienating him from his more liberal
contemporaries, and making him appear to belong to a less
flexible world-picture of the past, rather than the rapidly evolving
world of the 1860s and 1870s. Sitting in lonely Chelsea, Carlyle
must have felt that his career was both at its climax, and in its
decline, simultaneously. It was a mood which was to set the tone
for the rest of his life.

12

THE SEVENTIES

In 1870 Carlyle was seventy-five. He was always active and athletic, still tall and spare, his grizzled hair and beard plentiful, and the electric blue of his eyes never losing its piercing intensity. His cheeks were ruddy, his step rapid, and it was difficult to realise that the stooped figure with his deep resonant voice and emphatic manner, who could still talk in blazing monologue for hours at a time, captivating an audience and if need be simply bearing down the opposition, was a man who had been born in the previous century, who had been publishing for almost fifty years, and was now an old man. Carlyle himself had little trouble in realising this: his notes to Jane's letters, and his own jottings in the diaries he kept, increasingly dwell on his bitter loneliness, his desire to be reunited with Jane, the futility of living on in a world where he seemed more and more out of place.

Apart from his niece Mary's companionship, he had the relief of a large circle of local friends. Carlyle travelled as frequently as he could, in good weather, to the Ashburtons', to friends' country houses, above all to Scotland. His family ties were still strong, and his brother John (to whom he had always been close) visited him in Chelsea frequently. The circle of friends was no old man's, small and secure in its familiarity, but an exciting and expanding group of challenging people. In 1872, Emerson (who had spent little time with Carlyle, although they had spent a large part of their lifetimes in correspondence) visited Carlyle, and again in 1873. At the same time Charles Eliot Norton, who was to play a notable part in the editing and popularising of Carlyle's works, was a frequent caller. David Masson of Edinburgh, another important figure in the story of Carlyle's later reputation, was a frequent and favoured visitor.

Signs of Carlyle's popularity and influence were very tangibly to be seen in this last decade of his life. In 1874 the historian of Frederick the Great was rewarded by the Prussian Order of Merit, which he received with good grace, although he habitually shunned public recognitions of this kind. More notably, in 1874 Disraeli offered Carlyle a state pension, in a well-phrased letter which survives, with Carlyle's answer, in the Carlyle House in Chelsea. The suggestion was well put, and came along with a nomination for Carlyle to receive the Grand Cross of Bath, in both cases a fitting end to a notable career as a public figure: Carlyle declined both in a graceful letter and in private comment admired that 'Dizzy' (whom Carlyle lost no opportunity to ridicule in conversation) should have made such a magnanimous offer. Disraeli had in part offered the pension in order that Carlyle might enjoy an old age free of financial worries: in fact by this time Carlyle was financially quite independent, and could afford to stand on his own feet.

To retain his independence had always been one of Carlyle's greatest anxieties, from the early days when he had made a bad guest in the homes of Edward Irving, and the Buller family whose children he had tutored. Except in the homes of very close friends indeed Carlyle was always uncomfortable, and he hated to be obliged to anyone for money or kindness of any sort. By the 1870s his writing had prospered, and reprint had followed reprint of his most popular works. His account-books and cheque stubs, which survive in the National Library of Scotland in Edinburgh, amply prove his financial independence at this time. A lifelong opponent of railways, he had nevertheless invested cannily in railway stocks, which gave him a steady income, from which he maintained his very modest life-style in Chelsea, and did a great deal to help others in the form of quiet gifts and charity. Never lavish with his money, he was content to live in the cramped quarters of Chelsea all his life, with dark rooms and old-fashioned furniture, in unfashionable clothes still made by his tailor in Ecclefechan and to eat the simple food he had known in his youth. It was not meanness, nor the affectation of a rich man preserving the life-style of his youth. It was simply a lasting habit of carefulness with money which affluence could not change. Disraeli's offer might have been prompted by a suspicion that Carlyle required help even in his old age: the truth was that Carlyle needed no help, and valued his independence far more. And so the pension, and the decoration which would have accompanied it, were both politely refused.

One honour which, like the Prussian one, he did not refuse was the remarkable birthday gift which he received on 4 December 1875. He was eighty, definitely the Grand Old Man of British literature, and he received from his admirers a gift which must have touched him deeply—a gold medal and address of admiration signed by an illustrious circle of scientists, writers and public figures. It was almost fifty years since he had been instrumental in arranging the same gift to be sent to his Hero of his early years, Goethe, signed by a brilliant gathering of those who dominated the literary world of the earlier part of the century. Now, in the closing years of the same century, he had become the Hero. The medal and the address are in Chelsea, and the A-Z of famous men who signed it is dazzling, men like John Morley, David Masson, Charles and Erasmus Darwin, Browning, Tennyson, George Eliot, T. H. Huxley, Trollope—119 in all.

The previous month had seen the establishment of a transatlantic link which flourished in later years, in the presentation of an honorary LL.D. from Harvard. In 1866 Carlyle had declined a doctorate from Edinburgh, but now he accepted the tribute from Charles Eliot Norton's University: the gift was to be reciprocated by a valuable selection of books from Carlyle's own personal library, which was to cross the Atlantic to the Harvard Library. This doctorate was more than merely a token of admiration, for there was expressed in it a feeling for Carlyle's whole achievement which swamped the irritations which North Americans might well feel for Carlyle's insensitive comments on Americans in general, on the Civil War, on the Negro question. Emerson had spread Carlyle's fame as well as he could in half-a-century's propaganda, but the Harvard degree initiated a transatlantic interest in Carlyle which was to produce an able editor in Norton, a host of scholars in the twentieth century, and which was to culminate in the 1960s in Duke University with a transatlantic project to publish the collected Carlyle correspondence.

Fame, then, came easily and comfortably to Carlyle in this last decade. He became a lion, whom painters and sculptors pursued for sittings, grudgingly given and testily endured. In 1875 Boehm began a long series of sittings which resulted in the famous seated statue, often reproduced, which guards the entry to Cheyne Walk from the Albert Embankment in Chelsea, and which likewise looks down over Ecclefechan from the hill to the north of the village. Carefully dressed, his long slender fingers holding a pipe and a rough dressing-gown gathered round his shoulders, Carlyle sits on a chair with a heap of books under it, pensively looking into the distance. He looks old and tired. The same mood was captured by Robert Herdman in 1875, with a brilliant portrait which shows a stooping and exhausted Carlyle in a bottom corner of the dark canvas, his cheeks flushed and unnaturally red, and large eyes gazing sadly into the darkness of the surroundings. He looks as if he was waiting endlessly for something, which of course he was.

In his less pessimistic moods, Carlyle could still display extraordinary energy, which manifested itself mainly in his talk, but which was plainly visible from the most successful photographs, and from Millais' splendid portrait, begun in 1877 and never finished. Millais could not complete the portrait and abandoned it in disgust; the hands, for instance, are mere sketches as they sit folded over the head of Carlyle's cane. Yet the face has enormous power. The violet eyes bore into the viewer's, the arresting angle of the pose suggests the vigour of Carlyle's personality. Carlyle was captured often by the camera in different moods—increasingly often in the 1860s and 1870s as photography became more and more commonplace, and Carlyle more famous—yet his character leaps out from the canvas of Millais and Herdman as never on the photographic negative. In Millais we see the energetic Carlyle whose memory haunted young literary figures who had just spent a mesmeric afternoon in Chelsea. In Herdman we see the lonely man who closed the door on them, and returned to his memories in the house itself.

The closing decade of his life was marked by more than just public recognition and social contact: Carlyle published miscellaneous works on John Knox, on a proposal for a National Portrait Gallery of Scotland, and perhaps most importantly on the Early Kings of Norway. His interest in Scandinavian mythology had been a long-standing one, and his brother John and he had shared an interest in the figures and names of Norse legend. With the publication of *Early Kings of Norway* in mid-1875, Carlyle effectively ended his career as a published writer. Modern scholarship suggests that his interest was amateur, his information dubious; certainly the writing (which was largely dictated) lacks the power of any of his mature work, and *The Early Kings* is largely neglected.

Yet if the published work ended on this low key, the correspondence did not. Until late in the 1870s, Carlyle continued to keep in touch with family and friends, dictating when he had to, writing in blue pencil when he could, and sometimes scrawling a pitiful penmanship of his own, difficult for the recipient, and infuriating to the modern editor. Yet he worked on, for no matter how discouraged and lonely he became, he never lost the urge to commit his thoughts to paper in the immediacy of the situation of the correspondent addressing the unseen audience. In his public mood, as when he addressed a reply to Disraeli's offer of a pension and decoration, he wrote with formality, yet with a charm which the public phraseology of the letter could not conceal. In private, he could be charming, witty, sad, even acid according to his mood. Dull he never was.

Yet nothing could conceal from him, or from his friends, that his energies were slowly diminishing. He saw his friends dying with increasing frequency: the decade had begun with the loss in June 1870 of Charles Dickens, a close intimate of Carlyle, for each had admired the talent of the other, as well as preserving a close friendship. In 1876 it was the turn of Dickens' biographer John Forster: Carlyle noted that 'It is the end of a chapter in my life, which had lasted, with unwearied kindness and helpfulness wherever possible on Forster's part for forty years.' Two months later, Carlyle's brother Alexander died. In 1879, his brother John,

always his most intimate friend, along with his mother and with
Jane the person from whom he had least reserve, died after a
long illness in September.

Carlyle was now very weary. His relatives reported that he was
not suffering much pain, just weakness and a desire to be gone
from a world which seemed to have done with him. Nothing
could have been further from the case, in point of fact, for the
world was eagerly awaiting every scrap of news about him, and
everyone (including Queen Victoria) anxiously kept track of the
progress of the Sage of Chelsea. Throughout 1880 the state of
weakness prevailed. Carlyle read a lot; books which he had
known in his youth, and some he now read for the first time.
He annotated frequently, comparing the differences between his
elderly reactions and his youthful ones. Sitting in a large leather
chair, with a hinged book-rest, which Forster had thoughtfully
had made for him, Carlyle read and read incessantly, greeting
visitors with grave courtesy, kindly enquiring about his friends,
frankly bidding farewell to his guests with the thought that they
might never see him again. He did not sicken, he merely declined
steadily.

Early in 1881 the decline reached critical proportions. Even in
1880 Carlyle had been well enough to be driven out in his
carriage daily, and to take a lively interest in what was going on
around him. New Year's Day, 1881 was the last on which he had
strength for a drive outside the house in Cheyne Row; when he
re-entered it, it was for the last time. His bed was placed in the
upstairs drawing-room which Jane had created by knocking two
rooms together, and in which they had entertained their friends.
There Carlyle lay through the month of January, growing
steadily weaker, among the ghosts of his happier days. On the
last day of January his appointed biographer, Froude, came for a
formal farewell.

In February, it was obvious that the end was not far off.
Bulletins were posted at the door, the streets were hushed so as
not to disturb the sick man. At half-past-eight on the morning of
5 February 1881, he died.

Westminster Abbey was offered, of course, so that Carlyle

could be buried among the most famous of his contemporaries, and predecessors. At his explicit request, this was refused and his instructions obeyed. The coffin, completely plain except for a brass plate with his name and dates, was taken to Ecclefechan by train for 10 February, and with it went a small group of his closest intimates and friends. In Ecclefechan it was snowing, and the streets were dark as the carriages rattled through the streets to the graveyard where the Carlyle family were buried. The school bell, muffled, tolled the only sound as the inhabitants lined the way from station to graveyard.

At Carlyle's wish there was no service. The coffin was carried into the graveyard, where the family lair had been opened alongside the burial grounds of Carlyle's mother and father. The weather continued dark but, reporters noticed, as the coffin was lowered into the ground, the sun broke through and shone on the brass, and the fresh flowers. The earth was shovelled in, the visitors left, and silence fell on Ecclefechan. It might have seemed the end of the story of Carlyle. In fact the most controversial chapter was just beginning.

13

AFTERMATH

THE FIRST pang of regret had passed, and Edward Fitzgerald was able to look back on Carlyle's life quite dispassionately by May 1883 when he wrote to Charles Eliot Norton. At the beginning he had been, like many of his contemporaries, deeply moved by the prospect of losing the man he had come to revere as Prophet and Sage: Carlyle's death, long-awaited and clearly about to happen, had shocked him and many like him even so. Now, in 1883, he had time for a proper assessment, and this was provoked in part by Norton's publication of the Carlyle-Emerson correspondence.

'. . . I had most to learn of Emerson, and that all good: but Carlyle came out in somewhat of a new light to me also. Now we have him in his Jane's letters, as we had seen something of him before in the Reminiscences: but a yet more tragic Story; so tragic that I know not if it ought not to have been withheld from the Public: assuredly, it seems to me, ought to have been but half of the whole that now is. But I do not the less recognize Carlyle for more admirable than before—if for no other reason than his thus furnishing the world with weapons against himself which the World in general is glad to turn against him . . .'

These weapons for the world to turn against him were the posthumous papers and *Reminiscences* with which Carlyle had occupied himself in the closing years of his life. In themselves they were fascinating literary documents: published at the time they were, and in the format in which they were printed, they were literary dynamite which threatened to blow Carlyle's reputation as Sage and Prophet sky-high.

Fitzgerald was obviously moved by the fate of the reputation of Carlyle, and in the same letter to Norton he described a walk to Chelsea as a sort of pilgrimage to the memory of the departed Sage:

'. . . I wanted to see the Statue on the Chelsea Embankment which I had not yet seen: and the old no. 5 of Cheyne Row, which I had not seen for five and twenty years. The Statue I thought very good, though looking somewhat small and ill set-off by its dingy surroundings. And No. 5 (now 24), which had cost her so much of her Life, one may say, to make habitable for him, now all neglected, unswept, ungarnished, uninhabited, "TO LET". I cannot get it out of my head, the tarnished Scene of the Tragedy (one must call it) there enacted.

'Well, I was glad to get away from it, and the London of which it was a small part, and get down here to my own dull home, and by no means sorry not to be a Genius at such a Cost. "Parlons d'autres choses." '

Clearly something had happened to the Carlyle reputation in these two intervening years, between the hush over London to hear the latest news of the dying Sage, and the 'tarnished tragedy' over which people screwed up their faces as they walked in Chelsea.

Fitzgerald's letters themselves form one of the most interesting commentaries on this change as it took place. On 13 March 1881 he had written, also to Norton, of the shock of losing Carlyle. 'I have just got the Carlyle Reminiscences', he adds, 'which will take me some little time to read, impatient as I may be to read them. What I have read is of a stuff we can scarce find in any other Autobiographer: whether his Editor Froude has done quite well in publishing them as they are, and so soon, is another matter. Carlyle's Niece thinks, not quite.' This is the first reaction, of disquiet, to the publication of the *Reminiscences* in March 1881. Froude had had the edition prepared for some time, since receiving the manuscript in 1871, and published it very soon after the Sage's death. The newspapers were of course full of comment on Carlyle's career, and the *Reminiscences* were eagerly received. Initial comment, like Fitzgerald's here, was guarded. There was a shocked recognition of excessive, perhaps unpleasant frankness on the author's part. 'I can only say', wrote Fitzgerald at much the same

time to Anna Biddell, 'of Carlyle what you say; except that I do
not find the style "tiresome" any more than I did his Talk: which
it is, only put on Paper, quite fresh, from an Individual Man of
Genius, unlike almost all Autobiographic Memoirs. I doubt not
that he wrote it by way of some Employment, as well as (in his
Wife's case) some relief to his Feelings.' To Mrs Kemble, later in
March, he could be more categoric. 'You have, I suppose, the
Carlyle Reminiscences: of which I will say nothing except that
much as we outsiders gain by them, I think that, on the whole,
they had better have been kept unpublished, for some while at
least.' This is reinforced by a remark to W. F. Pollock: 'I suppose
that Carlyle amused himself, after just losing his Wife, with the
Records he has left: what he says of her seems a sort of penitential
glorification: what of others, just in general: but in neither case
to be made public, and so immediately after his Decease.'

Finally there is the considered judgement of April 1881. 'As
to Carlyle, I thought on my first reading that he must have been
égaré at the time of writing . . . I must think Carlyle's judgements
mostly, or mainly, true; but that he must have "lost his head" if
not when he recorded them, yet when he left them in any one's
hands to decide on their publication. Especially when not about
Public Men, but about their Families. It is slaying the Innocent
with the Guilty. But of all this you have doubtless heard in
London more than enough . . .'

More than enough controversy certainly was stirred up by
Froude's publication of the *Reminiscences*. The prohibition of the
Reminiscences will be remembered, the clear injunction not to
print without fit editing, which editing would perhaps be impossible after Carlyle was gone. The crucial words were a solemn
forbidding to '. . . *publish* this Bit of Writing *as it stands here*'.
Fit editing would perhaps affect nine-tenths of it, and Carlyle
saw himself as the only person able to do this. Yet on the same
page Carlyle admits to his own weakness for not destroying a
manuscript he plainly did not, at the time, intend for publication.

'I still mainly mean to *burn* this Book before my own departure;
but feel that I shall always have a kind of grudge to do it, and an
indolent excuse, "Not *yet*; wait, any day that can be done!"—and

that it *is* possible the thing *may* be left behind me, legible to interested survivors,—*friends* only, I will hope, and with *worthy* curiosity, not *un*worthy!'

Whatever he hoped would be the outcome, Carlyle did not consign his manuscript to the flames. Instead, he hesitated, changed his mind, finally gave up all responsibility and handed the task of deciding over to Froude. Froude described the incident in this paragraph from *My Relations with Carlyle*:

'It was in 1871, that suddenly, without a word of warning, without permission given or asked for, he one day brought to me a large parcel of papers. It contained a copy of the memoir which he had written of his wife, various other memoirs and fragments of biography, and a collection of his wife's letters to himself and other persons. He had put them together, he said, they were not completely prepared for publication, but he could do no more with them, nor could he tell what ought to be done with them. He gave them simply to me. Afterwards he seemed to have forgotten this, for he bequeathed them to me in his will. But at the time he said: "Take these for my sake; they are yours to publish or not publish, as you please, after I am gone. Do what you will. Read them and let me know whether you will take them on these terms." '

Froude had known Carlyle since being introduced to the Sage shortly after leaving University: his close friendship had first been with Jane, 'the most brilliant and interesting woman that I had ever fallen in with', but for Carlyle himself he could only have a more distant feeling: Carlyle he regarded '. . . with admiration too complete for pleasant social relationship'. The move to make this relation closer came from Carlyle in 1861. Flattered by this proof of the great man's attentions, Froude became more and more intimate and finally was the chosen biographer to whom Carlyle entrusted his documents ten years later.

Froude (as he made clear later in life, answering critics who had attacked him bitterly for the way he wrote of Carlyle) had not looked for this honour, indeed 'It happened that I had laid out my plans for the occupation of my later life in a way which would have been pleasant and profitable to me . . . To undertake it would

involve the sacrifice of all the arrangements which I had made.'
Yet so intensely did he admire Carlyle that he took on the duty
imposed on him, and published after Carlyle's death the *Reminiscences*, selections from the letters which he had inherited from
Carlyle, and his monumental four-volume biography which
remains one of the greatest ever written.

In admitting that it is so great, any reader speaks of its cumulative effect, its insight into the character of Carlyle, and its splendid
handling of an immense quantity of material to build up a
coherent picture of Carlyle and Jane. He does not, emphatically,
praise it for its accuracy, nor credit it as the ultimate unbiassed
picture of either of its main subjects.

To deal first with the question of accuracy, this was one of the
main weaknesses of which Froude was accused in publishing the
Reminiscences. His edition was unquestionably scandalous in its
editorial transcription, even after allowance is made for a crabbed
hand and a difficult manuscript. An edition of the complete text
of the *Reminiscences* from the original manuscript, currently under
preparation, lists pages of editorial mistakes committed by
Froude in transliteration from Carlyle's original. Some are
admittedly more serious than others. Froude simply had different
standards from many modern editors: if he saw a word which
began with a capital for no apparent reason (as many of Carlyle's
might seem to do) he thought nothing of 'normalising' it to
English usage. Ampersands became 'and', contractions were
expanded, 'mistakes' silently corrected. The text, in short, was
tidied up and no attempt made to transcribe the original *literatim*.
This method has its dangers, and more than once in so doing
Froude altered the tone, if not the meaning, of the original.

More serious, however, was his habit of altering words,
phrases or sentences. Sometimes he omitted portions, sometimes
added; sometimes words are re-arranged, sometimes the whole
sentence. Occasionally censorship removes a particularly sarcastic
or personal remark. The final result is closely related to the
original, but distinctively different. Froude's changes are massive
in number, though to be fair the trivial ones far outweigh the
serious.

Froude (as he explained to his readers in *My Relations with Carlyle*) surrendered the manuscript of the *Reminiscences* after its publication by him, and returned it to Mary Aitken, now Mary Aitken Carlyle (she had married her cousin, Alexander Carlyle, a great-nephew of Carlyle who had returned from Canada, where he was born). Finding out how substantially she could illustrate Froude's inaccuracies, Mrs Carlyle was quick to commission a further edition from Charles Eliot Norton, and this 'accurate' edition was published in 1887. Although greatly improved (a fact which it labours somewhat in introducing itself to the public) it is still far from exact: however, it was enough to discredit completely Froude's edition.

Editorial inaccuracy seems a strange basis for such a virulent attack on Froude, and indeed there was a deeper vein of resentment. Many (as will be gathered from Fitzgerald's letters) resented Froude's tactlessness, as they saw it, in publishing the *Reminiscences* so near to Carlyle's death, if at all. A thin-skinned work, full of little irritations and sarcasm forgivable to a man who has just lost his wife, and writing to relieve his feelings, seems strange when read almost twenty years later by a generation who have forgotten the circumstances under which it was written. There was much unpleasant personal sarcasm in the book: worse, there was indication of the strain which had existed in the Carlyle household, and which had been hidden from the outside world at large.

In *My Relations with Carlyle* Froude indicated with what surprise he had come across the deep undercurrents of tension in the Cheyne Row house. Particularly, as Jane's confidant, he had heard a good deal of Jane's jealousy of Lady Ashburton, who too clearly fascinated Carlyle. 'The vanity of the wisest will carry him far when he is flattered by a woman's attentions', noted Froude, perhaps unaware of how much his picture depended on Jane's own viewpoint, as confided to her serious-minded youthful worshipper. Clearly Froude did worship Carlyle, but he also worshipped Jane, and finding in Jane someone much closer to his own experience and social class, he was much readier to listen to her version of the facts, without the same critical frame of mind which he might bring to Carlyle's. To bring into public vision any hint of this quarrel, or indeed of any quarrel in the household of a man who was respected by the whole of Britain as a moral influence was to many bad taste, to more an insult to the memory of Carlyle.

Yet the problem went deeper still. Froude did not stop at the editing of the *Reminiscences*. Having interpreted his mandate from Carlyle as he did, and decided to publish, Froude prepared selections of letters (*Letters and Memorials of Jane Welsh Carlyle*) and the biography, which brought to the public attention the jealousies and tensions between the two, Carlyle's 'peasant treatment of his high-born wife' (or so Froude interpreted their different social origins) and—worst of all, from the point of view of Carlyle's admirers and relations—Froude brought to light the story of the Carlyles' supposed unfulfilled marriage. He reported in *My Relations with Carlyle* that Jane's confidante Geraldine Jewsbury had first brought the matter to his attention, that Carlyle was impotent, that Jane had tried her best to live with this situation, but '. . . his extraordinary temper was a consequence of his organisation'. Victimised by this temper, Froude thought he saw Jane sink into hypochondria. 'As he grew older and more famous, he had become more violent and overbearing. She had longed for children, and children were denied to her. This had been at the bottom of all the quarrels and all the unhappiness. Anger led to violence, and Jane reported that Carlyle used force on her, bruising her arms. Froude checked with Geraldine, who confirmed it, though admitting that 'Jane could be extremely provoking'. The more Froude discovered about his erstwhile hero and heroine, the more distressing it became for him. 'I found myself entangled in painful family differences of exactly the kind which I most disliked to hear of, and acquaintance with which I had always avoided. It was all left to my discretion, but how was my discretion to be exercised?' It was exercised—discreetly. The biography states some things, hints at more, gives the impression of tension without adequately expressing it. Froude's enemies easily pried open his gentlemanly reserve by attacking his accuracy (on which he was painfully vulnerable) and so forced him into publishing defences of himself. The arguments grew bitter, finally almost incredibly bitter, and Froude's defence in *My Relations with Carlyle* is so painful that his relatives declined to print all of it, so deeply had Froude been hurt. It was published posthumously. 'I have discharged my duty', he ended his manuscript, 'which was laid on me as faithfully as I could. I have nothing more to reveal, and, as far as I know, I have related exactly everything which bears on my relations with Carlyle and his history. This is all that I can do, and I have written this that those who care for me may have something to rely on if my honour and good faith are assailed after I am gone.' These words were written in 1887, after his publication of the *Life* (1882, 1884) and the other Carlylean works which he issued after Carlyle's death.

The violence of the controversy cast an immediate shadow on the memory of Carlyle. The battle was waged with an intensity which was almost embarrassingly personal. Here is David Alec Wilson, Carlyle's other major biographer, writing in his early 1898 volume, *Mr Froude and Carlyle*:

'. . . But nobody ever felt that he knew Mr Froude's "Thomas Carlyle", and all who knew well the Carlyle of real life say he is not to be seen in that book at all.

'Contemplating the long array of Mr. Froude's blunders, ranging from mere errors of punctuation in the quotations up to erroneous reports of conversations, erroneous statements as to Carlyle's attitude towards science and religion, and a completely mythical account of Carlyle's relations with his wife, the impartial critic is reluctantly driven to use very strong language indeed, and to declare that in historical fidelity Mr. Froude's account of Carlyle's life is inferior even to Mr. Froude's other writings.'

Wilson dismisses Froude's biography as '. . . a glorious opportunity for Boswellism', which is extremely unkind and unjustified. No more could we accept W. H. Dunn's comment, in his survey *Froude & Carlyle* (1930), that 'Froude's work emerges from the fires of controversy unscathed'. Far from it, both Froude and the biography are heavily marked by the dispute

Froude

Thomas Carlyle's niece Mary (later his housekeeper) and her cousin Alexander whom she married, and who was to be the editor of Carlyle's works

'A Chelsea Interior': Thomas and Jane Carlyle. After a painting by Robert Tait, 1857

Thomas Carlyle. Painting by J. Millais

Thomas Carlyle. Painting by Robert Herdman

On the steps of St. Brycedale's house, Kirkcaldy. (*Left to right*)
John Carlyle, Thomas Carlyle, Mary Aitken Carlyle, and Provost
Swan, now rich and famous, but in 1817 a pupil of Carlyle's in
Kirkcaldy Burgh School

Thomas Carlyle's funeral, 1881

which surrounded them in their time. Worse still, Carlyle too was marked by these arguments.

The more argument raged over Froude's biography, the more public attention was drawn to the private strains of life in the Carlyle home, the extent to which the moral Sage of Chelsea had been human after all. A morbid public interest was aroused in his unfaithful behaviour to his wife, his 'wife-beating' (a fiction which survives in the 1970s), his impotence, his temper. The very features which were weakest and the most vulnerable to criticism without 'fit editing' were brought most into prominence by the controversy which was, strictly, about editorial principles, but which bulked in the public eye as a biographical, not an editorial matter. The Chelsea home became not the home of a Sage so much as a Victorian peep-show, encouraging a cult of detail in books about Carlyle which helps, perhaps, to explain the enormous bulk of biographical material which surrounds the family. David Alec Wilson's classic biography, written consciously to correct Froude, occupies six substantial volumes, full of fascinating if undisciplined anecdote, half-justified by annotation, half by hearsay. Wylie and other early biographers added further detail, each one returning to Carlyle's early scenes of childhood to search for further detail, further scraps of evidence which might throw light on the facts in dispute. Even Carlyle's medical attendants were sought out. The unfortunate man who supplied Carlyle's truss (after a hernia) was solemnly interviewed, to glean what evidence posterity could of Carlyle's endowments. The craze rose to enormous proportions. When it subsided, as it inevitably did, it was difficult to see the reality which had existed behind the maze of disagreements. Perhaps the real Carlyles were most easily envisaged by reading Froude, but then Froude was discredited. Wilson was only gathering materials, Masson published a sane account in *Edinburgh Sketches and Memories* which took the reader only to 1834, and for the rest there was a bewildering number of shorter books by a variety of authors, some academic and some not. Some, like John Nichol, were splendidly abrasive in their criticism of Carlyle: some, like W. H. Wylie, all but revered the subject of the biography. Above all, an objective approach to the Sage of Ecclefechan or the Sage of Chelsea was difficult.

Another factor began to operate against the Sage. In his lifetime he had been admired enormously for his 'style', and the expression 'Carlylese' denoted a habit of writing which was frequently imitated, and which with its wealth of imagery and illustration, and its striking energy, captivated many young men who tried (mostly with dismal lack of success) to emulate it. When Carlyle was alive, he was able to supplement his written 'Carlylese' with his spoken utterance: in Fitzgerald's words, his style is his Talk, '... put on paper, quite fresh, from an Individual Man of Genius'. In Carlyle's presence people noticed how time flew by, how fluently Carlyle could illustrate his point in a torrent of monologue: if he wrote like this, he heaped example on example in a copious style which excited people in part by the abundance of its thought and illustration. It excited them, that is, while it was fresh, and while the author was living in London to act as an example of his style, a living proof that it was not affectation but a transmuted form of his usual speech. Without the author, Carlylese began to look like a tiresome relic of a bygone age. The German elements in his style, which had looked so exciting when Carlyle was himself introducing figures from German literature to the British public, seemed *passé* when several generations had passed. The strength of feeling evoked by the style in describing the French Revolution, a recent memory to many at the time of first publication, seemed forced and overdone by the end of the nineteenth, and still more in the twentieth century. The fantastic inversions, the Biblical and Miltonic allusions all palled, and people began to shun Carlyle's collected volumes as too long, too involved and too caught up with past events, past controversies, and a forgotten world-picture. He was perhaps admired by some for his intensity, by others for his moral earnestness. The public at large lost the habit of familiarity with the extraordinary richness of his work, its references not only to literatures (in Britain and abroad) but to historical subjects, and to moral, ethical and social questions. Safely relegated to the position of 'Sage', Carlyle became a figure of the nineteenth century who had been admired in his time, no doubt for good reasons, but whose fame belonged to his lifetime, and had been rudely shattered by scandal (the details of which quickly faded) after his death.

This is no longer true. Since the 1930s, Carlyle's reputation has slowly been restored among specialists, and is now re-emerging into general currency. The process was a slow one, for the recovery in the 1930s came just at a time when a dangerous equation was drawn between Carlyle's doctrines of hero-worship and the rise of fascism on the Continent. It was an easy equation to make, and it illustrates how difficult it is rightly to judge a man so original and copious as Carlyle. Take a passage like this one from *Heroes and Hero-Worship*, describing Mahomet's violent propagation of his religious beliefs:

'On the whole, a thing will propagate itself as it can . . . I care little about the sword: I will allow a thing to struggle for itself in this world, with any sword or tongue or implement it has, or can layhold of. We will let it preach, and pamphleteer, and fight and to the uttermost bestir itself, and do, beak and claws, whatsoever is in it; very sure that it will, in the long-run, conquer nothing which does not deserve to be conquered. What is better than itself, it cannot put away, but only what is worse. In this great Duel, Nature herself is umpire, and can do no wrong: the thing which is deepest-rooted in Nature, which we call *truest*, that thing and not the other will be found growing at last.'

Out of context, this passage comes gravely close to doing just what Carlyle's detractors claimed—advocating the use of force. Force for its own sake was justified, they would claim, since it would succeed. Might, in short, would be right. Put in context, it becomes part of the more familiar Carlylean message that the universe is sick, and that people need to realise the veracities of life in order to put society in order. In *Past and Present*, most notably, Carlyle is appalled by the unphilosophical attitude of his contemporaries to life, which they reduce to a matter of making money. 'The Universe is not made so; it is made otherwise than so,' he writes. 'The Man or nation of men that thinks it is made so, marches forward nothing doubting, step after step; but marches—whither we know!' Which is a circuitous way of saying that it marches to hell: where his contemporaries 'are now, very ominously, shuddering, reeling, and let us hope trying to recoil, on the cliff's edge!—'Everywhere Carlyle saw himself surrounded by 'the accursed quintessence of all sorts of Unbelief!' Lack of belief meant lack of ability properly to see the universe; more urgently, practically to recognise the hero. 'For if there is now no Hero, and the Histrio himself begin to be seen into, what hope is there for the seed of Adam here below? We are the doomed everlasting prey of the Quack; who, now in this guise, now in that, is to filch us, to pluck and eat us, by such modes as are convenient for him.' A proper attitude, then, is to be able to recognise the hero, and to know when to obey him. Perhaps Book III, chapter 13 of *Past and Present* is the clearest indication of what Carlyle felt in this matter. 'England will either learn to reverence its Heroes, and discriminate them from its Sham-Heroes and Valets and gas-filled Histrios; and to prize them as the audible God's-voice, amid all inane jargons and temporary market-cries, and to say to them with heart-loyalty, "Be ye King and Priest, and Gospel and Guidance for us": or else England will continue to worship new and ever-new forms of Quackhood,— and so, with what resiliences and rebounding matters little, go down to the Father of Quacks!'

In short, Carlyle was convinced that the road to ruin lay in not recognising heroes: the lesson was a hard one to learn, 'a lesson inclusive of all other lessons', but it led to '. . . finding of government by your Real-Superiors'. To obey such people is not something forced on us, but a necessity. 'When a world, not yet doomed for death, is rushing down to ever-deeper Baseness and Confusion, it is a dire Necessity of Nature's to bring in her ARISTOCRACIES, her BEST, even by forcible methods.' To such a person, Carlyle thinks the attitude of others should be— 'O, if thou really art my *Senior*, Seigneur, my *Elder*, Presbyter or Priest,—if thou art in very deed my *Wiser*, may a beneficient instinct lead and impel thee to "conquer" me, to command me! If thou do know better than I what is good and right, I conjure thee in the name of God, force me to do it; were it by never such brass collars, whips and handcuffs, leave me not to walk over precipices!' In conclusion, 'liberty requires new definitions'.

These passages amply illustrate why Carlyle should have been an unpopular thinker, and one accused of fascism. In the first place, the surface meaning of what he says is entirely concerned with ruling and force, and only a deeper considering will take into account the fact that the appeal to force is based on an acute consciousness of impending doom of England. In the second, the force is not to be applied by a person of superior military or political strength, but by a God-created and God-revealed Hero—whoever he may turn out to be. Might is not right in the sense that the strong man will conquer, but right in the sense that the strong man has been created by God to perform a function in society crucially requiring that function—and society's responsibility is to accept the rule of this Hero, not to abase itself before the superior strength of this Hero. The Hero is no strong-arm bully—frequently the reverse, as anyone acquainted with the lectures on *Heroes and Hero-Worship* will know. Further, the Hero is himself part of the God-created universe and subject to the controls and restraints put on everyone in that universe.

None of this, however, comes immediately to the attention of the reader of Carlyle, particularly one who is not acquainted with the other, earlier works from which this idea grew, from the ideas of self-cultivation expressed in Carlyle's translation of Goethe's *Meisters Wanderjahre*, from the social analyses of *Signs of the Times* of *Characteristics*, from the growing gloom concerning the state of early nineteenth-century society expressed since the writing of *The French Revolution*. What the reader sees most immediately is the call for strong rule, and absolute obedience to that rule. It makes an unattractive message for liberal-minded readers in the twentieth-century, just as it appalled his contemporaries when he took the stand he did on the negro question, or the Governor Eyre controversy.

Still worse, perhaps, for Carlyle's reputation in the twentieth century is the style in which his message is put across. Verbally it is an exciting style, and one which conveys the energy with which he talked himself. Its extraordinary system of punctuation is very much a guide to public declamation, the frequent use of colon or semi-colon a guide to when to pause, or take breath. The point was reinforced by Carlyle writing to the publishers of the 'Library edition' of his works in 1868, refusing to simplify the style of *Sartor Resartus*. This would, he said, '. . . in many cases considerably obscure the sense (or comprehensibility in reading): much better for the thing to stand as it is than *so*'. The capitalisation of nouns is an imitation from the German, not an absolute rule as in that language, but again a guide to emphasis, particularly in spoken form. 'Carlylese', as his contemporaries dubbed it, was exciting to hear read aloud, and particularly exciting to a generation who had heard the man himself speak, and who could relate the written style to its spoken original.

It is, however, a style which functions in large blocks. To make a point Carlyle will willingly write for many pages, using a variety of styles to make his emphases clear. He will adopt various *personae*, his own, that of 'Dryasdust' (the pedantic historian) or 'Sauertig', a fictional writer who is often speaking for Carlyle himself, or 'Teufelsdröckh' from *Sartor Resartus*. Each *persona* speaks in his own style, and in deliberate contrast comes the comment from the author, in a different style. The author himself may vary his manner of speaking, in meticulous historical narration, in semi-hysterical adjuration to his hero (be he Cromwell or Frederick) to heroic action, or condemnation of the villains for their villainy. The style can be quasi-biblical where necessary, or heavily influenced by the classics of English literature (as it was in the *Lectures on the History of Literature*). Whatever his method at the time, it is a method which takes time to achieve its effect. It is read by the page, and the internal echoings begin to make sense. Carlyle is fond of making a point early in the work he is writing, then alluding to it constantly in the remainder of the work. A case in point from the chapter 13 of Book III of *Past and Present*, quoted above, will illustrate this. Having stressed the necessity for England to learn to revere its heroes, Carlyle goes on:

'One thing I do know: Those Apes, chattering on the branches by the Dead Sea, never got it learned; but chatter there to this day.

To them no Moses need come a second time; a thousand Moses would be but so many painted Phantasms, interesting Fellow-Apes of a new strange aspect . . .'

The passage, by itself, is almost meaningless, and seems strange at a climactic point in the argument. Yet it refers back ten chapters, to Book III, chapter 3: there Carlyle repeats a Moslem tradition that Moses went to visit a tribe near the Dead Sea, and they did not listen to him with attention or respect, for which they were turned into Apes. 'They made no use of their souls; and so have lost them. Their worship on the Sabbath now is to roost there with unmusical screeches, and half-remember that they had souls.

'Didst thou never, O Traveller, fall-in with parties of this tribe? Me seems they are grown somewhat numerous in our day.'

The close inter-allusions of these passages give the total work a tautness which it would be difficult to achieve any other way: the more famous example in *The French Revolution* is Carlyle's habit of calling Robespierre the 'Sea-Green Incorruptible Robespierre', an allusion to his complexion which becomes a tag which pursues the unfortunate Robespierre throughout the history. The name is shortened to the 'Sea-Green Incorruptible', finally to the 'Sea-Green', and the reader understands perfectly— and his attitude to Robespierre is skilfully manipulated, not only by the choice of adjectives, but by the repetition which finally has the effect of making a joke of the description. It is a habit which we know Carlyle acquired from his family, who were famed throughout their district of Scotland for their facility of making nicknames, which stuck. In the context of the multiple volumes of *Cromwell* or *Frederick* the trick gives coherence to a long and sometimes dreary narrative. In extract, it seems as mannered as does Carlyle's choice of vocabulary and his contorted syntax.

Both these matters of style, then, operate against Carlyle in the twentieth century. The reader who is familiar with a wide band of Carlyle's work, as his contemporaries were bound to be, sees these style matters in the perspective of the total output of the Sage, and judges them accordingly. A modern reader, familiar perhaps only with extracts, or with one work, finds the mannered style repulsive. Similarly, familiar perhaps only with the more remarkable passages often quoted, on heroism, on slave-labour, on the Gospel of Work, the modern reader finds Carlyle out-of-touch, over emphatic on religious questions, illiberal, hopelessly narrow-minded. Again, perhaps the reaction follows from a limited acquaintance with the ideas which develop in Carlyle's writings.

Such, at any rate, are the main factors which operated against Carlyle, and which helped to explain why he was dismissed in the 1930s as a 'fascist' writer, advocating the unthinking use of force and the oppression of the weaker by the stronger. If, as has been argued, the misapprehensions expressed in this estimate emerge from a limited acquaintance with his work, then a proper critical estimate could only be made by a wide critical activity, properly assessing the growth of Carlyle's ideas and judging them in the light of their contemporary situation, as well as of modern scholarship.

This has been the story of Carlyle scholarship since the 1930s. The attempt to estimate Carlyle is still in progress, nor have many of the difficulties been overcome. Chief perhaps among the problems is the daunting weight of material which confronts any reader, the thirty volumes of H. D. Traill's Centenary edition which is still the standard one in use, despite the fact that it was completed before the end of the nineteenth century. Even it is not complete, for to it have to be added uncollected essays and lectures, and minor unfinished works such as the *History of German Literature*, or the so-called *Last Words of Thomas Carlyle*, including much important travel-writing, and the valuable *Wotton Reinfred*. To these volumes we add the forthcoming edition of the *Letters*, which will number at least as many again, and the bulk of material to be covered would give pause to any but the most devoted student.

Perhaps one answer to this problem will be in anthologising, and there are several examples available, from the early best-of-Carlyle sampling anthologies to more recent scholarly selections which look not for the 'best' in the sense of most memorable or best-written, but for a selection from the whole range of Carlyle's output which will most lucidly give the reader insight into the range of the thought embodied in Carlyle's developing work. No anthology, however, can bypass the problem that the cumulative effect is lost in a number of selections: the individual passages offer a rapid introduction, but they cannot match the Sage in his massive accumulation of evidence, his intentional self-repetition, his stylistic effects which subtly develop by variation as well as repetition.

If anthologies will make the work better known, perhaps stimulate readers to look more widely, then the work of scholarly criticism and biography will assist the reader to form this curiosity.

Of biographies there have been excellent ones since Wilson's monumental six-volume work of the 1920s and 1930s. Neff, Burdett, Symons and the two Hansons have given fine treatments, though always inadequately on the early years of Carlyle's life which have remained under-researched until recent years. Few biographers looked to the rich collection of original manuscript letters which are available, and which are still half-unpublished. The 'real' Carlyle, a figure whom several biographers have offered to present to their readers, has been slow to emerge.

Much important criticism of Carlyle began in the 1930s with Charles Frederick Harrold, an American scholar who patiently accumulated a massive work on Carlyle's debt to German literature and thought, through important social investigations by Raymond Williams, Basil Willey and John Holloway, to a recent upsurge of scholarly publishing in the United States by such critics as Professors Sanders, Tennyson, La Valley and Levine. The new interest shows no signs of waning: indeed the lists of dissertations completed or in progress show that in universities in Europe and the United States of America there is a growing interest which is leading to an increasingly specialised investigation into Carlyle's relationship to the authors of his time, and to an attempt to assemble the critical material for a proper assessment of Carlyle as a writer. Perhaps as the letters are published, this estimate will grow to be a more and more accurate one.

Yet between the resurgence of Carlyle's popularity in the

twentieth century and the reader lies the massive bulk of published work by Carlyle, and by scholars seeking to understand him. Perhaps what is first required to pursue his ideas through the necessary reading is an indication of the principal ideas in his work, and this is what the concluding chapter of this work seeks, briefly, to provide.

CARLYLE: A PICTURE

CARLYLE CAME, as we have seen, from a strong home background where the religion of the family was a basic fact in its existence, and where certain ideas were beyond argument. The family's Church was the Burgher Seceder one, devoted to individual liberty from state interference in religious matters. Clearly, from the *Reminiscences*, certain features of this Church were deeply engrained in Carlyle's mind.

I. A STRONG RELIGIOUS SENSE IN LIFE was necessary, for Carlyle as for his father. James Carlyle 'was Religious with the consent of his whole faculties', reason as well as emotion. His mind, 'thoroughly free and even incredulous', found it necessary to live consciously and continuously aware of its religious emotions, and obligations. This example, which he also gained from his mother, was the earliest and (one could argue) the most important influence on Carlyle's work. The French Revolution, the story of the Cromwellian wars, the description of the Court of Frederick the Great are all overshadowed by the inadequacy of the religious convictions of some of the main actors. In eighteenth-century France 'Faith is gone out; Scepticism is come in. Evil abounds and accumulates'. In *Heroes* we find Carlyle writing that 'Scepticism means not intellectual Doubt alone, but moral Doubt; all sorts of *in*fidelity, insincerity, spiritual paralysis'. A sense of religion is not even strictly defined in terms of the Christian Church, let alone the Burgher Seceder Church, for one of Carlyle's Heroes is Mahomet, who battled for the sake of his own religious convictions, and performed the task of a Hero nobly. The important point is to have an awareness of a greater dimension to life than the surface appearances, or the too-factual, over-mechanical approach induced by a rational philosophy. The too-mechanical approach to life is the nightmare producing the energy and emphasis of *Signs of the Times*.

The notably ironic praise for machinery at the beginning of the main part of the essay emphasises with much repetition how much the mechanism of the early nineteenth century has triumphed: 'We remove mountains, and make seas our smooth highway; nothing can resist us. We war with rude Nature; and, by our resistless engines, come off always victorious, and loaded with spoils.' The irony lasts only a short time. 'This condition of the two great departments of knowledge,—the outward, cultivated exclusively on mechanical principles; the inward, finally abandoned, because, cultivated on such principles, it is found to yield no result,—sufficiently indicates the intellectual bias of our time.' This bias is to fact, to mechanism. 'The truth is, men have lost their belief in the Invisible, and believe, and hope, and work only in the Visible; or, to speak in other words: This is not a Religious age.'

Carlyle has good reason for stressing the need for religion in an age which was too-obsessed by the mechanical, for his own religious struggles in his student years and afterwards had convinced him that a great deal of human suffering resulted from the habit of mind which produced the 'mechanical'. To give up the Christianity of his childhood had caused him grief, and had hurt his parents, but at the time he thought it was the only course he could follow. Afterwards, as we know, he reconstructed his own life-philosophy with some help from Goethe, and some from the recollected outlines of his childhood religion. Goethe, especially in *Meisters Wanderjahre*, stressed the necessity for the well-educated youth to be brought up with a sense of the sanctity of life, of a deeper mystery than he could immediately understand. This idea impressed Carlyle greatly, in a mood of despair induced by years of loneliness and frustration, and the absence of any strong religious impulse such as had made him happy when he was younger. The sense of purpose which he was given by Goethe was strengthened by influences from other German thinkers: from Kant, whose distinction between the different levels of existence and different means of apprehending them affected Carlyle deeply, and from Fichte and Novalis who likewise helped him believe that there was more to life than surface appearance.

The crucial moment is recorded in the three central chapters of *Sartor Resartus*. In the 'Everlasting NO', Carlyle emerged from his pessimism bred from a too-mechanical view of life. The chapter progresses from a fearful vision of the universe as 'one huge, dead, immeasurable Steam-engine, rolling on, in its dead indifference, to grind me limb from limb', to some sort of defiant stand against mere pessimism, a stand which is transformed gradually through the 'Centre of Indifference' to the 'Everlasting YEA' which incorporates at its heart the awareness that there is a deeper obligation in life, a religious obligation to participate and not merely to stand back in awe of a threatening universe. From 'a feeble unit in the middle of a threatening Infinitude', Carlyle gains new power to analyse his position and emerge with a positive message—'Love not Pleasure; love God'. Teufelsdröckh, and Carlyle with him, realises that the Christian message of the eighth century will not do for the eighteenth; instead of throwing it away, he turns his mind to re-defining it, 'to embody the divine Spirit of the Religion in a new Mythus, in a new vehicle and vesture, that our Souls, otherwise too like perishing, may live.' This done, Carlyle is able to re-enter the world after the symbolic soul-struggle of *Sartor Resartus*, while retaining the sense that life must include a sense of obligation to a religious power in life, and an awareness of more complexity in life, in interpersonal relations, in social obligations and intellectual argument than can be measured by mere mechanisms, or understood by appeal to appearances only. 'But indeed Conviction, were it never so excellent, is worthless till it convert itself into Conduct', concluded Carlyle in the 'Everlasting YEA', and in so doing introduced the second major element in his thinking.

2. THE IMPORTANCE OF ACTION. Again the *Reminiscences* of James Carlyle form our best starting-point.

'This great maxim of philosophy he had gathered by the

teaching of nature alone: That man was created to work, not to speculate, or feel, or dream. Accordingly he set his whole heart thitherwards: he did work wisely and unweariedly (*ohne Hast aber ohne Rast*), and perhaps *performed* more (with the tools he had) than any man I now know . . . His Life was "no idle tale", not a Lie, but a Truth, which whoso liked was welcome to come and examine. "An earnest toilsome life", which also *had* a serious issue.'

James Carlyle worked hard all his life for several reasons. One, the most obvious, was his poverty, for the *Reminiscences* make vividly clear the life conditions which had forced him to hunt rabbits for pennies when young, to work hard as stonemason to bring up a large family (and send two to University), and finally to work hard at farming in the 1820s and early 1830s when farming was at an unprofitable ebb. James Carlyle worked hard because he had to. More than that, he worked all his life because of his religious convictions; bred in a strongly Calvinistic theological system, he was acutely conscious all his life of a personal obligation to an all-seeing all-controlling God, to whom every action was accountable, and in whose eyes salvation had to be worked for, according to the rules and conditions of the Bible and the Church. An acute consciousness of this obligation nerved James Carlyle to action throughout his career, and much of the criticism levelled against him in the *Reminiscences* (Carlyle is just enough to show a rounded picture of the man, not just a pious eulogy written at the time of his death) is of his stern inflexible adherence to his code of duty and morals. If he was unapproachable and grim, it was because of his hard life, and his desire to live up to the high standards he thought were expected of him. Carlyle draws the comparison between Burns, incredibly gifted but ill-advised and ultimately misguided, and his own father, who '. . . was a man of Conduct, and Work keeps all right. What strange shapeable creatures we are.'

The Carlyle family, then, worked hard not just in the consciousness of the need to survive, but in the belief that this was part of their destiny. Carlyle was no exception to the family pattern. The serried ranks of his works are mute testimony to the vigour with which he wrote, first in order to make the money to survive, latterly with a driving energy which carried him through the seemingly impossible tasks of Cromwell and Frederick, while keeping up a huge acquaintance, writing letters widely, and helping friends and relatives in every possible way. Like his notable countryman, Sir Walter Scott, Carlyle amazed his friends and visitors by the amount of time he could spend in conversation, while they little realised that he had spent his morning in hard work, and could afford to take his leisure later in the day. The difference perhaps lay in Scott's amazing facility for writing well-ordered material, whereas Carlyle wrote with hesitation and with real effort, crossing out much of what he had written, occasionally committing large portions to the flames of his own accord, even without the unlucky help of Mill and Mrs Taylor. Certainly he fulfilled his father's promise, in his own personal achievement as a writer.

In this case, though, Carlyle wished to use his father as more than just a personal example to live up to. Carlyle came to commend, more and more, the 'Gospel of Work' to his generation as a means of recovery from what he plainly took to be their moral depravity. In 1831, with *Characteristics*, he was plainly launched as a social commentator of some force. That the times were out of joint he took to be self-evident, and that a change was necessary he demonstrated to be not necessarily a cataclysmic possibility (as it had been in 1789) but potentially a new beginning of better things:

'Nay, in the higher Literature of Germany, there already lies, for him that can read it, the beginning of a new revelation of the Godlike; as yet unrecognised by the mass of the world: but waiting there for recognition, and sure to find it when the fit hour comes. This age also is not wholly without its Prophets.'

The exhortation of the essay is not to acquiesce in a feeling that the times are sick, but to work for the betterment of these times.

'Do we not already know that the name of the Infinite is GOOD, is GOD? Here on Earth we are Soldiers, fighting in a foreign land; that understand not the plan of the campaign, and have no need to understand it; seeing well what is at our hand to be done.

Let us do it like Soldiers; with submission, with courage, with a heroic joy. "Whatsoever thy hand findeth to do, do it with all thy might." Behind us, behind each one of us, lie Six Thousand Years of human effort, human conquest: before us is the boundless Time, with its as yet uncreated and unconquered Continents and Eldorados, which we, even we, have to conquer, to create ...'

The Gospel of Work is strongly conceived of in Christian terms here, the language biblical, the underlying idea being this: we do not understand the reasons for life at present, so labour on meantime without the wider perspective, content in Christian resignation to work only. The viewpoint is the one Carlyle was shortly to describe in the memoir of his father. The gospel was an attractive one to his contemporaries, very definitely unsure of the short-term perspective, bewildered by a century of expansion which was happening too swiftly to be fully understood, surrounded by the activity of an industrial society which seemed to be expanding rapidly, yet at a terrible cost of human suffering for which there seemed to be no immediate explanation. To the people caught up in this struggle, the Gospel of Work was as appealing as it was to Teufelsdröckh at the end of the 'Everlasting YEA'. Saved from a Hell of impotent suffering in a machine Universe, Teufelsdröckh finds meaningful hope in the thought: 'I too could now say to myself: Be no longer a Chaos, but a World, or even Worldkin. Produce! Produce! Were it but the pitifullest infinitesmal fraction of a Product, produce it, in God's name! 'Tis the utmost thou hast in thee: out with it, then. Up, up!'

After blank despair, it was an exciting new start to a new life, and Carlyle gladly embraced it. For him, it was a solution to apparently insoluble problems. For others, it might be, too. For men like John Sterling, Christianity was an inducement to lead the best possible life and always to strive for the best—for this reason Carlyle admired him, and the admiration accompanies the personal affection behind the *Life of John Sterling*.

To be fully an answer to the world, the Gospel of Work was not enough. In his more mature works, Carlyle coupled it to another important idea, and transformed it to a conception which explains much of his political writing. This new idea is:

3. THE IMPORTANCE OF ORDER. The motivation behind James Carlyle's appetite for work seemed to his son to lie very much in the father's acceptance of a world-order in which the Gospel of Work played a prominent part. 'He was among the last of the true men, which Scotland (on the old system) produced, or can produce; a man healthy in body and in mind; fearing God, and diligently working in God's Earth with contentment, hope and unwearied resolution. *He* was never visited with Doubt; the old Theorem of the Universe was sufficient for him, and he worked well in it, and in all senses *successfully* and wisely as few now can do.' Living under the consciousness of an ordered world, in which he had a place to fulfil, James Carlyle provided an inspiration to his son. But it was a distant ideal. There is a clear note of wistfulness in this passage for a world where the old Theorem would be enough; that world is clearly past, for James Carlyle is produced as an example of the last of his kind—'Ultimus Romanorum', Carlyle explicitly calls him.

The new world lacked this order. Evidence was all around—nowhere more so than in the history of the French Revolution. Near the end of his history, Carlyle eloquently called for an ordered world where reconstruction could begin. The passage contains a *mélange* of ideas, all of them important in Carlyle's later work:

'Meanwhile we will hate Anarchy as Death, which it is; and the things worse than Anarchy shall be hated *more*. Surely Peace alone is fruitful. Anarchy is destruction; a burning up, say, of Shams and Insupportabilities; but which leaves Vacancy behind. Know this also, that out of a world of Unwise nothing but an Unwisdom can be made. Arrange it, constitution-build it, sift it through ballot-boxes as thou wilt, it is and remains an Unwisdom,—the new prey of new quacks and unclean things, the latter end of it slightly better than the beginning ... Let there be Order, were it under the Soldier's Sword; let there be Peace, that the bounty of the Heavens be not spilt; that what of Wisdom they do send us bring fruit in its season!'

Order will certainly bring about reconstruction, and it will allow the firm basis for building up a society which will function well—clearly the attraction for Carlyle in Frederick the Great's Prussia, or Cromwell's England. Carlyle's history is deliberately organised to show the disaster which follows on a lack of order, and the fruitless attempts to impose order on a situation which was more serious than the participants in it recognised.

Yet the quotation from *The French Revolution* illustrates that there is more to Order in Carlyle's mind than a mere imposition of a surface discipline and quiet in society—the sort of life which people attributed to fascist societies, when they equated Carlyle's social message with fascism. There are certain kinds of order, Carlyle insists, which cannot be brought about. These are the kinds which are slowly worked towards by the democratic means in use in Carlyle's own time.

Carlyle had lived through the Reform Agitation of 1830-1832, and expressed a profound contempt for the way in which the Reform was carried through. In subsequent years he maintained an attitude of contempt for Parliamentary procedures, and in such publications as *The Nigger Question* and the *Latter-Day Pamphlets* he was to show that he had little time for the established forms of democracy in use in his day. As early as *Signs of the Times* Carlyle had noticed that there were people who were more entitled to be listened to than others. 'For the plain truth, very plain, we think, is, that minds are opposed to minds in quite a different way [than mechanically]; and *one* man that has a higher Wisdom, hitherto unknown spiritual Truth in him, is stronger, not than ten men that have it not, or than ten thousand, but than *all* men that have it not.' It was to such that Carlyle commended his generation to pay attention, not the ballot-boxes of democratic votes. He plainly had little time for the votes of a public whom he considered ill-informed, and unable to base their judgements on a true assessment of the facts. The hero, by virtue of his God-given talents and his efforts to master the complexities of the situation, would be able to make the correct decision. Clearly, then, we must add to the importance of order, the inextricable further point:

4. THE PLACE OF THE HERO. Repeatedly we come across the idea in Carlyle's work that the hero is intended by divine law to be

head of the state, and entitled to obedience from the non-heroic majority. Only, he writes in *Sartor*, " . . . in such Obedience to the Heaven-chosen is Freedom so much as conceivable"; in *Chartism* that individual right is the "right of the ignorant man to be guided by the wiser, to be, gently or forcibly, held in the true course by him;" in the third of the *Latter-Day Pamphlets* that the horrendous task of clearing the mess of nineteenth-century England "is really a heroic work, and cannot be done by . . . dextrous talkers having the honour to be: it is a heavy and appalling work". Once again it is the magnitude of the problem, and a sense of the urgency of the search for a solution, which exaggerates Carlyle's answer to it. We must find heroes, and when found we must obey them.

To those who would interrupt that this Carlylean analysis is a gross violation of personal freedom if they do not accept the duty to work unquestioningly, even in a universe they do not understand, Carlyle abruptly replies in terms which make him doubly unpopular to modern liberals. His answer is that some people are born to slavery, that their inherited condition is low, their abilities low, and their voice worthless in democratic discussion. Such people are the prisoners lambasted in the *Model Prisons* section of the *Latter-Day Pamphlets*, such is frequently the condition of the Irish as Carlyle describes it, and the Negro workers in *The Nigger Question*. Carlyle accepted that it was part of the order of things that some people were born superior to others, and that it would be a fraud to pretend that everyone was equal and free.

'Slave or free is settled in Heaven for a man; acts of parliament attempting to settle it on earth for him, sometimes make sad work of it . . . Whom Heaven has made a slave, no parliament of men nor power that exists on Earth can render free. No; he is chained by fetters which parliaments with their millions cannot reach. You can label him free; yes, and it is but labelling him a solecism . . . Heroism, manful wisdom is not his: many things you can give him, but that thing never. Him the Supreme Powers marked in the making of him, *slave*; appointed him, at his and our peril not to command but to obey, in this world.'

This is from the sixth of the *Latter-Day Pamphlets*; in *The*

Nigger Question the language Carlyle used was to be more violent, the absolute condemnation of the Negro for failing to work more severe. Carlyle had by this time come completely to judge events by his own scale of measurement, which was the scale of a God-dominated universe where men were put to work. If they would not work, then they must be made to work, by the Hero or strong man. Not because he *is* strong, but because he is *right*. Again from the *Latter-Day Pamphlets*:

'Many men vote; but in the end, you will infallibly find, none counts except the few who were *in the right*. Unit of that class, against as many zeros as you like! If the King's thought *is* according to the will of God, or to the law appointed for this Universe, I can assure your Lordship the King will ultimately carry that, were he but one in it against the whole world.'

So Carlyle, ironically adopting the tone of one addressing a judge makes his point. Yet he was sufficient of a realist to see that his own way of thought would not instantly carry the mass of the population, indeed that even if a hero were found there would be no instant improvement.

'It is not by rude force, either of muscle or of will, that one man can govern twenty men, much more twenty millions of men. For the moment, if all twenty are stark against his resolution never so wise, the twenty for the moment must have their foolish way; the wise resolution, for the moment, cannot be carried.'

However, Carlyle's advice to the King or Governor is in most cases to ignore the protests of a majority if he thinks it is right, 'for in general it is but frothy folly and loud-blustering rant and wind'. Good rhetoric though this may be, it is not calculated to endear Carlyle as a political thinker to his contemporaries. Yet he would have ignored this thought, had it occurred to him, for his scale of measurement was related to the wider duties he saw in the world. 'Obedience,' he wrote in the ninth chapter of *Chartism*, 'little as many may consider that side of the matter, is the primary duty of man. No man but is bound indefeasably, with all force of obligation, to obey.' What interests Carlyle, and what he comes to press for with more and more urgency, is not a mechanism forcing people to obey, against their wills, but a parliamentary system which the nation will accept, and he proud to obey. In *Chartism*, for instance, he does not condemn the Chartist uprising for taking place, but marvels at the patience of the working classes. 'Not that Chartism now exists should provoke wonder; but that the invited hungry people should have sat eight years at such table ... patiently awaiting somewhat from the Name of a Reform Ministry, and not till after eight years have grown hopeless, this is the respectable side of the miracle.' The right of good government lies behind Carlyle's repeated attacks on what he took to be the inefficient administrations of his own time; the institution of government itself is not at fault. In the sixth lecture of *Heroes and Hero-Worship*, or *The Hero as King*, the Carlylean character through whom many of the author's thoughts are presented to us, muses as follows. 'Take my money, since you *can*, and it is so desirable to you; take it;—and take yourself away with it; and leave me alone to my work here. *I* am still here; can still work, after all the money you have taken from me!' The government does not stop the Carlylean good citizen from getting on with his duties of work. Rebellion comes, however, when the Government tries to take not only taxes, but freedom of thought. 'No; by God's help, no! You may take my purse; but I cannot have my moral Self annihilated. The purse is any Highwayman's who might meet me with a loaded pistol, but the Self is mine and God my Maker's; it is not yours; and I will resist you to the death, and revolt against you, and, on the whole, front all manner of extremities, accusations and confusions, in defence of that!' The position has changed little from that of the *Reminiscences* quoted earlier: alone in the universe with a personal obligation to work and justify one's existence to an all-seeing God, the individual clings to this right in the face of everything. Carlyle is articulating the protest of the individual in a century where the individual seems to have little chance to face up to corrupt government, and standing up for the rights—*not* of the individual alone, but of the individual in his proper relationship with the rest of the universe. It is a repetition, in less obscure terms, of the struggle Teufelsdröckh makes in the 'Everlasting

NO' to assert his 'ME': 'and then was it that my whole ME stood up, in native God-created majesty, and with emphasis recorded its Protest . . . "*I* am not thine, but Free, and forever hate thee!" '

The Carlylean Universe, then, is revealed as a place where disorder is a constant threat. As a social critic of the present, Carlyle does not hesitate to point to disorder in government at home and overseas. Abroad were the colonial troubles in Ireland, in the Governor Eyre question: at home there was poverty, social unrest, the nightmare picture of London slums painted in *Model Prisons*. As historian, Carlyle is quick to indicate points where disorder led to uprising, chaos, bloodshed—most noticeably, in the French Revolution, in Cromwell's England, in the badly governed provinces described in *Past and Present*. Even as literary critic, Carlyle immediately pinpoints the disorder inherent in late eighteenth-century criticism and thought—bankrupt as the result of a sceptical Enlightenment—and the wrong literary judgements which so easily could follow. This is the tone of the essay *State of German Literature*, which seeks to establish critical order by finding a new standard on which a nation's literary excellence could be judged—not by 'elegance', the French term, but by a new German excellence, much more acceptable to Carlyle, by earnestness.

Into this disorder, we have seen, there must be introduced some strong controlling force which will impose form and good management. Carlyle is realist enough to see that change will not come overnight, but he is insistent that some change is needed. To many, this is his chief value as a nineteenth-century writer, not that he proposed far-reaching changes, but that he drew the nation's attention to abuses, and put before the nation a picture which was so vividly drawn that most could not ignore it.

Having proposed an omnipotent God overseeing everything in His creation, and having directed men to obey this God, Carlyle finds it difficult to devise an infallible way to recognise the commands which come from God. The cleverest satires of extremes of Calvinism (such as James Hogg's *Confessions of a Justified Sinner*) attacked the system at this weak point, for the

Calvinist is as fallible as anyone in recognising the commandments he desperately wishes to obey. Hogg's hero, in the *Confessions*, is seduced by a devil who looks personable and speaks in the voice and accent of a Calvinist Christian. To the reader the perversion of Christian ideas in the Devil's mouth is obvious, but to Hogg's character it is invisible, and he is hypnotised into a career of murder and rape which ends (inevitably) with his damnation, Faust-like, to Hell. Hogg's attack is at its strongest because it does not depict the devil with cloven hooves and horns, but as a respectable, mild-mannered quasi-Christian. Hogg's countryman Carlyle saw many devils in this respectable disguise. *Chartism* and *Past and Present* gain a considerable amount of their power from their indignation against many of Carlyle's contemporaries who, although outwardly Christian, cause misery to millions by their behaviour. These are the people who treat their workers like cyphers or machines, the people who advocate the hated 'laissez-faire', 'As good as an *abdication* on the part of governors; an admission that they are henceforth incompetent to govern, that they are not there to govern at all, but to do—one knows not what!' And so society lurches on its unbalanced way, with 'Nakedness, hunger, distress of all kinds, death itself' a visible symptom—the words are Carlyle's, from *Chartism*. Without leaders, society was bound to flare up in trouble just such as the Chartist demands.

'If from this black unluminous unheeded *Inferno*, and Prison-house of souls in pain, there do flash up from time to time, some dismal wide-spread glare of Chartism or the like, notable to all, claiming remedy from all,—are we to regard it as more baleful than the quiet state, or rather as not so baleful?'

To Carlyle, the question was not a rhetorical one. It was something he experienced with personal involvement, not callous disengagement from the realities of suffering, or woolly-headed religiosity. As early as 1835 he could write to his brother John from London:

'This country I take to be on the edge of perilous, perhaps bloody) strife, confusion; it may be, dissolution and chaos: *rottenness* is written over it thro' every relation of man to man.

Is the End come then? It *is* coming, and was . . . Really these things give me great pain.'

The vision of the phoenix, arising fantastically transformed from the ashes of its former self, had been part of the artistic planning of the climax of *Sartor Resartus*, intended to indicate that the existing society had to be purged by fire and emerge in a new shape. From the moorland isolation in which the phoenix-symbol was developed this was fair comment, but from Chelsea this became personal commitment as Carlyle grew more and more involved with political figures (such as Mill) and espoused public causes. Everything served to reinforce his impression that the country—the world—needed a leader.

The leader, once found, would clearly (in Carlyle's view) need no encouragement, but would rise to the occasion and be acclaimed. An example clearly to emerge in Carlyle's own historical writing is Abbot Samson in *Past and Present.*

'What is to hinder this Samson from governing? There is in him what far transcends all apprenticeships; in the man himself there exists a model of governing, something to govern by! There exists in him a heart-abhorrence of whatever is incoherent, pusillanimous, unveracious, that is to say, chaotic, *un*governed; of the Devil, not of God. A man of this kind cannot help governing!'

Such a person, a 'born servant' of God, is what Carlyle earnestly commended to his age. His age was understandably bowled over by the rhetoric, but the practical application was inevitably the weakest point. Carlyle, satirised by Trollope as Dr Pessimist Anticant in *The Warden,*

'. . . instituted himself censor of all things in general, and began the great task of reprobating everything and everybody . . . This was not so well; and, to tell the truth [he] did not succeed in his undertaking. His theories were all beautiful, and the code of morals that he taught us certainly an improvement on the practices of the age. We all of us could, and many of us did learn much from the doctor when he chose to remain vague, mysterious and cloudy; but when he became practical, the charm was gone.'

Now of course this is not altogether fair, but it contains many shrewd points. Carlyle realised that times were changing, even when he seemed most keenly to advocate a return to impossible old values. At the beginning of the *Latter-Day Pamphlets* he vividly compares Britain in the early 1850s with France at the time of the erupting Revolution of 1789. '. . . New street-barricades, and new anarchies, still more scandalous if less sanguinary, must return and again return, till governing persons everywhere know and admit that'. If he repeatedly dismisses democracy as meaningless and uninformed (it is an overwhelming theme of the *Latter-Day Pamphlets*) it is with a historical perspective of the anarchy which resulted in the 1790s, not just with a distaste for the political crowds of the 1840s and 1850s. He is aware that a complex industrial society is emerging (he saw the possibilities of social abuse as early as 1829, and *Signs of the Times*) and his theories are changing in as complex a way. *Heroes and Hero-Worship*, for instance, puts forward the idea that heroes are emerging because the concept of heroism is changing with the times. The Hero as Man of Letters, for instance, is 'altogether a product of these new ages', and if literature is (as Carlyle claims later in the same lecture) 'an "apocalypse of Nature," a revealing of the "open secret" ' then it changes as does man's understanding of his environment—and throws up new heroes. These are Burns, Rousseau—unheroic men in many ways. To Carlyle ordinary people, hard-working (perhaps unremarkable) people were intensely interesting.

'The noble, silent men, scattered here and there, each in his own department; silently thinking, silently working; whom no Morning Newspaper makes mention of! They are the salt of the Earth. A country that has none or few of these is in a bad way.'

In this way, the desire for order in the Carlylean universe defines itself in a strange and complex manner. Indubitably Carlyle longed for some sort of reassertion of the order of the first world he had known, in the back streets of South-West Scotland. His essays return again and again to the theme of the noble working man, the man who remains uncorrupted, if provincial, and retains his nobility with his quiet innocence.

Carlyle's enormous admiration for silence is part of this feeling too: his early years were spent in a house where speech was not witty or copious, but earnest and occasionally violent. Some of his best work was done in the loneliness and silence of Craigenputtoch. To the mature Carlyle, living in a growing city—perhaps already visibly growing too fast to be understood or controlled—the silence and order of these early days must have seemed a distant but desirable ideal.

This is only one element in a complex feeling. Even a casual reading of the love letters which passed between Thomas and Jane before they finally chose to live in Edinburgh in 1826 or in London in 1834 shows that to neither was a solitary quiet existence ultimately satisfying. Jane's ideal home was a quiet well-run one where there was always a welcome interval of conversation and good company. Her husband would have added to this, large periods of quiet order for working in, and large periods set aside for talk and (sometimes in his case) denunciation. He needed the quiet as he needed the order for his own work and his own lifestyle. In 1849 he wrote:

'I used to think, having plenty to say was a good thing; but I find it now rather worse than having *nothing*, for that would at least leave one a quiet life. Heigho! There is a mass of mud and street-sweepings . . . and at what corner to *begin* is and has long been a desperate mystery! For most part I stand leaning on my shovel; looking at it with mere desperate dismay, unable to strike in anywhere with decision or fixed purpose.'

The longing for order was bound in with the compulsive desire to work and fulfil the obligation put on him by the memory of his father, and his other religious forebears. The chaos of the attic study in Cheyne Row (vividly captured by the remarkable photographs still on display there, showing Carlyle miserably burying his head in his hands among piles of notes as he labours with *Frederick*) was continually an affront to Carlyle's longing for order. To create order was to finish a 'task' or chosen piece of work, and hastily sweep aside the disorder and burn everything. If the manuscript was burned, like the hapless first volume of *The French Revolution*, the result could be disaster. To scholars seeking some sort of information on how the books were written the absence of notes and drafts can be irritating. But to Carlyle it represented order in his immediate universe, which he could (to some extent) achieve by his own efforts.

It was an extension of his personal conception of a disciplined life which he passionately recommended to his contemporaries. Order meant (of course) far more than trains running to time and streets being clean, though unkind critics who look in Carlyle for signs of proto-fascism could easily parody him in this way. Order was a society which was self-aware in terms of work and obligation, and which functioned to best effect inside a chosen framework. If the Negro workers upset the order then (as we have seen) the order was more important than their immediate welfare. Very early in his career Carlyle made up his mind on that point: at the climax of his sufferings Teufelsdröckh in *Sartor Resartus* asks himself (with sarcasm) 'Foolish soul! What Act of Legislature was there that *thou* shouldst be Happy? . . . There is in Man a HIGHER than Love of Happiness: he can do without Happiness, and instead thereof find Blessedness!' If he never quite found the first, Carlyle never gave up looking for the second, and trying to encourage his contemporaries to do the same.

The ordered universe, once achieved, subsumes the other desires Carlyle expresses in the sort of world-picture contained in his work, and outlined in this final essay. It is not a static picture of order, such as the early one which he sketched in his *Wotton Reinfred* of 1827. This fragment of novel tried to show order in terms of quiet middle-class intellectual *soirées*, of good conversation and careful self-analysis in country-houses with hard-thinking and hard-talking weekend houseparties. For the Buller family (Carlyle's first introduction to this level of society) and for the Jeffreys in Craigcrook (Carlyle's intimate friends in 1826-1828) this was the norm, but Carlyle (as we know from the *Reminiscences*) never felt at home in this sort of ordered universe. Even in the height of his London popularity, he detested 'literary' dinners where conversation was the obvious intention. Carlyle found he could not converse at these formal dinners. It was (for him) a false order.

His order is expressed in less social terms. It is a world of order achieved through suffering perhaps, certainly through effort. The effort is continuous on the part of each individual to to detect order and disorder in his own environment and if appropriate in others. To the silent working man, an object of Carlyle's admiration, order is to get on with his task. To politicians, castigated by Carlyle, order is to give up career politics and concentrate on finding some sort of order in the mess of Victorian society all around, clearly visible but ignored by many. This is one of the two principal dynamic features in Carlyle's view of an ordered world—his intense sympathy for suffering. He cared about the poor and the socially deprived, and his concern not only brought life to works like *Past and Present* and the *Latter-Day Pamphlets*, it communicated itself to other writings like *North and South*, and *Hard Times* where other people carried his ideas into another literary medium to find for them a wider (and perhaps a more enduring) public.

The other dynamic feature needs no underlining by now. The religious search for order was a thread in Carlyle's thought from his very earliest memories. From the calm, disciplined life of the church-going family in Ecclefechan his memories had been of order, of parents intensely conscious of a hierarchical universe and working to maximum advantage in it. He left this ordered world for the disorder of Enlightened Edinburgh, and his sufferings before he recovered his poise in *Sartor Resartus* must have convinced him how unsuitable a substitute freedom of thought was for a religious order. Personally and intellectually Carlyle knew real misery between 1810 and 1830, and the relief with which he produced the amalgam of religious belief and half-assimilated German philosophical ideas in the closing chapters of *Sartor Resartus* is quite visible. He achieved total happiness no more than did Teufelsdröckh, for he continued to be driven by dyspepsia, by nervous irritability and by a sense of obligation to work himself to the limit as scholar, and to talk and discuss and propagate ideas with equal energy.

The religious sense changed with Carlyle's own developing ideas. From a desperate desire to reachieve an earlier order, it changed to a strong duty-oriented belief (in *Sartor Resartus*), through the vision of *The French Revolution* where religion is the one barrier which separates society from total anarchy, the inevitable result of a sceptical eighteenth century, to the later social writings where religion is seen simultaneously in terms of individual obligation and social application. The religious sense behind the *Latter-Day Pamphlets* is firmly attributed to a sardonic observer, who uses it not as a personal *credo* (which Carlyle was still willing to do in his earlier historical works) but as a rhetorical weapon in demolishing the shams and injustices of the 1850s. The injunction in the 'Everlasting YEA', 'Love not Pleasure, love God!' could be interpreted in this fluid way, for Carlyle's own interests were fluid as his London period progressed.

Earlier the suggestion was made that religious freedom was no substitute for an ordered religious view of life. This is an important idea, for it is crucial to Thomas Carlyle's view of the religious universe, particularly as he remembered it from his father's own example.

'He was Religious with the consent of his whole faculties: without Reason he would have been nothing; indeed his habit of intellect was thoroughly free and even incredulous, and strongly enough did the daily example of this work afterwards on me . . . But he was in Annandale, and it was above fifty years ago; and a Gospel was still preached there to the heart of a man, in the tones of a man. Religion was the Pole-star for my Father: rude and uncultivated as he otherwise was, it made him and kept him "in all points a man".'

But that was Annandale, and fifty years ago—it is at this point that Carlyle's message becomes more than mere harking back to happy days before the Serpent. He realises that times change, and that people have to change with them. His father's Church was no longer in existence, as various schisms had been healed and branches of the Scottish Church reunited, before being again split in the great Disruption of 1843. In the later *Reminiscences* of Edward Irving Carlyle was to write nostalgically of the 'sacred lambencies, tongues of authentic flame from Heaven, which kindled what was best in one, what has not yet gone out', but he was also to admit that 'Irving and I were probably among the last products it delivered before gliding off, and then rushing off, into self-consciousness, arrogance, insincerity, jangle and vulgarity . . .'. To do him justice, Carlyle was not suggesting a return to a golden ideal world of Ecclefechan church-going, any more than he could resurrect Cromwell or Frederick the Great as cures for the ills of his time. The ills had changed, and so had the living conditions of the people who were suffering them. What had not changed, in Carlyle's opinion, was the individual obligation to an overall order, which no one could ignore. This is a personal matter, and niceties of Church doctrine do not affect it. This is the key which in part explains Carlyle's extraordinary devotion to the memory of his father's life-style, which he himself rejected very early on. The personal commitment behind the life-style was what Carlyle admired, in retrospect.

'*He* was never visited with Doubt; the old Theorem of the Universe was sufficient for him, and he worked well in it, and in all senses *successfully* and wisely as few now can do . . . Thus curiously enough, and blessedly, *he* stood a true man on the verge of the Old; while his son stands here lovingly surveying him on the verge of the New, and sees the possibility of also being true there. God make the possibility, blessed possibility, into a reality!'

It was by attitudes like this, and apothegms from Germany like 'Work, and Despair not!' that Carlyle convinced a whole generation of his Victorian contemporaries that he had an earnest message which might be relevant to them at a time of industrial unrest, social reform, and worryingly uncontrolled expansion of industry and exploitation of natural resources. It is difficult sometimes to realise the comprehensiveness of Carlyle's vision of the development of Victorian Britain. In 1825 he was visiting Birmingham at the height of its powers as an industrial city, the sky bright at night with the fire of the iron works, everywhere signs of industrial energy which astounded Carlyle even after months in London. In 1881, Carlyle was still in London, having outlived many of his most distinguished contemporaries and still preserved his status in people's minds as Sage of Chelsea. Since the popular success of 1837 and *The French Revolution* he had been more than a historian and essayist, though that was how he was catalogued in libraries. He had been a Sage in the full sense, offering an encouragement and example to his contemporaries as his own father had done to himself—and in quite as irrational a way.

The Carlyle style has of course dated badly. Its energy seems obstructed by its heavily biblical language, and its involved structures (often concealing irony) difficult to analyse without painful effort. His long life aggravated the problem as his output grew larger and larger. Many of the ideas most adapted to the extreme disorder and uncertainty of the society of his time seem most unattractive to modern ideas of civil liberty and equality. In short, the ranks of his collected works may seem an insuperable barrier to appreciating the 'message' of Carlyle. Perhaps this introduction to his thought has suggested the complexity of that message, and how it developed to meet the change not only in society over the better part of a century, but in its author whose circumstances changed from poverty and obscurity to world eminence as Sage of Chelsea.

Swinburne wrote in his elegy on the deaths of Thomas Carlyle and George Eliot of

> The stormy sophist with his mouth of thunder,
> Clothed with loud words and mantled with the might
> Of Darkness and magnificence of night,

and this undoubtedly is part of the importance of any assessment of Carlyle. Yet aside from the magnificence of the rhetoric there is the personal appeal he made to many of his contemporaries who found in him a person who worried about things which deserved attention, who drew the notice of the world to abuses too easily overlooked, and who tried to live a life which would be as exemplary as his own father's had been. George Eliot's own tribute sums it up simply: writing in *The Leader* of 27 October 1855 she said, 'There is hardly a superior or active mind of this generation that has not been modified by Carlyle's writings; there has hardly been an English book written for the last ten or twelve years that would not have been different if Carlyle had not lived.'

SELECTED REFERENCES AND NOTES

THIS CHAPTER is in no sense a complete guide to the reading matter available on the field covered by an introductory book. The reader who wishes to read further will find information to supplement this chapter in the revised *Cambridge Bibliography of English Literature*, vol. III (1969), in Carlisle Moore's chapter in *The English Romantic Poets and Essayists, A Review of Research and Criticism*, ed. C. W. and L. H. Houtchens (1966), and in R. L. Tarr's *A Check-list of English Language Articles on Thomas Carlyle: 1900-1965* (1972). Older, but still valuable works, are the standard bibliography by Isaac W. Dyer (1928, reprinted 1968), and its predecessor by R. H. Shepherd (1881). One of the most useful recent surveys of Carlyle scholarship occurs in the early chapters of J. Cabau, *Thomas Carlyle ou le Prométhée Enchaîné: Essai sur la genèse de l'oeuvre de 1795 à 1834* (1968).

As this book goes to press there appears a definitive bibliographical essay by G. B. Tennyson in *Victorian Prose, A Guide to Research* (1973), ed. D. J. De Laura. Professor Tennyson's pages on Thomas Carlyle (33-104) and Jane (105-111) are exhaustive: he admits to consulting over 1,200 items for his study, and they are comprehensively listed and estimated with charm and wit, and where necessary, acid comment. 'As we enter the decade of the centenary of Carlyle's death', writes Professor Tennyson on p. 35, 'and to within two and a half decades of the bicentennial of his birth, we can see Carlyle in perspective as neither madman nor inerrant pontiff, but as one of the enduring monuments of our literature who, quite simply, cannot be spared.'

In cataloguing manuscript sources the reader may begin by consulting the introductory volumes of each set of the Duke-

Edinburgh edition of the *Correspondence of Thomas and Jane Welsh Carlyle*: vols. I-IV were published in 1970; vols. V-VII due in 1975. The manuscripts covered by these volumes belong to the period 1809-1834, and with the publication of vols. VIII-IX will cover the period to 1837.

Many of the other manuscripts are published, in part or in whole: the reader who wishes to trace them is recommended to the Catalogue of Manuscripts of the British Museum Library, The Victoria and Albert Library, the Carlyle House, Chelsea, the Berg Library, New York, Yale and Duke University Libraries, and the Houghton Library, Harvard. A more comprehensive list is in Tennyson (cited above) pp. 35-38. All superlative collections, none can match that of the National Library of Scotland in Edinburgh, which has accumulated from a core of letters and manuscript amassed by Alexander Carlyle the most complete collection in the world, fully bound and catalogued and being increased as letters reach the market. In this venture (aggravated by the rising value of literary manuscripts on the open market) they are being helped by Edinburgh University Library, itself the possessor of a distinguished collection of correspondence, particularly Jane's.

For a useful iconography, 'The Principal Portraits, Statues, Busts, and Photographs of Thomas Carlyle' by J. A. S. Barrett, see Isaac Dyer's *Bibliography*, pp. 543-553.

Carlyle's works themselves may usefully be listed at this point, to offer the reader a chronology of the principal publications in his literary career:

1819 ff	miscellaneous articles
1822	translation of Legendre's *Geometry*
1824	translation of Goethe's *Wilhelm Meisters Lehrjahre*
1825	*Life of Schiller*
1827	*Specimens of German Romance* (including Goethe's *Wilhelm Meisters Wanderjahre*)
1836	*Sartor Resartus* (American edition) (published in magazine form in London in 1833-1834, in book form in London 1838)
1837	*The French Revolution*

1839   *Chartism*
1841   *Heroes and Hero-Worship*
1843   *Past and Present*
1845   *Oliver Cromwell's Letters and Speeches*
1850   *Latter-Day Pamphlets*
1851   *Life of John Sterling*
1853   *The Nigger Question*
1858-65 *History of Frederick the Great*
1866   *On the Choice of Books*
1867   *Shooting Niagara—And After?*
1875   *The Early Kings of Norway*
        Portraits of John Knox
1881   *Reminiscences* (posthumous)

For further details see 'A Chronology of Composition for Carlyle's Work, 1814-1833' in G. B. Tennyson, *Sartor called Resartus*, (1965), pp. 332-342.

The standard edition, most generally used in scholarship referring to Carlyle, is the Centenary edition edited by H. D. Traill (1896-1899). To this may be added supplementary volumes, such as *Collectanea Thomas Carlyle 1821-1855* (1903), *Last Words of Thomas Carlyle* (1892, reprinted 1972), *Two Notebooks of Thomas Carlyle* (1898), *Carlyle's Unfinished History of German Literature* (1951) and minor collections of more specialist interest. Hill Shine's list of *Carlyle's Early Reading to 1834* (1953), as the title suggests, allows the reader to follow the progress of Carlyle through his voluminous reading.

Readers who prefer to look at smaller collections will find anthologies and single editions of great value. C. F. Harrold's edition of *Sartor Resartus* (1937) has yet to be superseded for the completeness of its annotation; Froude's edition of the *Reminiscences* (1881), on the other hand, was rapidly superseded by Norton's (1888) and it in its turn is now out of print and replaced by a more complete edition in Everyman's University Library (1972). A full scholarly edition edited by E. Sharples is in preparation in the U.S.A. Considerable portions of Carlyle's work are available in Everyman's Library, including *Sartor, Heroes, Cromwell, Chartism, Past and Present, The French Revolution*, the

Reminiscences, and selections of *Essays*. An excellent introduction to Carlyle can be found in Alan Shelston's Penguin, *Thomas Carlyle, Selected Writings* (1971), or in G. B. Tennyson's *A Carlyle Reader* (1969). Julian Symons' selection for the Reynard Library (1955) is still a very attractive introduction.

Principal among the many works on Carlyle which could be recommended are Froude's biography (which is being re-issued in a one-volume abridgement by John Clubbe) and Emery Neff's *Carlyle* (1932), a perceptive and well-balanced introduction.

Chapter 1

The early life of Carlyle is surprisingly little researched, since interest has tended to focus on the period after Carlyle settled in London. Readers who wish full documentation of the early chapters of this book are invited to consult my doctoral dissertation 'Thomas Carlyle and Edinburgh, 1809-1834' (1970) in Edinburgh University Library. This attempts to relate Carlyle in detail to his family background, and to examine the strain which occurred in Carlyle's developing personality as his experience widened.

The Dumfriesshire environment may be best visualised with the aid of J. M. Sloan's well-illustrated and full *The Carlyle Country* (1904), which follows Carlyle through his different locations in Dumfriesshire, and speculates on the effect the changes may have had on him. A more comprehensive introduction is contained in the various *Statistical Accounts* (1792, 1845) of the parishes in which Carlyle lived. The circle in which he lived did not, as a rule, leave much impression on the pages of history, and so our picture has to be built up from stray references in other works. Materials for this may be found in Robert Herdman's notes of conversations made with Carlyle while the latter was sitting for his portrait in 1876, and published by me in *The Weekend Scotsman*, 12 August 1967, as 'Portrait of Carlyle'; in a letter from Carlyle to the Highland Society, November 1827, published in *Essays and Transactions of the Highland Society* VII (1829), 290-291, recently discovered by Miss Aileen Christianson; in the notes Carlyle left to Friedrich Althaus' biography

of him which was published in *Unsere Zeit in Leipsig* (1866)—
soon to be republished by John Clubbe; in *Homes and Haunts of
Thomas Carlyle* (1895); and in A. Steele's pamphlet on the
Ecclefechan Church, *The Story of a Hundred and Fifty Years*
(1910). A very large amount of secondary material will be found
in the Dumfries collection of the Ewart Public Library in
Dumfries. The main sources of information gleaned for conversational remarks made by Carlyle in later life are Sir C. G. Duffy,
Conversations with Carlyle (1892), William Allingham, *A Diary*
(1907), Francis Espinasse, *Literary Recollections and Sketches*
(1893) and Moncure Conway, *Autobiography* (1904).

For the Church history of the period the reader may consult
the comprehensive history by A. C. Cheyne (due for publication
in 1975), or those of J. H. S. Burleigh (1960), G. D. Henderson
(1936), D. Scott (1886), G. Struthers (1848) or J. McKerrow
(1841). I have traced Carlyle's relationship to the Burgher
Seceder Church in 'Carlyle and the Secession', *Records of the
Scottish Church History Society* 18, 1 (1972), 48-64, and the
effects of this on his religious thought in 'Carlyle's Religion—the
Scottish Sources' in a forthcoming *Festschrift for C. R. Sanders*
(1974), ed. J. Clubbe.

Chapter 2

From this point in the book the reader is directed to the
published letters of the Carlyles, of which volume One has some
bearing on the University years and immediately afterwards.
There is very ample documentation provided in the footnotes.

For Edinburgh itself there are numbers of introductions ranging
from the literary ones (*Humphry Clinker*, or the tours of either
Boswell or Johnson) to the more factual accounts of R. W.
Chambers (1824) and the excellent *Making of Classical Edinburgh*
published by A. J. Youngson (1966). The standard works by
which one may gain insight into the literary forces of the period
include *The Autobiography of Alexander Carlyle of Inveresk* (1910,
re-edited by James Kinsley 1973), J. G. Lockhart's *Peter's Letters
to his Kinsfolk* (1819), the *Memorials* and *Journals* of Henry
Cockburn (1856, 1874), A. Somerville's *My Own Life and Times*

1741-1814 (1861), and more recent studies such as John Clive's *Scotch Reviewers* (1957) and Elsie Swann, *Christopher North* (1934). The reference to Engels may be followed up in *The Condition of the Working Classes in England*, ed. Henderson and Chaloner (1958), p. 41.

The history of the University of Edinburgh is contained in a recent brief work by D. B. Horn (1967), but in more detail in A. Grant's *The Story of the University of Edinburgh during its First 300 Years* (1884). An important source, quoted several times, is Thomas Murray's *Autobiographical Notes* (1911). David Masson's *Edinburgh Sketches and Memories* (1892), although superseded in many ways, is still a pioneer account of this period of Carlyle's life.

Carlyle's address to the students on his installation as rector was published in 1866 under the title *On the Choice of Books*: his late discussions of science with John Tyndall are included in the latter's 'Personal Recollections of Carlyle', *Fortnightly Review* 277 (1890), 5-32.

Finally a central book on this period with wide-ranging implications throughout this study is G. E. Davie, *The Democratic Intellect* (1961). Dr Davie's Rhind Lecture at Dundee (1973) carries his argument further.

Chapter 3

The reader who has sampled widely the books recommended so far will be in a better position to follow the course of Carlyle's development in this period of his changing attitude to the ministry, and to religion, both of which are treated in my article 'Carlyle's Religion—the Scottish Sources' (*supra*) and in my 'Carlyle's Borrowings from the Theological Library, Edinburgh University', *The Bibliotheck* V, 5 (1969), 165-168. The stress under which Carlyle laboured is explored in J. L. Halliday's 'psychosomatic biography', *Mr Carlyle my Patient* (1949), and in a yet more narrow and extraordinary study by S. Sagar, *Round by Repentance Hill* (1930), where Carlyle is presented as the peasant who has lost his priest, and yearns for strong spiritual guidance. A great deal has been written about Carlyle's religion: arguably

most of it with grossly insufficient detailed study of the early belief
in which Carlyle was strongly formed. An exception must be
made for C. F. Harrold's early article 'The Nature of Carlyle's
Calvinism', *Studies in Philology* 33, 3 (1936), 475-486 and for
Carlisle Moore's '*Sartor Resartus*, The Problem of Carlyle's
"Conversion"', *PMLA* 70 (1955), 662-681 and 'The Persistence
of Carlyle's "Everlasting Yea"', *Modern Philology* 54 (1957),
187-196.

Frederick Harrison's acid review is quoted from *On the Choice
of Books* (1903). Finally the quotation in which Carlyle describes
his late friend is taken from my 'Thomas Carlyle and George
Cron', *Notes and Queries* 18, 5 (1971), 183-185, and the details
about Carlyle's work on Pictet from my 'Carlyle, Pictet and
Jeffrey Again', *The Bibliotheck* 7, 1 (1974), 1-16.

Chapter 4

With the appearance of Jane comes reference to a considerable
amount of published literature concerning the two Carlyles, most
importantly their correspondence, of which part was published
by Alexander Carlyle as *The Love Letters of Thomas and Jane
Welsh Carlyle* (1909). Jane's own *Letters and Memorials* were
prepared by Carlyle for publication by Froude (1883), and her
Early Letters by D. G. Ritchie (1889). All her remaining letters
are, of course, scheduled for inclusion in the Duke-Edinburgh
edition.

An exhaustive and carefully researched book on Jane is that
of Lawrence and Elisabeth Hanson, *Necessary Evil* (1952): more
recent, and more superficial, is J. S. Collis' *The Carlyles* (1971).
Several biographical studies and works of fiction based on Jane
are in preparation.

Carlyle's growing involvement with continental literature is the
subject of several excellent studies, notably L. Cazamian's
Carlyle (1913) (English version 1932), J.-M. Carré's *Goethe en
Angleterre* (1920), René Wellek's *Immanuel Kant in England*
(1931) and *A History of Modern Criticism* (1955-1966), and (so
far the finest in this field) C. F. Harrold, *Carlyle and German
Thought 1819-1834* (1934). In a different field is an equally fine

book which has set new standards in the criticism of Carlyle in relation to other literatures: G. B. Tennyson's *Sartor called Resartus* (1965) which traces the origin and growth of the ideas in *Sartor Resartus* both in Carlyle's own mind, and in the work of literature which emerged from this process. Tennyson's work has been followed by other important scholarship: J. Cabau, *Carlyle ou le Prométhée Enchaîné* (1968), G. Levine, *The Boundaries of Fiction* (1968), A. J. Lavalley, *Carlyle and the Idea of the Modern* (1968), which studies Carlyle's prophetic literature in relation to Blake, Nietzsche and Marx, J. P. Siegel's volume on Carlyle in the 'Critical Heritage' series, which puts Carlyle in the context of the critical responses of his contemporaries (1971), and a book which fits no category neatly, E. W. Marrs' *The Letters of Thomas Carlyle to his Brother Alexander, with Related Family Letters* (1968), a magnificent collection of family papers (surviving largely in Canada) with explanatory text and annotation. All are central to an attempt to understand the totality of Carlyle's thought: all have some useful bearing on the early struggle taking place in Carlyle's mind at this time.

Comely Bank lay outside the city boundaries of Edinburgh, and little is known of it apart from its pleasant pastoral conditions. On literary conditions at the time, much useful information is in Ian Jack, *English Literature 1815-1832* (Oxford History of English Literature, vol. X, 1963). Minor additions can be made from the 'Reminiscences of a Town Clerk' in *The Book of the Old Edinburgh Club* 14 (1925), 156, and from the letters of Sir Walter Scott written at this period, edited by H. J. Grierson *et al.* (1936).

Chapter 5

In addition to Elsie Swann's *Christopher North*, the reader may consult Henry Cockburn's *Life of Jeffrey* (1852), and for a very full account of the literary life of Edinburgh, Edgar Johnson's monumental life of Scott (1971). Masson's *Edinburgh Sketches and Memories* deals in some detail with the life in Comely Bank, as does vol. IV of the *Letters*.

More details of life in that period come from Carlyle's own account of 'Christopher North' (in *Reminiscences*, Everyman editions, reprinted from Alexander Carlyle's published version in *The Nineteenth Century and After* (1920)). The speculation on the cost of living is difficult to prove by documentation: the principal printed source to which one can appeal for information, apart from Masson's *Edinburgh Sketches and Memories,* is B. Mitchell and P. Dean, *Abstract of British Historical Statistics* (1962).

The extracts from *Wotton Reinfred* are taken from its published form in *Last Words of Thomas Carlyle* (1892): they can be supplemented with the excerpt, 'Sir Gideon Dunn', which escaped publishing in this collection. I have included it in 'Carlyle and Sir Gideon Dunn', *English Language Notes* 9, 3 (1972), 185-191.

Chapter 6

In this chapter an essential guide is the fascinating chapter 'Dumfries' in the *Statistical Account of Scotland* (1845): each chapter is by a different author (the minister of the parish described) and the man who wrote this one gives a vivid account not only of life in the area, but of the cholera outbreak in 1831-1832 which so alarmed the Carlyles while they were in far-off London. The Ewart Library, Dumfries will also provide essential local records for the Craigenputtoch area. For Edward Irving, and further information on him, the reader is referred to A. L. Drummond's general study, *Edward Irving and his Circle* (1937), and Gordon Strachan's more specialist *Edward Irving and the Pentecostal Church* (1973). An illustration of how the religious background shared by Irving and Carlyle might affect their attitude to art, and their consequent credibility to a non-Scottish audience, is to be found in my 'Irving, Carlyle and the Stage', *Studies in Scottish Literature* 8, 3 (1971) 166-173. At this stage in his career Carlyle made a brief but important contact with the Saint-Simonian radicals in France, and despite a lofty injunction from his admired Goethe to have nothing to do with them, for some time did all he could to acquaint himself with their 'Christian socialism'. See H. Shine, *Carlyle and the Saint-Simonians* (1941), and K. J. Fielding, 'Carlyle and the Saint-Simonians (1830-1832):

New Considerations', in the *Festschrift for C. R. Sanders* (1974) already referred to. Carlyle's whole changing social attitude, and growing conviction that he had a worthwhile new social message, emerges fascinatingly from his letters: his growing intimacy with John Stuart Mill can be seen interestingly mirrored in Mill's *Autobiography* (completed edition, 1924) and further in J. Hamburger, *Intellectuals in Politics: John Stuart Mill and the Philosophic Radicals* (1965).

Chapter 7

The *ménage* in Chelsea is the subject of intensive study in Thea Holme's entertaining *The Carlyles at Home* (1965): as curatrix of the Carlyle house in Chelsea, Mrs Holme had access to the letters and papers to describe fully the extraordinary mixture of happiness and disaster in Cheyne Row. More detail about the area in which the Carlyle's lived can be found in Mrs Holme's *Chelsea* (1972), in which the historical associations of the area (which fascinated both Carlyles) may be traced. R. Blunt's *The Carlyles' Chelsea Home* (1895) adds a valuable dimension of the local rector who knew the Carlyles in residence, and knew what happened after Carlyle's death to the house in Cheyne Row. After being let to an eccentric lady who filled the house with dozens of pet cats, it was bought for the nation by the Carlyle House Memorial Trust and restored as a museum.

The catalogues of both Carlyle houses, in Ecclefechan and Chelsea, are out of print: the latter, however, is being prepared in a new edition, since extensive reconstruction and alteration has lately taken place in the property itself. The house and street are little changed, although an intrusive brick church at the top of the street has spoiled its unity of style. Leigh Hunt's house, two minutes' walk away, is marked by a plaque, as is the Carlyle House itself (now administered by the National Trust). For details of Irving's London career, the reader should consult Drummond's *Edward Irving and his Circle* (1937), already referred to: for Leigh Hunt a standard work would be E. Blunden, *Leigh Hunt* (1930).

Chapters 8 and 9

Here many of the previous books referred to may be consulted in continuation, such as the Blunt and Holme books on Chelsea, and *Homes and Haunts of Thomas Carlyle*. The standard edition of *Past and Present*, excellently edited by Richard Altick, is in the series of Riverside editions (1965), and the reader is also recommended to G. Calder, *The Writing of 'Past and Present'* (1949). Carlyle's own essay 'On History' (1830) was supplemented by his 'On History Again' (1833). An illustration of his search for materials for Cromwell in private houses, and his subsequent gift of an essay on these materials, may be found in my article 'Carlyle, Cromwell and Kimbolton', *The Bibliotheck* 5, (1970), 246-252. The 'Squire Papers' first appeared in an article in *Fraser's Magazine* for December 1847: they appear in the third and subsequent editions of Carlyle's *Cromwell* (1850 ff), with Carlyle's own explanatory note of 7 May 1849. For more details see *Carlyle's Cromwell*, ed. S. C. Lomas (1904). Jane's very amusing begging letter for more housekeeping money, the 'Budget of a *Femme Incomprise*', can be read in Froude's *Thomas Carlyle, A History of his Life in London* (1884), II, 162 ff. On *The Nigger Question* there is much polemical writing on both sides, one of the most recent, as well as the most reasonable, being E. R. August's interesting pairing, *Carlyle, 'The Nigger Question', Mill, 'The Negro Question'* in the Crofts library (1971). My own article 'Carlyle and the Negro Question Again', which tries to put Carlyle's attitude in the perspective of the ideas of his childhood environment, appears in *Criticism* 8, 3 (1971), 279-290. The lecture of Grierson on *Carlyle and Hitler* is well known; it dates from 1931 and was published in 1933.

Chapter 10

The expression 'Latent sadism' comes from A. Shelston's commentary in his *Thomas Carlyle, Selected Writings* (1971), p. 283. Jane's encounter with the income tax authorities is detailed in Thea Holme's *The Carlyles at Home* (1965) pp. 142-145. Mrs Jellyby is the character whose weak philanthropism is described in *Bleak House*, but arguably she is not the only such character in a plot where people too easily overlook suffering at close quarters for more distant, if more spectacular, suffering. Much of Carlyle's travel documentary diary-keeping is published: see, for instance, his 'Excursion, Futile Enough, to Paris; Autumn 1851', in *Last Words of Thomas Carlyle* (1892), pp. 149-191, and his various travels to Germany.

Chapter 11

The Rectorial election and installation were widely reported in the press at the time: there is a good account in A. Smith, *Last Leaves* (1868). The address itself is published as *On the Choice of Books* (1866). Tyndall's article 'Some Personal Recollections of Carlyle' gives valuable detail not only on this, but on the period immediately surrounding Jane's death, when Tyndall did a great deal to shield Carlyle from the worst of the strain he might otherwise have had to face—above all the possibility that Jane would have had to undergo autopsy, since the cause of death was unknown. Many hoary stories about this period and afterwards stem from Frank Harris' 'Talks with Carlyle' (1911). Harris repeats (he tells us) table-talk from physicians who examined Jane after death, and who had attended her before that. The distasteful controversy between Froude and Carlyle, including the controversial editing of the *Reminiscences* as well as the questions of health and temperament, is surveyed in W. H. Dunn's *Froude and Carlyle* (1930), and in E. Sharples' doctoral dissertation for the University of Rochester (1964). When Carlyle's journal entries are occasionally quoted, they come from the text of Froude's biography: Froude had access to the whole of Carlyle's manuscript journal, which is now in private hands and not available for publication. See my 'James Barrett and Carlyle's *Journal*', *Notes and Queries* 17, 1 (1970), 19-21. On the Governor Eyre controversy, see Ian Gregor's fine introduction to his edition of Matthew Arnold's *Culture and Anarchy* (1971).

Chapters 12 and 13

Edward Fitzgerald's *Letters* (1960) are a mine of information on literary events at the time: they serve to illuminate much of the feeling which surrounded the major literary events. The reader might also consult W. H. Dunn's *Life of Froude* (1961-1963), and the selections in J. P. Siegel's 'Carlyle' volume in the *Critical Heritage* series (1971).

Chapter 14 and after

The specialised reading has now all appeared, in so far as it is possible to mention so much in such a short and selective list. There are obvious omissions, and a few extra books should certainly be recommended, such as M. Storrs, *The Relation of Carlyle to Kant and Fichte* (1929), H. Shine, *Carlyle's Fusion of Poetry, History and Religion by 1834* (1938), C. R. Sanders' article 'Thomas Carlyle as Editor and Critic of Literary Letters', *Emory University Quarterly* 20 (1964), J. H. Buckley, *The Victorian Temper* (1951), J. Holloway, *The Victorian Sage* (1953), R. Williams, *Culture and Society, 1780-1950* (1958), A. A. Ikeler, *Puritan Temper and Transcendental Faith* (1972), G. Brooks, *The Rhetorical Form of 'Sartor Resartus'* (1972), and M. Goldberg, *Carlyle and Dickens* (1972).

Last, but not least, mention should be made of the pamphlets, occasional papers and published lectures on Carlyle appearing from the Carlyle Society of Edinburgh, which still flourishes. Some of its publications, such as David Daiches' *Carlyle and the Victorian Dilemma* (1963), are miniature classics. The other Carlyle Society (in London) is long defunct: the Edinburgh one continues to grow. It might have pleased Carlyle to regard this as a Sign of the Times.

INDEX